W9-CDU-582

3-19.63   (62-18616)   Trayrham
11-11-63

Spain and the Great Powers, 1936-1941

946,681
P

SPAIN and the GREAT POWERS 1936-1941

by Dante A. Puzzo

1962 NEW YORK AND LONDON

COLUMBIA UNIVERSITY PRESS

WINGATE COLLEGE LIBRARY
WINGATE, N. C.

In memory of

LOUIS PUZZO *and*

MARY BELMONTE PUZZO

COPYRIGHT © 1962 COLUMBIA UNIVERSITY PRESS

LIBRARY OF CONGRESS CATALOG CARD NUMBER: 62-18616

MANUFACTURED IN THE UNITED STATES OF AMERICA

Preface

FOR all its blood, cruelty, intrigue, and corruption, there was something pure about the Spanish war. The enthusiasm it engendered was a springtime that briefly loosened the wintry grip of a world grown old and weary and cynical. As did no other event of our time, it caught the conscience of a generation.

From the initial uprising in Morocco to the virtual abandonment of "Operation Isabella-Felix" Spain was at or near the center of world interest. This is an account of how a vertebrate Spain succumbed to an invertebrate diplomacy, of how a democratic republic was made into an Axis satellite. In treating of matters so emotionally evocative, it would be fatuous, or worse, to pretend to an Olympian detachment. I believe with Gaetano Salvemini that it is not necessary to don the frayed mask of "objectivity" to write good history. What is needed is a respect for fact and right reason.

Two decades of formal study leave their imprint on a person. They leave, also, an appreciation for the many dedicated teachers and scholars who have helped to inform one's mind and heart. But each of us has a particular teacher who excites a special admiration and affection, who through the years remains "my old professor." I want here to acknowledge my unpayable debt to J. Fred Rippy, Professor Emeritus at the University of Chicago. Much of what is meritorious in the pages which follow should be attributed

21061

to his influence. The errors of fact and interpretation are, of course, strictly my own.

For their many kindnesses and considerable help, I thank the people at the Columbia University Press, particularly Mr. Robert Gravallese and Miss Joan Teitel. For the comfort of his furry presence amidst the clutter of my desk while I wrote this book, I thank T. C. For her encouragement, patience, and indispensable help, I thank my wife.

DANTE A. PUZZO

New York City
April, 1962

Contents

I

The Spanish Background

THAT the Spanish conquistadores should have constituted
the vanguard of that movement in modern history known as the
"Expansion of Europe" is somewhat anomalous. For Spain can be
properly described as the Tibet of Europe. Behind the granite
heights of the Pyrenees, Spain, 194,783 square miles of arid plateaux
and sun-filled plains, is a land apart, not of Europe nor yet of Africa, but a land driven in upon itself, isolated and remote. The rise
of Spain was truly phenomenal. In the century and a half following the conquest of Granada (1492)—the last Moorish stronghold
on the Iberian Peninsula—Spaniards established an empire that
stretched over half the globe and included most of the New World.
But the decline of Spain was equally rapid and not less far-reaching.
The destruction of the Armada in 1588 and the defeat at Rocroi
in 1643 marked its beginning. The French Revolution found Spain
a weak and backward country, her days of greatness long since
past, her possessions pawns in the game of empire now played by
others.

However, the French invasion of 1808 sucked Spain into the
vortex of a continent in great motion and change. The constitution of 1812, the abortive First Spanish Republic of the seventies,
the philosophic orientation and ideas of Miguel Unamuno, Joaquín
Costa, Francisco Ferrer, and others of the "Generation of '98,"
can be traced back to the impact of Napoleonic France on an isolated, stagnant Spain. This is not to say that the coming of the
Bourbons in 1700 and the Enlightenment had not affected Spanish
life and thought. It is only to emphasize that the active forces of

the nineteenth century, upon entering Spain, redefined and re-
vitalized those earlier transpyrenean influences. They served, too, to
infuse with fresh meaning ancient traditions and practices—in-
digenous expressions of freedom—which had persisted here and
there in Spanish society through the centuries. With modern notions of liberty and democracy came power looms for the mills
of Barcelona. With science and rationalism came machinery for
the mines and shops of the Asturias and the Basque regions. Inevitably the crust of old Spain began to crack and to fall away.
Then, against a background of defeat in war and the loss of Spain's
last vestiges of empire, the attack of the "Generation of '98" on
the ineptitude, the corruption, and the anachronistic prerogatives
of an ancient ruling class acquired a cogency that forced a re-
examination of traditional attitudes and loyalties.

Spain entered the twentieth century beset by vast political, economic, and social problems. With republican sentiment growing
among the middle classes and the peasant masses as well, the position of the monarchy was increasingly insecure. The prestige of
the army and of the officer caste in particular being greatly
diminished by defeat in the American war, there was a clamor
for modernization of the military institutions of the nation. The
demand for the secularization of education epitomized the widespread criticism of the power and influence of the Spanish Church.
Liberal sentiment was manifested, too, in the demand for greater
political and civil rights and for freedom of the press. The conflict
of interests between agriculture and incipient industry posed serious
political problems, as did the struggle between Castilian centralism
and Catalan and Basque regionalism. The rapid growth of trade
unionism raised the question of its proper place in Spanish economic life, a question complicated by the simultaneous rise of socialism and anarchism as important mass movements. However,
significant and vexatious as these problems were, they remained
distinctly secondary to the problem of the land.

The economic life of Spain is centered in crops and herds, with
mining and manufacturing important but essentially peripheral ac-

tivities. In a population of some twenty-five millions in 1936 there were more than fifteen millions on the land. In times past, Spanish politics reflected the conflict of interests between agriculturalists and stock-breeders. The latter, predominantly Castilian and organized into the famous sheep-farmers' guild known as the *Mesta*, enjoyed a preeminent influence in the councils of state from the middle of the fifteenth to the middle of the nineteenth century. As a result entire provinces in Spain were stripped of vegetation by the "sheep's corrosive tooth," with desiccation and depopulation following.[2] In more recent times, agriculturalists and stock-breeders have joined together against the menace to their interests represented by mine-owners and manufacturers. Disputes involving tariff policies and the great question of Castilian centralism as against Catalan and Basque regionalism, while influenced by discrepant historical traditions, variant customs and speech, and sheer sentiment, find their premises, nonetheless, in the unresolved conflict between agrarianism and industrialism.

However, the land problem in Spain—ownership, distribution, systems of tenure, the uses to which land is put, the matters of rainfall, irrigation, relative fertility, and soil erosion—transcends in complexity the ancient conflict between Castilian stock-breeder and Andalusian agriculturalist or the new dichotomy of agrarian Castile and industrial Catalonia.

In Galicia, in the northwest of Spain, land was held or subleased in such small allotments that the peasant was reduced to sheer subsistence farming, growing all his food and, in some districts, making his own clothing and household articles. In order to earn the money to pay rents and taxes, the Galician peasant would journey to other parts of Spain to help with the harvest.

In the south of Spain, in Andalusia, vast estates of thousands of acres were the rule, with some three-fourths of the peasantry without a fistful of earth to call their own.[3] In the early 1930s the life of the *braceros*, or landless farm workers, was mean and difficult in the extreme. Idle for about half the year, and earning from three to six pesetas for a working day of from eight to twelve hours during the remaining months, their lot was wretched poverty, chronic hunger, disease, and demoralization.[4] These conditions and not the "Moorish blood" of the Andalusian peasant or the "mañana" propensities of the stereotyped Spaniard account for the near suspension of life reported by travelers in the more remote districts of Andalusia.

Between the minifundia of Galicia and the latifundia of Andalusia were to be found the peasant communities of the northern part of Old Castile, the Asturias, the Basque regions, of which Navarra is the most easternly and the least Basque in sentiment, Pyrenean Aragón, and part of Catalonia. In these northern, mountainous districts of Spain, which enjoy adequate rainfall and generally good soils, small peasant holdings were sufficient to sustain a modestly prosperous standard of rural life. Systems of land tenure included individual peasant holdings, family proprietorships, community proprietorships unchanged since the early Middle Ages, and share-cropping, the most widespread and least satisfactory type being the *rabassa morte* in Catalonia. Under the terms of the *rabassa morte* the *rabassaire* possessed the right to cultivate a piece of land after the payment of a lump sum down and the promise of a quarter, a third, or half the yield, depending on local conditions, to be delivered to the proprietor, until such time as three-quarters of the planted vines had died. The land would then revert to the proprietor and a new contract would have to be negotiated. Because it takes six or seven years for young vines to become productive and because the average life of the American vines introduced into Catalonia in the 1890s after the phylloxera plague had destroyed the native vines[5] is only about twenty-five years, it is apparent that the *rabassaire* found himself in an uncertain situation.[6]

Beyond the Tagus river south and west toward New Castile and Extremadura the annual rainfall amounts to less than twenty inches (as against between forty-five to eighty inches in Galicia and in some parts of the northern, mountainous regions) and the soil is thin and poor.[7] In these central regions of Spain the number of peasant proprietors was considerably smaller than in the north while *latifundios* were not as prevalent as in Andalusia. However, in those parts of Extremadura where stock-breeding continued important vast estates predominated as in Andalusia. By and large, throughout central Spain the peasants lived in abject poverty. In Extremadura the lot of the *yuntero*, the landless peasant whose only resource was a team of ploughing mules or oxen with which he journeyed from estate to estate in search of work, was most precarious.

The only region in Spain where the peasant could be counted prosperous and content (save the more modest prosperity of many peasant communities in the north of Spain, particularly in Navarra) was the Levante, which contained the provinces of Valencia and Murcia. It is an almost rainless area, but the soil consists of deposits washed down from the central tableland and is remarkably fertile. However, only the peasant who possessed a plot of land in one of the *vegas*, or irrigated districts, could be counted prosperous. The *vegas* constituted the most productive agricultural districts in all Europe, yielding three to five harvests in a single year.[8] The Valencian or Murcian peasant who worked the land of the surrounding dry, unwatered plain, and he was in the majority, suffered a poverty differing only in detail from that of the Andalusian *bracero* or Extremaduran *yuntero*.

The land problem in Spain had profoundly important social and political implications. In more than half of Spain's provinces only 2 per cent of the people owned more than 65 per cent of the land while more than 75 per cent of the people owned less than 5 per cent of the land as recently as 1931.[9] Among a people described by an eminent Spaniard [10] "as a '*pueblo*' people, an agricultural race of rural temperament," great discontent and unrest on the one hand and fear and repression on the other were the inevitable concomitants of such vast economic disparities.

The history of Spain is replete with risings and revolts. In the main these have emanated from the pueblo, from the mass in the lump without the leaven of an interested, directorial class, for nowhere in Europe is the mass of people so profoundly self-conscious, so morally integrated, and at the same time so isolated from the life and thought of the ruling classes.[11] Risings of the *Comuneros* in defense of the *concejo abierto* and *cabildo*, organs of self-government in medieval Spanish towns and villages, risings amongst the Catalans and Basques in defense of their *fueros*, or local liberties, the expulsion of the Moriscos in 1609, an action that received its force from the will of the people and was successful despite the opposition of the great landlords who had found in the Moriscos a source of cheap, servile labor,[12] the surging forth of the Spanish people (except in Catalonia) in support of the Bourbons against the Austrian Archduke Charles during the War of the Spanish Succession when the latter was favored by the Spanish aristocracy and episcopacy, all attested to the capacity for militant action of the Spanish pueblo. The heroic uprising of the Spanish masses against Napoleon gave guerrilla war its name. The spontaneous mass movment in defense of the Republic in July, 1936, was to demonstrate anew the profound self-consciousness and moral cohesion of the Spanish folk.

Yet, magnificent as these sporadic bursts of energy were, they meant little in terms of the betterment of Spanish life. The virtues of the Spanish pueblo were also its defects. Folk loyalties were symptoms of an essential conservatism just as the wide gulf that separated the masses from the ruling classes was the mark of social stagnation. And, objectively, given the limited industrial development of Spain, the Spanish peasant could not follow his northern European counterpart to the city. Forced to remain on the land and to endure a crushing poverty, his estrangement from the life above him became virtually complete.

Spanish publicists—from the priest Juan de Mariana in the sixteenth century through the eighteenth century economist Gaspar Melchor de Jovellanos to the "Generation of '98"—had addressed themselves to the agrarian and other economic ills which afflicted Spain and had come forth with brilliant diagnoses and bold remedies. Moreover, from the Throne and from the Cortes had come promises of and plans for land reform. There had been no dearth of ideas and good intentions. However, precious little of all this had been translated into practical achievement. For, in the view of the Spanish grandees and landlords—and in the end it was their opinions which mattered—the effective solution of the land problem lay in the establishment and steady strengthening of the *Guardia Civil* and in the bringing to perfection the techniques of power of the cacique.

The Civil Guard, a para-military, rural constabulary, was organized in 1844. It took the place of the local militias which in many instances had proved politically unreliable. The original purpose of the Civil Guard was to put down banditry, principally in the south of Spain. It should be remembered, however, that this was when banditry was at least in part a manifestation of peasant intransigence, a species of peasant revolt not confined to Spain but found wherever extreme poverty and ruthless oppression coexisted. The character of Andalusian banditry was to change in later years, becoming to a great extent but another instrument in the apparatus of power of the cacique.[13] For the maintenance of order in the rural areas of Spain the Civil Guard was peculiarly well suited. In personnel and organization it was probably the most reliable and efficient of the various branches of the Spanish military establishment. It selected its recruits with care, subjected them to a rigorous discipline, imbued them with an *esprit de corps,* and thereupon established them in barracks far from their native villages. Armed with rifles and later with machine guns, never permitted to leave the barracks unarmed or alone, forbidden to marry women of the village or even to fraternize with the villagers, the gray-clad troopers with the black, odd-shaped, patent-leather hats constituted a veritable army of occupation. For the maintenance of order in the rural areas of Spain the Civil Guard was peculiarly well suited, indeed, but at the price of the unflagging hatred of the peasant population.[14]

The cacique was the political "boss" in rural Spain. An insight into his role is gleaned when it is recalled that the word is of Indian origin and that, at the time of the *Conquista*, the Spaniards, through what amounted to a system of intimidation and bribery, availed themselves of the authority and prestige of various Indian chiefs and headmen, or caciques, to insure the tranquillity of the natives while Spanish power was being consolidated. Thus the cacique served as the intermediary between the white conquerors and the native masses. This is not to suggest that the Spaniards, in organizing the Conquest in this fashion, were political innovators. This system was already old at the time of Rome. (In more recent times, it was used with singular success by the British in India.) However, it does not appear in modern Europe, at least in developed form, until the advent of political democracy and the enfranchisement of the masses. The Spanish cacique, usually a local landlord, was distinguished by the nearly complete success he achieved in corrupting and negating what little democracy there was in the Spanish countryside. Like every "boss," he built his "machine" by an adroit manipulation of public apathy and individual fear, through fraudulent elections, corruption, and force. Able to dispense favors and to set aside legitimate claims with equal facility, to threaten with immediate reprisals any one who dared to oppose him (in addition to the punitive powers of the Civil Guard and the local courts the cacique could turn against any recalcitrant the fists, knives, and guns of his private gang of ruffians), the cacique was the substantive power behind the façade of constituted civil and legal authority. Of course, like Iago, he put money in his purse and in the purses of his friends. Quite outrageously. But he was the indispensable agent of the government in Madrid.

With poverty and hunger, the ubiquitous Civil Guard and the omnipotent cacique the sure tokens of his lot, it would be assumed that the Spanish peasant, particularly the Andalusian, would have been persuaded that the prospect of a better life did not exist. In times past he had found solace and considerable support in the Church, especially among the lower clergy who had often fought at his side against oppressive landlords and foreign usurpers. How-

ever, by the middle of the nineteenth century, the social force of
the Spanish Church was largely spent and the Spanish peasant,
particularly in the south and along the Mediterranean coast, increasingly sought inspiration and support in ideas and programs
not those of Spanish Catholicism. It is important to appreciate the
extent and the finality of the estrangement of the Spanish masses
from Spanish Catholicism because from it dates the advent and
vigorous development of anarchism in Spain. This movement, although an importation from abroad, came in time to express the
individualistic temperament and quixotism of many Spaniards. Indeed, in Spain anarchism found its natural habitat.[15]

The Spanish Church had been truly great, reaching the apogee
of its spiritual and intellectual vigor in the era of Spanish ascend-
ancy, that is, almost the span of the sixteenth and seventeenth
centuries. By 1650, with Spain in decline, the power of the Spanish
Church to originate, to inspire, and to lead had begun to wane.
With the coming of the twentieth century, while it remained in
possession of considerable wealth (however, the nature of its property holdings had changed during the previous decades and from
the single largest landowner it had become the single largest capitalist in Spain) [16] and while it continued to be the decisive influence
in both lower and higher education, the Church ceased to be, in
significant measure, the locus of the spiritual values of the Spanish
people. In many villages of New Castile, for example, only about
5 per cent of the people attended Mass.[17] In Andalusia but 1 per
cent of the male population attended Mass.[18] Irreligion was widespread in Madrid, and even more so in Barcelona and Valencia.[19]
In one Madrid parish, a rich and fashionable one at that, 25 per cent
of the children born were not baptized.[20] Civil marriages and civil
funerals were not uncommon and among the less sophisticated as
well as among the intelligentsia a frank skepticism was voiced regarding many dogmas of the Church.[21]

Many factors had been at work to bring about this estrangement
of the Spanish people from the Spanish Church but not the least
important was the unwillingness or the inability of Spanish

Catholicism to initiate a program of social reform that, attuned to modern realities, might serve to alleviate the desperate poverty of the masses and at the same time to rekindle in the Church its sense of mission. Little was attempted and less accomplished along the lines of Catholic social action pursued in other parts of Europe following the appearance, in 1891, of Pope Leo XIII's encyclical, *Rerum Novarum.* By forsaking its historic, albeit desultory, role of popular champion and aligning itself unreservedly with the ruling classes, the Spanish Church ceased to have vital meaning in the day-to-day experiences of a large segment of the population. Franz Borkenau put it: "The Spanish masses have relinquished the Spanish Church, not because they have lost the traditional religious fervour of the Spanish race, but because the Spanish Church has lost it. . . ." [22]

On September 28, 1864, in St. Martin's Hall in London, the First International was founded. The socialist movement, having established from divers elements a coherent body of doctrine, entered a period of practical achievement that was to make it a significant force in the political life of modern Europe. Socialism, of course, was to adapt itself to the temperament, the cultural traditions, the political institutions, and the economic circumstances of the various peoples among whom it came to be an important influence. It, nevertheless, was to continue to exhibit a doctrinal consistency, a fundamental rationale, that owed much to the philosophic synthesis that was Marxism. During the middle decades of the nineteenth century socialism reached Spain and soon gained an important following, largely in Castile and other regions of central Spain. However, almost from the beginning, Spanish socialism was forced to compete as a mass movement with anarchism. For on entering Spain anarchism achieved its broadest success. Neither in Russia nor in Italy, the only other European nations where it was important, did anarchism win the wide acceptance that it gained in Spain. It was particularly strong in the south among the peasant masses of Andalusia, along the Mediterranean coast among the most wretched peasants of Murcia and Valencia, and among the industrial workers of Catalonia.

While notions of the inherent goodness of man and of the essentially coercive nature of institutionalized authority, especially that of the State, can be traced back through the Enlightenment and the Middle Ages to the early Christians, the Essenes, and even the Sophists of ancient Greece, the modern anarchist movement, reaffirming these concepts and postulating others, can be said to have begun with the English social reformer, William Godwin (1756–1836). However, it was not so much from Godwin nor from the French Utopians who followed him as from Mikhail Bakunin (1814–1876) that Spanish anarchism received its original impetus. The Russian aristocrat turned revolutionist brought to anarchism a militant atheism, collectivist principles of social organization, and the frank advocacy of violence in the destruction of the existing social order. His ideas were introduced into Spain by Giuseppe Fanelli, an Italian architect and engineer who had been converted to anarchism by Bakunin himself and who, in 1868, went forth to proselytize the Spaniards. There was considerable doctrinal affinity between Bakuninist anarchism and Marxist socialism and the followers of both had joined together in the establishment of the First International. However, basic differences existed between them concerning such important matters as party organization and discipline, the nature of and approach to political activity, and ultimate expectations with respect to the society of the future. In the final analysis, the cleavage between the Marxists and the Bakuninists—that was soon to result in open antagonism—reflected the fact that while the Marxists thought and acted in terms of the politically advanced, industrially developed social order of northern Europe, the Bakuninists shaped their ideas to the needs and hopes of the economically backward, ruthlessly oppressed peasant masses of southern and eastern Europe.

In a nation such as Spain, so little affected by the industrial revolution, without an important middle class, without firm traditions of political democracy and civil liberty, still agrarian, illiterate, and socially inert, the anarchism of Bakunin supplied the exigent demand of a wretchedly poor and cruelly oppressed yet intelligent and resentful peasantry for a viable faith. Simplicity and agelessness marked these men and time and technique had little or no meaning in their lives. One great blow and there would be an end to tyranny and the triumph of a brotherhood that was as much of the pristine past as of the future. For Spanish anarchism thought and acted not in terms of modern industrial society, but in terms of the land, the village, small-scale manufacturing, and simple and direct relationships. It was motivated at least as much by a sense of injustice and outrage, by concern for the moral regeneration of society, as by the desire for material betterment and progress.[23] These atavistic, moralistic attitudes of Spanish anarchism were to prove extremely significant when, in July, 1936, Spain was engulfed by civil war and the Spanish government had to work the political wizardry of permitting sufficient scope to the revolutionary forces which constituted its principal support while at the same time achieving enough social cohesion in its rear to enable it to wage war effectively.

The Italian political scientist, Gaetano Mosca, believed that the measure and vitality of the "civilization" of a community lay, quintessentially, in its legal processes—its system of jurisprudence, the independence enjoyed by the judiciary, the swift and equitable administration of justice, and the vigilant protection of the legal rights of the individual. He held, further, that the principal menace to the establishment and maintenance of a truly civilized legal order in society arose from the single greatest repository of armed power within society, the army. The need for some sort of military power being imperative, it devolves upon the community, if it would establish or would preserve the essential elements of civilized life, to seek a political formula that insures the national defense and the maintenance of internal order but prevents the subversion of the law by this armed and organized force.[24]

The history of modern Spain is replete with *pronunciamientos,*

or uprisings of the army chiefs and their regiments against constituted authority. For in modern Spain the political formula of
which Mosca spoke has never been found. Since the middle decades
of the nineteenth century the army in Spain has constituted an
imperium in imperio and has acted as the ultimate arbiter of the
political destinies of the nation. To make matters worse, Spanish
officers, as a body, were ill-trained, ignorant, and avid for the
spoils that power brings. They resembled more the condottieri of
Renaissance Italy than the officer corps of a modern European
army.

The Spanish officer class was composed, in the main, of sons
of aristocrats and landlords. Yet promotion from the ranks, if
rare, was not impossible. Over the years the number of *oficiales
de cuchara* ("spoon-officers," as they were popularly called because as privates they had eaten with large spoons from a common
dish) [25] was not unimpressive. However, whether a gentleman-
officer or a "spoon-officer," the Spanish officer exhibited all the
arrogance and none of the technical proficiency and conspicuous
success in war of the Prussian Junker. Of doubtful value in the
event of war, the Spanish officer was less a soldier and more a
racketeering police agent. Although budgetary appropriations for
the military establishment were consistently adequate to provide
Spain with respectable military strength, the army (and the navy)
suffered from acute shortages of artillery, transport, and other
necessary equipment, corruption and peculation being rife in high
places. Moreover, the number of officers far exceeded the real needs
of the Spanish army. In 1931 there were 21,000 officers in the
Spanish army or as many as comprised the German officer corps
at the outbreak of the First World War.[26] This plethora of officers was a permanent characteristic of the modern Spanish army,
there being, over the years, approximately one officer, active or
reserve, to every six enlisted men.[27] Suffering from poor and insufficient professional training and lacking even the rudiments of
a general education, the Spanish officer cut a sorry figure. Yet, ar-
rogant, vain, fustian in speech and manner, he was extremely caste-

WINGATE COLLEGE LIBRARY
WINGATE, N. C.

conscious, clinging tenaciously to his numerous privileges and many immunities. He claimed the right, until 1931, to try in military courts civilians who had offended the honor of the army!

J. Álvarez del Vayo, who as the son of a Spanish general was reared in the atmosphere of the barracks, said of the Spanish officer class:

In the Infantry Academy of Toledo they had a custom of physically nailing to the wall the textbook on the last subject passed, a formal declaration that the recent graduate would never open a serious book again in his lifetime. This helps explain the general lack of culture of the Spanish officer, the catastrophic effects of which have always made themselves felt in Spanish politics. The average officer, not knowing anything about anything, has no interest in life other than his career; he cannot, as in other countries, make a success in business or take up a different profession. As a consequence, holding his position, winning promotion in the Army, and the aggrandizement of the Army itself, become his supreme objectives; and he is always disposed to follow the first dictator who reduces by half the budgetary allowance for education and other social institutions in order to increase three-fold the appropriation for the Army. . . . This, rather than a spirit of romantic adventure, is the reason why *pronunciamiento* is a Spanish word and, what is worse, a typically Spanish vice.[28]

It should be noted that the Spanish army had not always been what it had become. In past centuries the Spanish army had possessed first-rate equipment, excellent organization, discipline, and morale. Its fighting qualities had made Spain the most formidable military power in Europe. Moreover, from the sixteenth century to the Napoleonic Wars and for a brief time thereafter Spanish military traditions were at least as democratic as those of other European armies.[29] However, by the close of the seventeenth century Spanish military power was at an end. By the last of the Carlist Wars the democratic traditions of the Spanish military had all but vanished, having succumbed to the general malaise of Spanish society.[30]

The only two important foreign conflicts in which the Spanish army has engaged since the Napoleonic Wars, the war against the United States in 1898 and the operations in Morocco from 1909 to 1926, were ignominious failures as military enterprises. The former resulted in the final expulsion of Spain from the Western Hemisphere while the latter saw Spain victorious over Abd-el-Krim in Morocco only because of the active support of the French army. After these events, the decline in prestige of the Spanish officer class was precipitous. Throughout Spain a clamor arose against the ineptitude, the technical incompetence, the vainglory and arrogance of the generals. In such circumstances it was inevitable that the virtually autonomous status of the military hierarchy in Spanish society would come under attack, exacerbating the antipathy and distrust between the people and the army.

And the army? Well, it nursed its resentment and prepared its revenge. The last *pronunciamiento* had not yet been heard in Spain.

Much of the criticism leveled against the army, as well as against the Church and the monarchy, came from the small but highly articulate liberal movement. Spanish liberalism, like Spanish socialism but unlike Spanish anarchism, had few important peculiarly Hispanic characteristics. The main structure of its ideas and methods was built of European timber. During the enlightened reign of Charles III (1759–1788) much of the political and economic thought of the philosophes had entered Spain. With the coming of the French Revolution and the wars of Napoleon, Spain increasingly felt the impact of liberal thought. The constitution of 1812 and the revolt of the Spanish army at Cádiz in 1820 were inspired by liberal ideas. It was during this period, too, that Freemasonry won an important following in Spain. By the middle of the nineteenth century Spanish liberalism was in violent conflict with the Spanish Church as well as with the traditional monarchy. It attacked the political power of the hierarchy, the great wealth of the Orders, particularly that of the Jesuits (it was during this period that the Spanish Church lost its preeminent economic position as a landowner and regained it as a capitalist), and the virtual monopoly of education enjoyed by the Catholic Church. With the establishment of the First Spanish Republic following the army revolt against Queen Isabel in 1868, liberalism was momentarily triumphant in Spain.

The Spanish Republic of the seventies proved abortive, however, for the liberal movement failed to sink its roots deeply into the soil of Spain. It remained what it always had been, a small, artic-ulate movement of middle-class lawyers, doctors, teachers, writers, journalists, and other intellectuals, some merchants, and a few generals and politicians. The weakness of the liberal movement was the weakness of the middle classes in Spain and this, in turn, reflected the slow, tenuous development of Spanish capitalism. Not only was capitalism late in appearing, it was largely restricted to the outlying regions of Spain, to a few districts in Catalonia, the Asturias, and the Basque country. Politically dominant Castile proved well-nigh impervious to the establishment of capitalistic institutions. The result was that Spain, unlike England, France, Germany, and even Italy, could not assimilate and form into a new and coherent social order the enterprise, the technique, the acquisitive psychology, the materialism and progressivism, and the concomitant political and intellectual tendencies of modern capi-talistic society.

Unable to impose its values on Spanish society, incapable of founding a broadly significant political movement among the Spanish masses, ever something of a pariah among the vested in-stitutions of Spain, Spanish capitalism nevertheless managed to maintain itself and even to expand the scope of its activities. Of the many factors which contributed to this steady if painfully slow development of Spanish capitalism three are of particular im-portance. First, capitalism was the carrier of modern industry and technology to Spain. To the extent that machines and other ap-purtenances of modern life appeared in Spain, Spanish capitalism prospered not merely in the monetary sense but also in the more important regard that its organization, its institutions, and its spirit, albeit minimally, came to impinge on the whole of Spanish life. After all, even in the days of the political predominance of the *Mesta*, Castile had found it impossible to neglect utterly the interests of important commercial centers in Spain.[31] Secondly, Spanish capitalists, eschewing the rigors of competitive enterprise and banding together in monopolies and quasi-monopolies, achieved sufficient unity of purpose to constitute a powerful lobby in Spanish politics. As a consequence, they were often able to barter their political support for economic concessions from Madrid. Finally, the Spanish economy was appendant in certain vital respects to the advanced industrialism of Western Europe. In mining, in public utilities and transport, in the armaments industries, such was the extent of foreign holdings that the situation approached colonialism.[32] Thus, "Spanish capitalism" was in significant measure but European capitalism in Spain.

As has been noted, Spanish capitalistic enterprises were mainly concentrated in the outlying regions of the nation. Catalonia, for example, accounted for only 10 per cent of Spanish agricultural production but for more than 85 per cent of Spanish industrial production.[33] While the manufacture of textiles was largely in the hands of Catalans, the iron and steel industry was controlled by Basques. The mines and mills of Guipúzcoa and Vizcaya could supply, by 1932, Spain's normal requirements of certain industrial products sevenfold, according to a statement made in the Cortes by Indalecio Prieto, the Socialist leader.[34]

In the period between the First World War and the Spanish Civil War the two most prominent figures in Spanish capitalism were Francisco Cambó and Juan March Ordinas, the one a Catalan and the other a Majorcan. Both men played important roles in the political as well as the economic life of Spain. Cambó controlled the huge power company, Compañía Hispano-americana de Electricidad (linked with British interests in Argentina in the Primitiva Gas Company of Buenos Aires),[35] that declared profits of almost 105 million gold pesetas in 1930.[36] At the same time, Cambó was the leader of the Lliga Catalana (Catalan League), dominated by Catalan industrialists and manufacturers but supported by a part of the Catalan middle class. Important in both Catalan and Spanish politics, it sought to influence the economic and tariff policies of

Madrid. The League was politically conservative and only moderately separatist. March, whose holdings in tobacco, oil, and shipping made him one of the wealthiest men in Spain and, perhaps, in Europe, preferred to play a less conspicuous and more devious political role. The old Majorcan smuggler had a natural propensity for clandestine operations. From 1931 to the revolt of the generals in July, 1936, his vast fortune was a many-pronged weapon aimed at the vitals of the Republic.[37]

The mineral wealth of Spain is both considerable and varied. Throughout the Peninsula are important deposits of iron, coal, copper, tin, lead, tungsten, pyrites, and manganese. Spain and Italy between them enjoy a virtual monopoly of the world's supply of mercury, the district of Almadén in Spain being by far the single largest producer of this industrially important mineral. The economic eclipse of Spain, first by the Netherlands, then by England, France, and other European nations, was not, then, implicit in a paucity of primary materials necessary to the emergence of a modern industrial civilization, as might be said of the decline of Italy following the Renaissance. While the rapid disintegration of Spanish power in the late seventeenth century is not susceptible of simple analysis, it is abundantly evident that political and semi-political factors militated against the effectual utilization of considerable natural resources.[38] Politically dominant, agrarian Castile had set its face against the future.

In more recent times, Madrid has been content to allow foreign capitalists to develop and to control important mining and industrial enterprises in Spain. Perhaps the best copper to be found anywhere in Europe is located in the Spanish province of Huelva. By 1930 the British Rio Tinto Company possessed some 32,000 acres of mining land in this region with capital assets estimated at more that £3,750,000.[39] A group of foreign financiers—Belgians, Frenchmen, Englishmen, and Canadians—controlled a number of Catalan hydroelectric power plants which together supplied about 80 per cent of the hydroelectric power needs of the region. This international combination was known as the Canadiense, its parent firm being registered in Toronto as the Barcelona Power, Light, and Traction Company.[40] The United States-controlled International Telegraph and Telephone Corporation owned and operated the Spanish telephone system. In this connection it should be noted that while the total of United States investments in Europe decreased by about $100,000,000 from 1929 to 1936 the total of United States investments in Spain increased from $72,230,000 to $80,533,000 during the same period.[41] The British Vickers-Armstrong firm indirectly controlled Constructora Naval, a Spanish company that for a time enjoyed a monopoly of warship construction in Spain.[42]

Foreign control of valuable industrial property in Spain was not a negligible factor in Spanish politics. The maintenance and expansion of these holdings, their possible redivision, the further penetration of the Spanish economy by foreign capitalistic interests were matters of considerable importance both in Madrid and in the chancelleries of Europe, as events during the Spanish Civil War and the Second World War were to demonstrate.

In the thirty or forty years prior to the Civil War there were in Spain only two politico-social movements which could be described as mass organizations existing outside the traditional institutional pattern of Spanish society. These were anarchism with its loosely associated anarcho-syndicalist labor organization, the Confederación Nacional del Trabajo (National Confederation of Labor, known simply as the C.N.T.) and socialism with its closely affiliated labor organization, the Unión General de Trabajadores (General Union of Workers, known simply as the U.G.T.). Within the traditional institutional pattern of Spanish society Catholicism, of course, continued to command the support of millions of Spaniards. However, their adherence to Catholicism was essentially formal, a conditioned reflex, as it were, to venerable symbols, rites, and ceremonies. As has been noted, Catholicism, as a dynamic and meaningful social movement, did not exist in modern Spain save, perhaps, in the Basque regions where in Guipúzcoa and Vizcaya it was moderately progressive and in Álava and particularly Navarra it was fiercely traditional.

Anarcho-syndicalism developed from the union of anarchist ideology with syndicalist conceptions of labor organization and action. These conceptions had first arisen out of the intellectual and social fermentation in France toward the fin-de-siècle, their chief exponent being Fernand Pelloutier. Pelloutier, an anarchist, taught that all workers should be united in a single labor organization, that the social struggle should be confined to the economic arena, that the principal weapon of the working classes should be the "strike," general, violent, and conclusive. While Pelloutier's ideas were not profoundly original, being implicit in anarchist ideology, his formulation of them guided the organization of the first French labor syndicates. From France syndicalist ideas reached Spain and Italy and even the United States where a syndicalist labor organization known as the Industrial Workers of the World flourished for a time. In Spain syndicalism achieved considerable success, becoming the organizational expression of anarchism in the Spanish trade union movement. It was particularly strong among the workers of Catalonia where anarchist traditions, separatist sentiments, and the insensate violence of the social struggle precluded the growth of socialism.

Spanish socialism, like Spanish liberalism, lacked the *hispanidad*, the cult of courage, of self and selflessness, the moral fervor and desperate violence, of anarchism. Well-organized and disciplined and active politically, it was more distinctly European. Its leadership was largely Castilian and centralist Castile could see in the Catalan nuptials of Bakunin and Pelloutier only an illicit act. Strongest in central Spain, particularly in Madrid, where there was little industry, weakest in Catalonia where industry predominated, moderately successful in the Asturias and the Basque regions where mining and manufacturing flourished but where, particularly among the Basques, Catholic and separatist sentiments persisted, Spanish socialism was built upon the shifting sands of a backward,

almost pre-capitalistic economic order. In this regard it shared the
limitations and weaknesses of Spanish liberalism. Yet, unlike liberalism, socialism had been able to build a mass movement in Spain,
an achievement greatly facilitated by the absence of other viable
social movements. For socialism appealed to those elements of the
Spanish working classes who, turning from a Catholicism devoid
of social vitality and meaning and spurning the heroics and per-
sonalism of anarchism, saw in Marxism the one coherent, practical
embodiment of their needs and hopes.

From the days of Pablo Iglesias, one of the founders of Spanish
socialism, to those of Francisco Largo Caballero, Indalecio Prieto,
and Julián Besteiro, the leaders of Spanish socialism on the eve
of the Civil War, the main thrust of the socialist movement was
increasingly reformist. In this respect, as in others, it paralleled
the political evolution of the other socialist parties of Europe.
Thus, while it continued to use the language of revolution and
to engage in verbal tilts with the liberal Republicans, it stead-
fastly adhered to the Second (Socialist) International and, in the
main, to parliamentary methods.

Left extremists who disagreed with the methods and aims of
the Socialist party founded, soon after the Russian Revolution, the
Spanish Communist party. And, in turn, disgruntled communists,
along with certain anarchist elements, organized the (Trotskyist)
Left Communist party. However, communism, of whatever de-
scription, was a negligible factor in Spanish politics and in the
Spanish labor movement until the outbreak of the Civil War.[43]

The principal organizations of the Right in Spanish politics on
the eve of the Civil War were the Communión Tradicionalista
(Traditionalist Communion or simply Traditionists), whose
strength lay among the Carlists of Navarra and in their armed
bands known as *requetés;* the Confederación Española de Derechas
Autónomas (Spanish Confederation of Autonomous Right Parties
and known simply as the CEDA), whose leader was José María
Gil Robles, an inveterate schemer whose role in Spanish politics
was not unlike that of Franz von Papen in Germany during the

winter of 1932–1933; and the Falange Española (Spanish Phalanx), organized in 1932 by José Antonio Primo de Rivera, the son of the former dictator, and composed largely of the *señorito* element (or "gilded youth") of the Andalusian cities and of Madrid. The Communión Tradicionalista or the Carlists reflected the conservatism and Catholicism of the isolated mountaineers of Navarra and was important only because of the fighting qualities of the *requetés*. The CEDA was a hodge-podge of conservative elements whose nucleus was the Acción Popular (Popular Action Party) of Gil Robles and whose common denominator was fear of the social change posited by the existence of the Republic. Notwithstanding the influence that fascism, especially the clerical fascism of Dollfuss' Austria, exercised on Gil Robles' thinking, the CEDA remained essentially negative in its program, centrifugal in its organization, and incapable of effective political action. The Falange Española was frankly fascist, finding its archetype in Mussolini's Italy. However, the Falange Española, even after it had merged with other fascist groups in 1934 to become the Falange Española de las Juntas de Ofensiva Nacional—Sindicalista (the Spanish Phalanx of the Councils of the National-Syndicalist Offensive, but known simply as the Falange), remained small and unimportant until the beginning of the Civil War. For fascism, depending for mass support on a large, disgruntled middle class, could not flourish in Spain.

Thus the attack upon the Republic, when it came, did not and could not come from Spanish fascism, from a vast, embittered, militant middle class thrown against an abortive socialist revolution; it came from the semi-feudal, traditional centers of power in Spain. The army was the hinge on which the political destinies of the nation hung. Its leading generals, José Sanjurjo, Emilio Mola, Miguel Cabanellas, Manuel Goded, and Francisco Franco, as well as the Unión Militar Española (Spanish Military Union, a secret organization of army officers) were determined to preserve the traditional powers and prerogatives of the army against the encroaching antimilitarism of the Republic. The army found natural allies in the episcopacy, the landed aristocracy, business and financial circles, and politicians such as José María Gil Robles, José Antonio Primo de Rivera, and José Calvo Sotelo. Calvo Sotelo, who had been minister of finance during the dictatorship of Primo de Rivera and was now a member of the Cortes, emerged as the leading civilian opponent of the Republic. A particularly able and energetic man, he sought to weld into a single, compact force the various elements of the Spanish Right which were violently opposed to the Republic.[44] His activities involved important persons both within and outside Spain.[45]

The assassination of Calvo Sotelo in the early morning of July 13, 1936, served ostensibly as the occasion for the long-prepared revolt of the generals.

II

The Spanish Republic and the Revolt of the Generals

ON January 28, 1930, Don Miguel Primo de Rivera, having lost the confidence of the king and of the military caste whose support had enabled him to establish his dictatorship six years and four months earlier, proffered his resignation and left Spain. On March 16, 1930, the corpulent Andalusian died in Paris. The last year of his rule had been marked by increasing economic difficulties and by growing unrest. The decline of the peseta to a point lower than at any time since the beginning of the century had preceded the fall of the dictator. The collapse of the dictatorship, moreover, presaged the end of the monarchy. The army officers who had forsaken the dictator would not now give their support to his royal master.

By making Primo de Rivera the scapegoat for the ills of Spain Alfonso XIII had hoped to preserve the throne for himself and his dynasty. What he gained was but a short-term lease on the Escorial. After the municipal elections of April 12, 1931, which declared beyond cavil the republican sentiments of a majority of Spaniards, Alfonso found it expedient to leave Spain forthwith.

At two o'clock in the morning of Wednesday, April 15, 1931, the provisional government of the Second Spanish Republic formally took office. The ancient throne had fallen with little violence and less bloodshed.

The life of the Second Spanish Republic was short and tempestuous. The eight-year period between April, 1931, when the Re-

public was proclaimed, and April, 1939, when the organized resistance of the Republican armies came to an end, can be divided
into four distinct phases. The first phase continued somewhat
more than two years, closing with the general elections of November 19, 1933. During this time Spain was ruled by a coalition
of conservative and moderately liberal republicans. Among them
were Niceto Alcalá Zamora, a lawyer of Andalusian birth and a
staunch Catholic, a former minister of the old monarchy and the
first president of the new Republic; Alejandro Lerroux, a Catalan
politician who through the alchemy of his oratory had been able
to transmute fine phrases into high office and material wealth;
Miguel Maura, a man of wealth and conservative temperament
whose family originally hailed from Majorca but was now en-
rolled in the new Castilian nobility; Fernando de los Ríos, the
scion of an intellectual family and himself a professor at the University of Granada; Santiago Casares Quiroga, a hard-bitten,
veteran politician from Galicia with an almost puritanical devotion
to duty; Luis Nicolau d'Olwer, a Catalan intellectual who was an
authority on medieval churches; and Manuel Azaña.

Manuel Azaña was indubitably the moving spirit, as well as the
leading figure, of this first republican coalition. Urbane, well-
educated, an excellent orator, Azaña embodied most of the virtues
and many of the failings of the Spanish, middle-class intellectual.
He was intelligent, strong-willed, and honest, yet in his vision of
Spain he was a political romantic. For his approach to Spanish
politics was predicated on the existence of a modern, economically
developed, politically advanced Spain, a Spain in which a large,
alert middle class stood as the guarantor of civil liberty and parliamentary democracy. Like another famous Spaniard (but with his
gaze fixed on the future rather than on the past), he persisted in
tilting with windmills. A good Voltairean, he seemed more concerned with exorcising the spirit of feudal Catholicism from Spain
with his fountain pen than with ameliorating the hard lot of the
peasant and the worker through basic land and economic reforms.
When events convinced him, at long last, that his conception of

Spanish political reality had been a delusion and a snare, he fell into an almost morbid apathy.

The principal achievement of the first two years of the Republic was the formulation and adoption of the Republican constitution by the Constituent Cortes. The constitution of 1931 was a remarkable document. It bore the mark of the Azañan dream in that it seemed, with one magnificent gesture, to transform Spain from a backward, semi-feudal nation into a modern, progressive, democratic state.[3] It began: "Spain is a democratic Republic of workers of all classes, organized in a regime of liberty and justice."[4] It continued: "the powers of all its organs [of government] emanate from the people."[5] "All Spaniards are equal before the law."[6] "The Spanish State has no official religion."[7] "Spain renounces war as an instrument of national policy."[8] It continued in a vein reminiscent of the high idealism that animated the framers of the Weimar constitution of the German Republic and of the humanitarianism and pacifist sentiments of contemporary statesmen such as the Frenchman, Aristide Briand, the German, Gustav Stresemann, and the American, Frank Kellogg.

However, certain proposals which had been put before the Constituent Cortes had aroused acrimonious and protracted debate. This was particularly true of matters which pertained to the role of the Church in the new Spain. As finally adopted, Article 26 of the constitution declared that "all religious confessions are to be considered as Associations subject to a special law."[9] It declared further that "the State, the regions, the provinces, and the municipalities will not maintain, favor, nor economically assist religious institutions, associations, and churches."[10] It added that "payment of the clergy [by the State] will cease within a period of two years."[11] Moreover, it ordered dissolved those religious orders which require a vow of obedience to an authority other than the legitimate authority of the State (to wit: the Society of Jesus). "Their property is to be nationalized and used for charitable and educational purposes."[12]

However, the next article stated that "liberty of conscience and the right to profess and freely practice any religion are guaranteed in Spain provided public morals are not offended." [13]

Work, in its diverse forms, was held to be a social obligation, enjoying the protection of the laws.[14] "The Republic guarantees to all workers the conditions necessary to a dignified existence." [15]

Primary education was to be compulsory and free.[16] Instruction was to be secular and inspired by "ideals of human solidarity." [17] But the State recognized the right of the churches to teach their respective doctrines in their own establishments, subject to inspection by the State.[18]

Having continued at its task throughout the summer and fall, the Constituent Cortes ratified the constitution on December 9, 1931.

However, precious little of this fundamental law was translated into living reality in the months and years which followed. The peasant masses of Andalusia and Extremadura, the miners of the Asturias, the industrial workers of Barcelona and Bilbao could find but cold comfort in this house of words. Yet, by and large, conservative and Catholic elements in the population viewed the republican constitution with distrust. They saw it as an "enabling act" which must eventually result in the complete subversion of the old way of life. Article 26 of the constitution, in particular, outraged the sensibilities of devout Catholics.

On August 10, 1932, General José Sanjurjo led a revolt against the Republic. The insurrection was quickly and easily suppressed by the government. But the abortive uprising was an earnest of the bitter, sanguinary struggle to come.

On November 19, 1933, thanks to the votes of the newly enfranchised women of Spain, to the outraged sensibilities of Catholics, and to the political indifference of the peasant masses, particularly in those regions where anarchist influence was strongest, the Right won the general elections. The second phase of the history of the Republic endured from November 19, 1933 to February 16, 1936, at which time the recently formed Frente Popular (Popular Front) triumphed at the polls. During this period Spain was ruled by a coalition of crypto-monarchists, quasi-fascists, and conservative republicans. The foremost leaders of the coalition were Alejandro Lerroux, whose demagogy and forensic skill have already been noted and who now served as popular ballast in the new government; Calvo Sotelo, the former finance minister under Primo de Rivera and an unregenerate monarchist; and José María Gil Robles, the leader of Acción Popular. Inasmuch as Acción Popular constituted the core of the Confederación Española de Derechas Autónomas which controlled 110 seats in the new Cortes and was thus the single largest element in the governmental coalition, Gil Robles occupied a position on the Right analogous to that recently held by Manuel Azaña on the Left.

Clever rather than intelligent, bold in speech but hesitant in action, an inveterate schemer, Gil Robles sought power not like a lion but like a jackal. Yet for all his infernal cunning, the essence of his plan was simple enough. Unable to gain the premiership for himself, largely because of the personal animosity of President Alcalá Zamora, Gil Robles aimed to reduce the incumbent premier (who was, usually, Lerroux or, occasionally, a nonentity such as Ricardo Samper or Joaquín Chapaprieta) to a puppet. With the premier dependent on the parliamentary support of the CEDA, Gil Robles could effectually obstruct any program of action that the government might seek to realize. At the same time, Gil Robles could turn the Cortes into a public platform from which he could denounce the weakness, the incompetence, the lack of purpose of the government and, by implication, of the Republic itself. Confusion would give way to despair and despair to demoralization. First from the CEDA, then from the general public the cry would come for a "strong" leader, for a "strong" government. Thereupon Gil Robles could emerge in the panoply of the *jefe*, the "strong" leader, who would set things right again. The petty machinations of Alcalá Zamora would have come to nought. The lawyer from Córdoba would now have to summon the lawyer from Salamanca to the premiership. Wearing the toga of legitimate authority, Gil Robles could proceed to a fundamental revision of the constitution, thus destroying the substance while maintaining the form of the Republic.[19]

Confident, clever, forever scheming, Gil Robles bided his time. It never came. Lerroux was to head six different Cabinets while Gil Robles' silent revolution died in embryo.

As the failure of Azaña "to make the revolution" had led first to confusion and apathy and, ultimately, to a growing militancy on the extreme Left, so the failure of Gil Robles "to make the counter-revolution" led the Right to forsake indirect in favor of direct and violent means of destroying the Republic. The apostle of direct action against the Republic was Calvo Sotelo, the leading figure in the monarchist Renovación Española (Spanish Regeneration Party) whose nominal leader was Antonio Goicoechea. Calvo Sotelo and Gil Robles represented divergent political tendencies within the Spanish Right. However, as time passed and his quest for power continued futile, Gil Robles himself, frustrated and embittered, increasingly evinced a more militant attitude.

Thus the Right, seeking to set aside the modest reforms of the previous two years which it saw as dangerous precedents, interpreted the constitution and governed with a cavalier disregard for the proprieties of good government. The Cortes amnestied the Sanjurjo rebels and at the same time restored the death penalty to Spanish law. The provisions of the constitution which dealt with educational and land reform were not enforced. But a law was enacted that provided for the restitution of confiscated Church properties. Not satisfied with this, devout Catholics raised a clamor for a concordat with the Vatican. Meanwhile, in the conservative press an attack was launched against the limited autonomy that the Republic permitted the Catalans and Basques. To make matters worse, the effects of the world-wide economic depression were particularly severe in Spain and the Spanish masses suffered grievously. Thus, coupled with political repression went economic hardship. These were the "two black years" of the Spanish Republic.

In October, 1934, insurrectionary strikes occurred in Madrid and Barcelona. At the same time, the miners of the Asturias, members of the socialistic U.G.T. in the main, rose in revolt. In Madrid and Barcelona the government easily suppressed the poorly prepared workers. However, in the Asturias bitter and sanguinary fighting ensued. Lerroux appointed Generals Francisco Franco and Manuel Goded his military advisers. Franco persuaded the government to dispatch African contingents to the Asturias.[20] Legionnaires and Moors commanded by General López Ochoa carried terror into the Asturian towns and villages. Thousands were killed, thousands wounded, thousands beaten and tortured, thousands more imprisoned.[21] The hard-fighting miners were crushed. The Moors were back in Spain for the first time since 1492 and in the Asturias which they had never conquered. The military lessons of this brief but bloody struggle were not lost upon Franco and the army chiefs who in less than two years were themselves to revolt, relying to a great extent on the fighting qualities of these same Legionnaires and Moors.

It would appear that the time was propitious for the Right, seizing on the Asturian revolt as a pretext, to proceed to the outright destruction of the Republic and to the establishment of a dictatorship. But the dictatorship would need a dictator—there was the rub. Gil Robles was the logical choice and he was available, of course, but he was not acceptable to important elements of the conservative coalition. President Alcalá Zamora had successfully kept Gil Robles from the premiership. He could hardly be expected to countenance now the elevation of Gil Robles to supreme authority. Moreover, Alejandro Lerroux and his Radical Party, although they had permitted themselves to be manipulated and used by Gil Robles, demurred at the prospect of complete political oblivion. Lerroux had not pursued a political career for some thirty years not to have learned that the principal business of a politician is to remain in office. To make matters worse, Gil Robles had failed to achieve a satisfactory measure of agreement with Calvo Sotelo, Antonio Goicoechea, and the monarchists. Discrepant political approaches continued to keep them apart, a situa-

tion exacerbated, at the level of personalities, by the mutual dis-
like between Gil Robles and Goicoechea.[22] Of decisive importance
was the fact that Gil Robles and the CEDA did not enjoy the full
confidence of the army chiefs.[23] Thus, while the time was propitious
for a coup d'état, the other elements necessary to its success—
unity of purpose, a common approach, organizational coordination, effective liaison with the military, an able and trusted leader
—were lacking.

The inability of the Right to make a fist and strike gave the
Left an opportunity to recover from the defeat and demoralization
of these "black years." The struggle in the Asturias had witnessed
the first feeble attempts at working-class unity.[24] Now the courage, strength, and incipient unity which had come out of that
struggle served to rally the forces of the Left. As the truth about
the Asturias penetrated the official censorship the Left wove it into
an epic, replete with heroes and martyrs. Asturias became a household word in the tenements and hovels of Spain. The poignancy
and meaning which attended the word were accentuated by the
fact that thousands of Spaniards remained in exile and tens of
thousands still languished in prison.[25] The working classes, through
their political parties and labor organizations, came together in
a new and stronger unity and sought, too, closer ties with the liberal
middle classes which had become alarmed by the attempt of the
Lerroux–Gil Robles combination to undo all that had been
achieved in the period following April, 1931. The seeds of the
Frente Popular were germinant.

There is no real evidence to support the contention advanced
by some writers[26] that the political phenomenon that arose in
Europe in the mid-thirties and went by the name of the "Popular
Front" received its original impetus, its organizational structure,
and its program from Moscow through the agency of the Third
International. The origins of the Popular Front were considerably
more complex and infinitely less sinister than this view suggests.
The rise of fascism in Italy, the advent to power of Adolf Hitler
in Germany, the brutal suppression of the Austrian Socialists by

the Dollfuss government in February, 1934, the fascist-inspired
riots in Paris on February 6, 1934, which turned on the Stavisky
affair, the general disintegration of democratic institutions in much
of central and eastern Europe under the impact of the Great Depression, and the continued drift toward a second world war were
among the causative factors in the formation of the Popular Front.
Thus, while it is extremely doubtful that the French (or Spanish)
Communist party would have adhered to the Popular Front agreement without the sanction of the Comintern, the sources from
which the movement sprang were broader and deeper than a
Kremlin directive. Moscow's support of the Popular Front reflected a realistic appraisal of the domestic political situation in
Western Europe as well as a concern for its own interests.

It is not entirely coincidental that the birthplace of modern
European democracy should witness the first manifestation of
that alert solidarity that led directly to the establishment of the
Popular Front. The attempt of the Croix de Feu (Cross of Fire,
a fascist organization led by Lieutenant Colonel François de la
Rocque) and the Jeunesses Patriotes (Young Patriots, also a fascist
organization and led by the perfumer François Coty) to turn the
public clamor that arose after the financial trumpery involving
Serge Stavisky and a minister of the government had become
known into an attack against parliamentary democracy evoked a
vigorous response from the French working classes. A twenty-
four hour general strike called on February 12, 1934, was widely
supported by French working-class parties and organizations.[27]
The attempt of fascist elements to discredit and to overthrow
parliamentary democracy in France was frustrated. However, the
February riots had dramatically defined the danger that confronted the Republic and the French Left in particular. In the
months to come the French Left was to seek strength and security
in unity. With the conclusion of a pact between the Socialists
and Communists on July 27, 1934, impetus was given to the formation of a people's front. The Front Populaire, a political alliance
of the Socialists led by Léon Blum, the Communists led by Maurice

Thorez, and the Radical Socialists led by Édouard Daladier, won the general elections of April 26 and May 3, 1936, Léon Blum becoming Premier on June 4, 1936.

In the period following the Asturian revolt the Spanish working-class and middle-class leaders also turned to the expedient of a people's front to secure themselves against the repression and terror of the Lerroux–Gil Robles regime. While the Seventh World Congress of the Third International, held in Moscow in the summer of 1935, enthusiastically endorsed the idea of a popular front of proletarian and middle-class parties,[28] it is fatuous to conclude from this, as, for example, G. M. Godden does,[29] that the Spanish Communist party (which lacked a mass following and was without important influence) was the catalyst in the political chemistry that was to produce the Frente Popular. Given the historic ideological affinities between the Spanish and French middle classes, between Spanish and French socialism, it is more reasonable to suppose that if outside influences were determinative in the formation of the Frente Popular, their source was in Paris, not in Moscow. However, while the idea of a popular front probably originated among the French Left and while it undoubtedly exercised considerable influence on Spanish political developments during 1935, it is equally certain that the Frente Popular was essentially a Spanish response to a complex and increasingly dangerous situation within Spain itself. As has been noted, after the Asturian revolt, the Socialists and Communists strengthened the ties between them and moved closer to the liberal middle classes. Moreover, many anarchists, notwithstanding the anathema pronounced on parliamentary political activity by the Federación Anarquista Ibérica (Iberian Anarchist Federation, the controlling organ of Spanish anarchism and known simply as the F.A.I.), displayed a growing solidarity with the other sections of the Spanish Left. Thus, the Frente Popular was not a "plot to seize power" but an instrument for political survival that arose, Phoenix-like, out of the precarious situation in which the Left found itself after the failure of the Asturian revolt.

On October 20, 1935, in the Campo de Comillas, just outside
Madrid, some four hundred thousand Spaniards—men, women,
and children—gathered from all parts of Spain to hear Manuel
Azaña make a speech.[30] It was a huge, impressive demonstration
of the strength of republican sentiment in Spain. It made clear
that the Spanish people were keenly aware of the threat to the
Republic that came from the Spanish Right and that they were
prepared to defend the Republic against its enemies.

On January 16, 1936, one month to the day before the date
set for the general elections, the Izquierda Republicana (Republi-
can Left party) led by Manuel Azaña, the Unión Republicana
(Republican Union party) led by Martínez Barrio who had broken
with Lerroux and the Radical party but who stood to the right of
Azaña, the Esquerra Catalana (Catalan Left party) led by Luis
Companys and representative of the Catalan middle classes and
their autonomist aspirations, the Spanish Socialist party led by
Francisco Largo Caballero (Left), Indalecio Prieto (Center), and
Julián Besteiro (Right), the Spanish Communist party led by José
Diaz, and small splinter groups such as the Partido Obrero de
Unificación Marxista (Workers' party of Marxist Unification,
popularly known as the POUM) led by Joaquín Maurin and
Andrés Nin formally banded together in the Frente Popular. The
POUM soon withdrew from the coalition. The Anarchists never
adhered to it, but thousands of Anarchists nevertheless were to
cast their votes for its candidates.

The program of the Frente Popular expressed the aim of the
Left to fulfill the promise of the Republic as embodied in the constitution of 1931. It pledged the Frente Popular to grant immediate
amnesty to the tens of thousands of political prisoners, to insist
on the reinstatement with compensation of workers discharged
from their jobs for political reasons, to restore the statutes of the
autonomous regions which had been guaranteed by the constitution but which had been repealed by the Lerroux–Gil Robles
regime, to implement the educational program envisaged by the
constitution, to reorganize the military establishment and the ad-

ministration of justice, to protect trade and small industry, to further agrarian reform, to establish a program of public works, and to enact minimum wage laws and other social legislation. Yet it expressly disavowed class measures, per se, as being incompatible with democratic liberty. It did not propose to collectivize industrial property and the land, or even to nationalize the Bank of Spain. So little imbued with class spirit was the program of the Frente Popular that even the principle of unemployment relief was repudiated! [31]

The program of the Frente Popular was certainly not communistic, nor even moderately socialistic; it was Azañan. Its spirit was not that of Stalin and the Dictatorship of the Proletariat but rather of Roosevelt and the New Deal with the added ingredient of French anti-clericalism. But the Spanish Right saw the program of the Frente Popular as the forceful implementation of the constitution and, for the Right, the constitution remained in 1936 what it had been in 1931—an "enabling act" that would lead to the destruction of "the traditional Spain."

The general elections of February 16, 1936, perhaps the most significant and fateful in the history of Spain, were held under the auspices of a government headed by Manuel Portela Valladares, a man of Rightist sympathies and nominally a member of Lerroux's Radical party. Most of the governors and mayors were men of the Right. In many parts of rural Spain the cacique remained omnipotent. What is more, the rich contributed their money, the Church its powerful influence to the campaign of the Right. While the Left had depleted its funds to succor the thousands of its adherents held in jail and thus had little money with which to wage the electoral campaign,[32] the Right was so prodigal of its ample resources that even Constancia de la Mora's Andalusian maid received twenty-five pesetas for her vote from a CEDA canvasser.[33] The clergy, in the main, openly supported the Right. The Bishop of Barcelona publicly declared: "It is sinful to vote for the Popular Front. A vote for the conservative candidate is a vote for Christ." [34] So great were the advantages enjoyed by the Right that Manuel Azaña at one time considered boycotting the elections rather than suffering inevitable defeat.[35]

However, when the polls closed and the votes were counted, it was found that the Frente Popular had won an impressive victory, garnering 258 of a total of 473 seats in the new Cortes.[36] The popular vote for the Frente Popular was 4,206,156 (including the 132,247 ballots cast for the Basque Nationalists) as compared with 3,783,601 for the Right and 681,047 for the Center parties.[37] The Socialists with 89 deputies constituted the single largest group within the Left coalition. However, the Socialists and Communists combined controlled but 103 seats in the new Cortes or less than half of all the seats held by adherents of the Frente Popular. Assured of the support of the other middle-class parties, Azaña's Republican Left party with 82 deputies dominated the Left coalition. Down to July, 1936, or until the outbreak of the Civil War, not one Socialist or Communist held a post in the cabinet.[38]

The triumph of the Left was not only electoral but politico-psychological as well. It attested to the prevailing republican and progressive sentiments of the mass of the people. The Republic was in the hands of its friends again. Unless there was a serious rift in the Left coalition the realization of the objectives for which the Republic had been established could not again be hindered, deferred, and then abandoned. Significantly, the Center parties had virtually disappeared. Lerroux's Radical party, for example, had been reduced from 101 to 8 deputies in the Cortes.[39] While the Right had fared better, Gil Robles' CEDA retaining 98 seats in the new Cortes, it had waged a campaign characterized by a frank contempt for republican ideals and democratic sensibilities.[40] Thus, the bitter animosity of the CEDA toward the Republic itself had been fully revealed. Unable to control and to subvert the Republic from within, henceforth the Right could hope only to destroy it from without. In this bipolarization of Spanish politics during the winter of 1935–36 there inhered both the politico-psychological victory of the Frente Popular and the tragedy of contemporary Spain. The Left now became the symbol and the instrument of the Republic while the Right, ultimately frustrated in its attempt to subvert the Republic during the "black years" and decisively defeated at the polls in 1936, would turn to conspiracy and violence and finally civil war. Gil Robles, the papier-mâché *jefe* would give away to Francisco Franco, the iron caudillo.

Was the Left (and therefore the Republic) aware of its peril? While among the political leaders and the people there was manifest an uneasiness about the future, little was actually done to forestall a Rightist coup d'état. The electoral victory had a different meaning for each political group and mutual distrust pervaded the Left coalition. Thus, the menace of a *pronunciamiento* was viewed with only one eye, as it were, or, perhaps, in the words of Constancia de la Mora, with "criminal carelessness and lethargy." [41]

The new Cortes was largely composed of middle-class elements, including some 130 lawyers, 34 professors, 31 doctors, 23 writers, and 20 engineers.[42] It evinced a moderate attitude and a reluctance to confront the exigencies of the times. "Azaña and his cabinet still worshipped legality, still believed in making haste slowly." [43] They seemed less concerned with the imminent threat from the Right than with the Left Socialists who affected the accents and airs of militant revolutionists. And, in turn, the Left Socialists, misconceiving the danger from the Right,[44] persisted in viewing the Azaña Republicans as the "class enemy."

The third phase in the history of the Second Spanish Republic, spanning the five months from February 16, to July 17, 1936, was marked by the conspiratorial activities of the Right, acts of violence by *Falangistas*, and incessant strikes led by Socialists and anarchists. Of salient importance was the tragic inability of the Azañan Republicans on the one hand and the Socialists on the other to transmute the electoral agreement that was the Frente Popular into a political compact from which could come a government of the united Left. The moderate Socialists led by Indalecio Prieto were in favor of joining forces with Azaña and the liberal middle classes in such a government, but the Left Socialists led by Francisco Largo Caballero were opposed to it.[45] Largo Caballero's powerful influence within the Socialist movement was enough to insure that a government of the united Left would not be formed in time to forestall a Rightist coup d'état.

The reasons which prompted Largo Caballero to take the position he did remain somewhat obscure. Yet, this much is certain: he disliked Azaña and distrusted the republicanism of the Spanish middle classes. This was, perhaps, natural, given the fact that Largo Caballero was of working-class origin and had spent most of his 68 years in the labor movement. Bourgeois intellectuals with a European outlook were an alien species to the onetime Madrid plasterer who had not learned to read and write until he was twenty-four. Then, too, Largo Caballero was probably influenced by the apolitical intransigence of the anarcho-syndicalists. As secretary of the Unión General de Trabajadores he could not appear less zealous a champion of the interests of the workers than his anarchist rivals of the Confederación Nacional del Trabajo. Moreover, Largo Caballero might have been swayed by the idle talk in the Madrid cafés that cast him in the role of the Spanish Lenin with Azaña as his Kerensky. Here was tragicomedy. Unaware that "politics is the art of the possible," Largo Caballero, a trade-unionist masquerading as a revolutionist, threatened a revolution that he did not prepare and that, objectively, was impossible of realization. Meanwhile, he did nothing to help Azaña thwart the planned revolt of the generals. Azaña himself did little more than transfer leading military dissidents to commands on the Canaries and Balearics. Largo Caballero's failure to divest himself of a revolutionary attitude and to join with the middle-class liberals in a common defense of the Republic, the liberals' complacent inactivity in the face of the imminent danger from the Right, and Azaña's fear and loathing of Largo Caballero (Azaña when President was as determined to keep Largo Caballero from the premiership as Alcalá Zamora had been Gil Robles) [46] left the Republic open to the blow that was soon to come.

There is no substantial evidence to support the contention of writers such as Robert Sencourt [47] that the Communists (either Spanish or Russian) were planning an insurrection against the Republic and that the revolt of the generals was simply anticipatory and preventive. Until the outbreak of the Civil War the Spanish Communists were numerically insignificant. Furthermore, they were without important influence in the labor movement, in the government, and, of course, in the army. Revolt in such circumstances would have been quixotic in the extreme. At this time, moreover, far from contemplating an uprising, they were advocating and pursuing a policy of collaboration with Azaña and the middle-class liberals.[48]

Concerning the plans and aspirations of Soviet Russia with respect to Spain, it must be remembered that at this time (the spring and summer of 1936) Soviet Russia had deferred its hopes of world revolution and, through the Comintern, was committed to the support of the Popular Front movement.[49]

W. G. Krivitsky, the Chief of the Soviet Military Intelligence in Western Europe until his defection from the Russian service (and therefore in a postion both to know and to reveal what the Russians were about in Spain), has written:

At the first thunder of guns beyond the Pyrenees, I [Krivitsky was at his headquarters in The Hague] dispatched an agent to Hendaye on the French-Spanish border, and another to Lisbon, to organize a secret information service in the Franco territory.

These were merely routine measures. *I had received no instructions from Moscow in regard to Spain, and at the time there was no contact beween my agents and the Madrid government.* As the responsible head of its European Intelligence Service, I was simply securing general information for relaying to the Kremlin.

Our agents in Berlin and Rome, Hamburg and Genoa, Bremen and Naples, duly reported to us the powerful aid that Franco was receiving from Italy and Germany. This information I dispatched to Moscow, where it was received in silence. *I still got no secret instructions regarding Spain.* Publicly also the Soviet government had nothing to say.

The Comintern, of course, made a great deal of noise, but none of us practical men took that seriously. . . .

In Spain itself the shouts of the Comintern were still more futile, for the number of its adherents there was almost infinitesimal—*only 3,000 men in the Communist Party all told. Spanish trade unions and all the strong revolutionary groupings, syndicalist, anarchist, Party of Marxist Unity, and Socialist, remained obstinately anti-Communist. The Spanish Republic, after five years of existence, still refused to recognize the Soviet government and had no diplomatic relations with Moscow.*[50]

The notion that the Spanish Communist party, either with or without the connivance of Soviet Russia, was preparing an uprising against the Spanish Republic during the summer of 1936 must be dismissed as sheer fascist propaganda.

But, then, were not the anarchists and the Left Socialists fomenting strikes and forever proclaiming the imminent triumph of the revolution? The anarchists had a "barricade" psychology and spoke the language of revolt in season and out. Frozen in a posture of defiance, they were boisterous, turbulent, and troublesome always, effective revolutionists never. Thus it had been under the monarchy, thus it had been under the dictatorship, and so it was under the Republic. It was only after the revolt of the generals that the anarchists seized the opportunity created by that event to implement their notions of "libertarian communism," and then only in Catalonia where they were strongest.

The Left Socialists were content to wait until Azaña and the middle-class liberals had demonstrated their inability to solve Spain's problems before assuming power themselves and establishing a socialistic regime.[51] But the time was not yet.[52] If Largo Caballero had been actively preparing a revolt during the summer of 1936, he must have proceeded in such a circumspect fashion that no evidence of his secret labors remains today. This is incredible, particularly when it is remembered that Largo Caballero and his followers played incessantly on the trumpet of their predestined victory. In the end, however, the Socialists, like the anarchists, had to await the revolt of the generals before they could begin to translate their words into deeds.

Concerning strikes and disorders in the period preceding the military insurrection, they were, to begin with, exaggerated in the conservative press in Spain and abroad as to frequency and intensity.[53] Moreover, they reflected the long-deferred hopes of the peasants for land and of the workers for better wages and were not revolutionary in the political sense of the term. Finally, they were to a considerable extent the work of fascist agents-provocateurs who thereby sought to embarrass and to discredit the Republic.[54]

The revolt of the generals, then, was not an attempt to forestall a Communist, a Socialist, or an anarchist insurrection, for such a danger did not exist in Spain during the summer of 1936. It did not seek to bring an end to intolerable conditions of disorder and violence, because the Republic essentially maintained order and on the occasions when it was infracted the open hand of the Right was as visible as the clenched fist of the Left. It was not a spontaneous uprising of patriots heartsick at the desecration of the traditional values of Spain, because the traditional values of Spain, if not the traditional privileges of certain classes of Spaniards, were quite safe in the hands of such men as Azaña, Casares Quiroga, Prieto, and Largo Caballero. The revolt of the generals was the consummation of a plot that stretched back through the months and years, that crossed frontiers and spanned the seas, that sought the destruction of the Republic at almost any price.

It has already been noted that the Spanish Right, despite the differences which divided monarchists and republicans, civilian politicians and army generals, agrarians and industrialists, clericals and freemasons, traditionalists and fascists, was united to this end: to seize control of the State and to transform the "immaculate Republic" into the "emasculated Republic," and failing in this, to assail the power of the State and to destroy the Republic bodily. The first tactic had been employed by the Lerroux–Gil Robles regime during the "two black years" and had eventuated in complete fiasco with the triumph of the Frente Popular at the polls on February 16, 1936. Among the Right there had been important elements, particularly in monarchical and military circles, which had taken a dim view of this approach from the beginning. They favored direct action, relying on the army and the traditional *pronunciamiento* and, to the extent that it might prove necessary, on the assistance of foreign powers which, in the rapidly changing diplomatic and strategic situation in Europe and the Mediterranean, might see in a friendly Spain a useful adjunct to their larger purposes.

At four o'clock in the afternoon of March 31, 1934, some two years and four months before the Franco uprising, Antonio Goicoechea, the leader of the monarchist Renovación Española, Señores Olazábal and Lizarra, representatives of the Carlist Comunión Tradicionalista, and Lieutenant General Emilio Barrera met in Rome with Benito Mussolini, the head of the Italian government, and Marshal Italo Balbo. Mussolini inquired of the Spanish delegation as to the political situation within Spain, the condition and aspirations of the Spanish army and navy, and the hopes and plans of the monarchist parties. After being enlightened on these matters by the Spaniards, Mussolini declared:

1. That he was ready to help with the necessary measures of assistance the two parties in opposition to the regime obtaining in Spain, in the task of overthrowing it and substituting it by a Regency which would prepare the complete restoration of the Monarchy; this declaration was solemnly repeated by Signor Mussolini three times, and those assembled received it with the natural manifestations of esteem and gratitude;

2. That as a practical demonstration and as a proof of his intentions he was ready to supply them immediately with 20,000 rifles; 20,000 hand-grenades; 200 machine-guns; and 1,500,000 *pesetas* in cash;

3. That such help was merely of an initial nature and would be opportunely completed with greater measures, according as the work achieved justified this and circumstances made it necessary.

Thereupon arrangements were made for the disposition of the arms and funds in Spain.[55]

In 1934 Mussolini was stirring the embers of an old fire. His interest in the Iberian Peninsula went back to the early years of his regime and the nearly simultaneous establishment of the Primo de Rivera dictatorship in Spain. From the autumn of 1923, and seizing on the controversy concerning the international administration of Tangier, Mussolini had striven to establish a bond of common interest between Italy and Spain. The racial, cultural, religious, and historical affinities of the two peoples became the theme of public orations and newspaper articles in both Rome and Madrid. Victor Emmanuel and Alfonso exchanged royal visits. On the occasion of King Alfonso's visit to Rome in November, 1923, the Spaniard proved lavish with the coin of flattery, introducing Primo de Rivera as "his own Mussolini." [56] Relations between the two states were most cordial. Considering that Spanish foreign policy had hitherto reflected Spain's economic and military dependence on Great Britain and France (they were her best customers and France was her recent ally against Abd-el-Krim in Morocco), Mussolini scored an impressive diplomatic success when, in 1926, Italy and Spain signed a treaty of friendship. Primo de Rivera, moreover, agreed to permit the Italians to establish a naval base in the Balearic Islands.[57] However, inasmuch as Italy's military position precluded an open affront to Great Britain and France in the Mediterranean at this time, the Italians prudently kept the project abeyant.[58] Before a propitious time could arrive, however, Primo de Rivera fell from power and subsequently the Second Spanish Republic came into being. Thereupon Italian-Spanish relations rapidly deteriorated, although furtive contact between the Italian government and the Spanish military was maintained. Meanwhile, the Japanese had invaded and conquered Manchuria and the Third Reich had been erected on the ruins of the Weimar Republic. The international situation was in flux. What with Italian plans for an attack on Ethiopia well advanced and *Mare Nostrum* increasingly a possibility the Duce seized the opportunity presented by the visit of the Spanish monarchist leaders to Rome in March, 1934, to bring to flame again his designs in Spain.

German interest in Spain was both strategic and economic. The penetration of the Spanish economy by German capital and the exploitation of Spanish mineral resources for the ends of German

rearmament were important considerations in the determination
of German policy. In a speech at Würzburg on June 27, 1937, almost a year after Franco had raised the banner of revolt, Hitler
declared: "Germany needs iron ore. That is why we need a
Nationalist Government in Spain, so that we may be able to buy
Spanish ore." [59] However, the strategic possibilities inherent in the
establishment of a fascist regime in Madrid entered at least as im-
portunely into the calculations of the Wilhelmstrasse as economic
matters. A Spain tied to German and Italy by ideological, diplomatic, military, and economic bonds could prove of decisive importance in reducing France to military impotence and rendering
Great Britain incapable of effective defense in the Mediterranean.[60]

The identity of interests between Germans and Spaniards vis-
à-vis the French in the European power-struggle stretches back to
the time when Hapsburgs ruled in both Vienna and Madrid. The
battle of Rocroi (1643) marked the end of Spanish and the beginning of French military hegemony. Down through the years
many Spaniards continued to cherish the memory of the great days
of Spain and of the old imperial ties. German statesmen were not
unaware of Spanish pride and sentimentality nor were they obliv-
ious of Spain's historic role in the containment of French power.
It will be remembered that the candidacy of a Hohenzollern prince
for the Spanish throne furnished the occasion for the Franco-
Prussian War of 1870–71.

During the First World War Spain remained neutral, but the
sympathies of Spaniards with respect to the belligerents were
sharply divided. The military caste, the ecclesiastical hierarchy, and
the landed aristocracy, in the main, favored Germany and Austria-
Hungary which they regarded as the respositories of traditional
values. The intelligentsia, the liberal middle classes, the parties of
the Left, and the manufacturers and industrialists of Barcelona and
Bilbao, by and large, favored France and England, capitalistic democracies with which they had many ideological affinities and strong
economic ties.[61] King Alfonso quipped at the time: "Only myself

and the *canaille* are on the side of the Allies." [62] However, Alfonso's attitude did not render him impervious to the influence of the highly placed Spanish Germanophiles, nor to the blandishments of the Germans themselves. The German Admiral Wilhelm Canaris managed to establish a network of spies and agents throughout Spain. The assistance rendered by the Spaniards in the refueling and resupplying of German submarines was an important factor in the success of German naval operations in the Atlantic and especially in the Mediterranean. Juan March, on his part, reaped a fortune from these clandestine activities.[63]

After the defeat of Germany, Canaris continued to fish in Spanish waters. In secret defiance of the Treaty of Versailles, he arranged with the Echevarrieta shipyards in Cádiz for the construction of submarines to be delivered to Germany.[64] Following the establishment of the Third Reich, German activity in Spain increased enormously, becoming a bold, vast, and coordinated effort to win a position of influence in Spanish affairs.[65] For the furtherance of German ambitions in Europe would be greatly facilitated by a Spain friendly to Germany and hostile to France. As E. N. Dzelepy, the French writer on international relations, put it:

It is certainly not due to chance that Spain has always been involved in one way or the other in all the hostile enterprises of German imperialism against France. . . .

On the eve of new aggression Germany automatically returns to the methods which she used formerly in similar cases. In the last resort the diplomacy of the Third Reich is doing nothing more than picking up once more the thread of Bismarckian and Wilhelmian foreign policy. What Bismarck tried to do with the diplomatic means of his epoch, the use of monarchial influence, Hitler is trying to do to-day with more modern diplomatic means—anti-bolshevist "mysticism."

Only the form of things has changed; the substance remains the same. To-day, as in the past, Germany's object is to isolate France, to keep her tied down within her frontiers, and to paralyse any possible action on her part in favour of her Central European allies and of Russia in the more than probable event of German aggression aiming at a reversal of the state of affairs brought about by the victory of the Allies, and at a readjustment of European frontiers.[66]

The recrudescence of the latent sense of mission, of dominion and empire of the Spaniard, particularly of the aristocrat and soldier, could be exploited by the Nazis not only against France but against England as well. For the animus of the Dons against the Island Empire whose forces were encamped on Gibraltar was deep-going and enduring. The desire to repossess Gibraltar has been voiced by every Spanish government and it transcends in sentimental significance the rivalry of Spain and France in Morocco. As G. T. Garratt has written:

So far as the reactionary parties in Spain have a foreign policy, it is based on the historical hatred of England, and on the desire to regain Gibraltar, as a matter of national prestige. This formed the mental background of the Spanish aristocracy; of the great landlords, like the Dukes of Peñaranda and Medina Celi; of the Catholic bishops and the leaders of the Church; of the Carlists, of the Army officers.[67]

The Germans, and the Italians as well, found the Spanish conservative press a convenient medium for the dissemination of their ideas.[68] However, in their efforts to bring Spain within the orbit of German influence, the Nazis were not content with evocations of pride and sentiment out of the Spanish past nor with descriptions of the wonders of the New Germany. They did not neglect more prosaic matters. The large German colony in Spain was honeycombed with Nazi agents, many in the guise of exiles.[69] The German Embassy and Consulates in Spain functioned as centers for the distribution of money, guns, and propaganda materials throughout the Republic, disposing of nearly three million pesetas for political purposes in 1935 alone.[70] Meanwhile, the Ibero-American Institute in Berlin, with General Wilhelm Faupel as its president, became an important bridge between the Nazi leaders in Germany and dissident Spaniards.[71] In February, 1936, General Sanjurjo together with José Antonio Primo de Rivera visited the Reich.[72] Ostensibly in Germany for a winter-sports holiday at Partenkirchen, they stayed at the Kaiserhof in Berlin, a hotel reserved for guests of the German government.[73] Admiral Canaris personally conducted General Sanjurjo on a tour of German arms-factories.[74]

The Spaniard gained more than an insight into the productive capacity and military might of the New Germany during his "wintersports holiday." Sanjurjo left the Reich with the promise of German support for the contemplated military insurrection against the Spanish Republic, including German aircraft to be used in transporting troops from Morocco to Spain if it should develop that the Spanish fleet remained loyal to the Republic.[75]

While Italian and German connivance in the revolt of the Spanish generals admits of no decent doubt, it should not be inferred from this that the military insurrection was planned, prepared, and set in motion by the dictators in Rome and Berlin, the Spanish conspirators being but pawns on the chessboard of European *Machtpolitik*. The Spanish generals, as well as other important figures who were privy to the conspiracy, believed that the coup d'état would meet with quick and easy success.[76] The tradition of the *pronunciamiento*, that arrogated to the army the role of ultimate arbiter in Spanish politics, assumed the political apathy or incapacity of the people. The establishment of the Republic, the armed revolt of the Asturian miners, the growing strength and militancy of the proletarian organizations within Spain, and the emergence of the Frente Popular had served to modify somewhat the traditional contempt of the Spanish ruling class for the masses. But the Spanish ruling class had not lost faith in itself. It was not ready to seek its salvation in subserviency to the aims and purposes of foreign powers. In the view of the Spanish conspirators the support of Italy and Germany would facilitate preparations for the revolt and, if the contingency should arise, would supply the margin of moral and material assistance that would insure the success of the enterprise, but without divesting it of its primarily and essentially Spanish character.[77]

Subsequent developments were to prove the generals wrong. The unexpectedly stubborn defense of the Republic by the people rendered the generals hostages to fortune. The *pronunicamiento* was metamorphosed into an Italo-German invasion of Spain.

The first attempt to negate the victory of the Frente Popular and to supplant the Republic by a dictatorship occurred in the early hours of February 17, 1936. It came in the form of identical proposals made to Señor Portela Valladares, the incumbent premier, first by the would-be Jefe and then by the destined-to-be Caudillo. One year after the general elections and with Spain riven by war, Portela Valladares declared at a meeting at the Cortes in Valencia: "At four in the morning on the day after the elections I was visited by Señor Gil Robles, who proposed that I should assume dictatorial powers, and who offered me the support of all the groups defeated in the elections. At seven that evening the same suggestion was made to me by General Franco himself." [78]

Señor Portela Valladares' testimony is corroborated by Joaquín Arrarás, General Franco's official biographer. Arrarás reports that the very evening of the general elections, Sunday, February 16, 1936, General Franco attempted to persuade General Pozas, the director of the Civil Guard, that the popular manifestations of joy at the triumph of the Frente Popular constituted a serious menace to public order. General Pozas dismissed Franco's fears as unfounded. Whereupon, at three o'clock in the morning, Franco called on the minister of war, General Molero, and suggested that he urge the Cabinet to proclaim a "state of war." Molero asked Franco whether he had conferred with the Premier on this matter. Franco replied that he intended to speak with the Premier immediately. The next day the Cabinet decided to proclaim a "state of war" throughout Spain. Franco, as chief of staff (to which post he had been elevated by Gil Robles when the latter was minister of war), conferred with the commanding generals and prepared the necessary orders. His labors were interrupted by an urgent message from Portela Valladares informing him that the president of the Republic, Niceto Alcalá Zamora, would not countenance a proclamation of a "state of war" as he considered it a provocation to the people.

"And what do you think?" asked Franco of the Premier.

"I obey the orders of Alcalá Zamora," answered Portela Valladares.

Undaunted, Franco urged the Premier to declare a "state of war," notwithstanding the opposition of the President. Franco reminded Portela Valladares that he, as premier, had authority over General Pozas and the instruments of state power. The Premier equivocated, asking for time in which to ponder the matter.

However, when General Pozas threatened that "the civil guard will oppose any uprising on the part of the military," Franco and his henchmen knew that for the nonce they had been thwarted.[79]

They bided their time, confident that it would come.

One of the first orders given by Manuel Azaña upon assuming the premiership for a second time sent General Franco as military commander to the Canary Islands and General Goded, who had stood close to Franco during the events described above,[80] as military commander to the Balearic Islands. It was hoped that by removing these ringleaders from Madrid the threat of a coup d'état would subside. This was a feeble gesture at best and one that proved a harbinger of the indecision and weakness with which the Republican government met the growing menace of armed revolt.

Before he left Madrid for the Canary Islands Franco conferred with General Mola and other army chiefs. Plans were discussed which would enable the army to be ready to meet any "emergency." Franco talked, too, with José Antonio Primo de Rivera who informed the future Caudillo of the strength that the Falange Española could muster in Madrid and in the provinces at a "given moment." Franco, moreover, arranged to be kept fully informed concerning future developments in the Peninsula.[81]

Thus, the web of conspiracy reached from the capital to the outlying possessions of Spain and involved besides Franco, Goded, and Mola, Generals Sanjurjo (the ranking officer in the Spanish Army but now an exile in Portugal), Cabanellas, Fanjul, and Queipo de Llano, the financier Juan March, and the politicians Calvo Sotelo, Gil Robles, and José Antonio Primo de Rivera, as well as a number of less important figures. The conspirators believed that they could rely on the Unión Militar Española, the army, the Foreign Legion, and the Moorish levies, as well as the Carlist *requetés*, elements of the Civil Guard, and, perhaps, the *señoritos* of the Falange Española, whose leader, José Antonio Primo de Rivera, was soon to be confined in the Alicante Prison.

With the departure of General Franco for the Canary Islands, General Mola (perhaps the most capable of them all) [82] was entrusted with the task of coordinating the activities of the far-flung conspirators. However, because of the prestige that accrued to him as the senior officer in the Spanish Army and as the leader of the abortive uprising of August 10, 1932, General Sanjurjo, on May 29, 1936, was formally given the leadership of this second insurrectionary movement.[83]

The revolt was tentatively set for some time between June 24 and 29, 1936, St. John's and St. Peter's days respectively, for the generals were imbued with a consecratory sense of mission.[84] However, on the advice of General Mola, it was postponed until after the middle of July.[85] Meanwhile, preparations were pushed to completion.

Early in July, General Franco, who had won his first military laurels in Morocco and who continued to enjoy considerable prestige there, was informed that he had been chosen to lead the forces in Africa.[86] It was a vitally important assignment and pregnant with future significance.

The plan of revolt was a simple one. It called for simultaneous risings of the garrisons in the principal cities of Spain in the Moroccan Protectorate. Morocco was to serve, initially, as the base of operations for the insurrectionary movement. It contained the hard-bitten, professional soldiers of the Foreign Legion and the excellent fighters of the Moorish levies. Moreover, there was little to fear from the politically untutored and unorganized populace. It was entrusted to Lieutenant Colonel Juan Yagüe to raise the banner of revolt among the Legionnaires and Moors. Yagüe's action was to be the signal for the general revolt.[87] Thereupon, Franco, flying in from the Canary Islands, would assume command of the Moroccan forces. Ferrying them across the Straits of Gibraltar, he would join with Queipo de Llano who, meanwhile, would have secured control over Sevilla, Cádiz, and the region of southern Andalusia. Synchronizing their actions, Fanjul in Madrid, Goded in Barcelona (having flown in from the Balearic Islands), Cabanellas in Zaragoza, and Mola in the North among the *requetés* would lead the garrisons out of their barracks and establish military rule in these leading centers of Spain. If Fanjul should fail in Madrid (this was a distinct possibility since it was the seat of the government and the population might well prove hostile), then Franco and Queipo de Llano from the south and Mola, Cabanellas, and Goded from the north and east would rapidly converge on the city and force its surrender. Whereupon, Sanjurjo, flying in from Portugal, would be acclaimed the head of the Spanish government.[88]

The plan was simple enough, and not too many difficulties were envisaged. The generals expected the revolt to have succeeded, the Republic overthrown, and a military dictatorship established by July 22.[89]

Now the time was come. Luis Bolin, a Spanish writer living in England and an agent of the conspirators, rented an airplane from the Olley Company in London. On July 11, 1936, he engaged Captain Bebb, an English pilot, to fly the airplane to the Canary Islands and from there to transport "a certain person" to Tetuán in Spanish Morocco. Bolin persuaded an English friend, Major Hugh Pollard,[90] his daughter, Diana, and her friend, Dorothy Watson, to accompany Captain Bebb in the guise of tourists so that the presence of the airplane in Las Palmas would not arouse suspicion.[91]

Two days later, on July 13, 1936, Calvo Sotelo was assassinated in Madrid (in retaliation for the murder of Lieutenant Castillo of the Assault Guards, a Socialist). Calvo Sotelo's violent death was to be publicly seized upon by the conspirators as justification for their "spontaneous" uprising.

On July 17, 1936, Lieutenant Colonel Yagüe raised the banner of revolt in Morocco. This was the prearranged signal. Queipo de Llano, Fanjul, Goded, Cabanellas, Mola, and the others did what was expected of them, or sought to. Franco landed at Tetuán at seven o'clock in the morning of July 19, 1936, and immediately assumed

command of the Moroccan forces. That evening he addressed Spain
by radio:

On taking over the command of this glorious and patriotic army
here in Tetuán, I send to the loyal garrisons and their country the
most enthusiastic greetings. Spain has been saved. You may pride your-
selves on being Spaniards.

Have blind faith. Never doubt. Gather energy, without pausing,
for the nation demands it. The movement is marching on. There is no
human force which will stop it. I greet you with a strong and hearty
embrace. Long live Spain! [92]

The fourth and final phase of the Second Spanish Republic, its
death agony, had begun.

III
The Generals Receive
Foreign Assistance

THE first reaction of the Spanish government to the news that the army had revolted in Morocco was one of indignation tempered by confidence. On the morning of July 18, 1936, the Madrid Radio announced:

A new criminal plot against the Republic has been frustrated. The Government did not wish to address itself to the nation until it had obtained exact information about the event and had put into execution urgent and relentless measures in order to combat it.

A part of the Army that represents Spain in Morocco has arisen in arms against the Republic, rebelling against its own fatherland and perpetrating a shameful and criminal act of rebellion against legally constituted authority. The Government declares that the movement is exclusively limited to certain cities in the zone of the Protectorate and that no one, absolutely no one, in the Peninsula has joined in this absurd undertaking. On the contrary, the Spanish people have reacted unanimously and with profound indignation against the reprehensible attempt already frustrated in its incipience. . . .

The Government of the Republic dominates the situation and affirms that it will not be long in announcing to the public that it has restored normality.[1]

However, the next twenty-four hours were to make it abundantly clear that the "absurd undertaking" had become a most formidable military insurrection. From cities and towns throughout Spain came reports of rebellious generals leading their Myrmidonian soldiery into the streets, proclaiming martial law, and seizing and shooting

Republican provincial officials. In Pamplona, the capital of Navarra, the rebels met with no resistance and were immediately successful. In Zaragoza, in Aragón, in Burgos, in Old Castile, and in Cádiz, Sevilla, Jerez de la Frontera, Córdoba, and Granada, in the south, they easily subdued the poorly armed workers who tried to resist them. Most ominously, General Franco succeeded in ferrying hundreds of Legionnaires and Moors from Morocco to the mainland.

The government, meanwhile, remained loath to open the arsenals and distribute arms to the workers, despite the insistent demands of Largo Caballero, Prieto, and other working-class leaders. It confronted the crisis like a somnambulist, wide-eyed but unseeing, its confident air as unreal as a shadow in a dream.

The passivity of the government is almost inexplicable in view of the fact that only a few weeks earlier Premier Casares Quiroga had informed the Cortes that the government was not only aware that the Right was preparing an insurrection but was acquainted in detail with the plan of the projected revolt.[2] Inasmuch as the government had done virtually nothing to forestall the expected blow and even now remained strangely inert, it would seem that Casares Quiroga either had grossly exaggerated what Madrid had really known of the plan or was guilty of a tranquil optimism that bordered on criminal negligence. While precise information regarding the conspiracy might not have been available to the government and therefore the exact time and place of the first blow might have come as a surprise to Madrid, there can be no doubt that the Azaña–Casares Quiroga regime, as well as the general public, knew that an uprising was imminent. Constancia de la Mora, whose husband, Ignacio Hidalgo de Cisneros, was at the time the second-in-command of the air force and aide-de-camp to the minister of war, wrote of the last days before the military revolt:

Madrid was on tenterhooks. . . . We sat up many a night beside the telephone, waiting for the terrible news that the Madrid garrison, or some other garrison, had risen against the Republic. And every morning, after such a sleepless night, Ignacio would go off to the War

Ministry and beg his immediate superior, the War Minister and Premier since Azaña's election to the Presidency, Casares Quiroga, to act.

But Casares would laugh. "You're an alarmist, Cisneros," he would tell Ignacio, "I have everything under control. I consult with the other Ministers. We consider we have taken the steps to insure the safety of the Republic."

"But the street fighting!"

"Gangs of toughs," Casares would reply; "the police can handle them."

Once Ignacio went with some other friends, who agreed with him that the Republic must act swiftly to preserve itself, to visit Azaña—to beg him to use his influence with the Cabinet.

Ignacio had expected to find the man who made the great speech of 1935, the man who had been imprisoned by Gil Robles. But Azaña had changed. Secure in his beautiful little presidential palace, once the King's property, Azaña had lost touch with the people. Remote, disinterested, he had already sunk into the lethargy that was later to overcome him completely.

"The Republic is sufficiently protected," Azaña told Ignacio coldly.

"But the generals who have been transferred to the islands, like Francisco Franco and Goded, still command troops. The only effect of transferring them is to make them think they are regarded as traitors and to force them to act quickly!"

"The Cabinet is in full control of the situation." It was Azaña's last word on the matter.[3]

Azaña's air of serenity and Casares Quiroga's easy optimism must appear, in the light of subsequent events, to have been sheer folly or worse. Yet, both Azaña and Casares Quiroga were able men and sincere democrats. It was not that they had come to love the Republic less but that they had come to fear the extreme Left at least as much, if not more, than they did the extreme Right. Their attitude during the weeks and days before the outbreak of civil war was eloquent of the predicament in which the moderate Republicans found themselves. How was it possible to preserve the liberal, middle-class Republic in a situation rapidly deteriorating into a trial of strength between rebellious generals and revolutionary workers? Azaña and Casares Quiroga had hoped to keep the fac-

tional strife from flaring into civil war, trusting that time and an
enlightened public opinion would safeguard the Republic against
its enemies.[4] However admirable such a course might appear as
a theoretical solution of an arduous political problem, it was bound
to flounder and to come to nothing against the hard reality of
Spanish politics which since the elections of February 16, 1936,
reflected an increasingly bitter bipolarization around the extreme
Right and the extreme Left. Azaña and Casares Quiroga, believing
that intervention on one side against the other would serve only
to exacerbate the factional strife, sought to remain impartial. However, they succeeded not in ameliorating the situation but only in
losing control over it. The revolt of the generals proclaimed the
bankruptcy of their hopes.

Yet, when confronted by military insurrection on the one hand
and a general strike and the demand that the workers be armed
on the other, the moderate Republicans still sought to temporize,
to steer a middle course between the Scylla of surrender to armed
rebels and the Charybdis of submission to armed supporters. Casares
Quiroga, disliked by both the Right and the Left and discredited
by the recent turn of events, resigned as premier on the night of
July 19, 1936. Thereupon, President Azaña asked Martínez Barrio
to form a new government, one that would include Felipe Sánchez
Román (a brilliant lawyer and a Left Republican who had refused
to adhere to the Frente Popular agreement, deeming it too radical)
and General Emilio Mola (who at that very moment was advancing
at the head of rebellious soldiers and *requetés* from Pamplona toward Madrid).[5] Señor Martínez Barrio's government proved to be
the shortest-lived in Spanish history, lasting only three hours. It
collapsed like an empty sack, for the Azañan maneuver evoked only
the contemptuous indifference of the rebellious generals while it
aroused the militant hostility of the proletarian parties. Largo Caballero declared that the workers were unalterably opposed to the
scheme and were prepared to use violence to thwart it.[6] Martínez
Barrio was succeeded by José Giral, a professor of pharmaceutical
chemistry and a devoted follower of President Azaña. The Giral

government, which was to endure until September 4, 1936, when Largo Caballero became premier, was composed of the close friends and followers of Manuel Azaña. In effect, the President was his own premier.

Meanwhile, events attendant upon the spreading military insurrection were to force Azaña's hand. He was, albeit reluctantly, to accede to the demands of the proletarian leaders that arms be given to the workers and that the defense of the Republic be swiftly organized. The heroic response of the Spanish masses to the military revolt, the very successes of the workers' militias against the rebels in such important centers as Madrid, Barcelona, Bilbao, and Valencia, carried the government along in its wake and was the decisive element in the determination of the government to defend the Republic.

Particularly severe fighting was in progress in Barcelona. The grim Barcelonese struggled with prodigious valor against General Goded's heavily-armed soldiers and succeeded, with the support of loyal units of the Civil Guard commanded by Colonel Aranguren, in crushing the rebellion by July 22, 1936. Goded himself was captured and summarily executed. In Madrid, too, the populace gained the victory. This had important psychological as well as practical results, for the loss of Madrid, the capital of Spain and the traditional objective of every insurrectionary movement, would probably have led to the swift collapse of Republican resistance. As it happened, Madrid was to become the bulwark and the symbol of the Republican defense. General Fanjul had sought to lead the Madrid garrison into the streets but instead had found himself beseiged in the Montaña barracks by thousands of armed workers. When loyal artillerists began to fire shells into the barracks, the position of the rebels became hopeless. But for hours heavy fighting continued until, with a reckless disregard for their own lives, the workers stormed and captured the barracks. Fanjul was taken prisoner and later shared Goded's fate. From other parts of Spain, from the Asturias in the north to Valencia on the Mediterranean, came reports which revealed that the earlier rebel successes were being counterbalanced by loyalist victories. Moreover, it developed that the greater part of the air force and navy had kept faith with the Republic. General Franco was now experiencing great difficulty in ferrying troops from Morocco to the mainland as Republican air and sea power in the Straits of Gibraltar increasingly made itself felt. The government had already released the soldiers under the command of rebel generals from their military oaths. Now teeth began to grow in the government's jaw. Going beyond Casares Quiroga's platonic gesture, Giral ordered the arsenals opened and arms distributed to the workers. Soon a number of cities and towns which had fallen to the rebels were recaptured by the hastily-formed columns of workers' militias which fanned out from Madrid, Barcelona, and other loyalist strongholds. Meanwhile, the general strike continued.

The Madrid government had acted tardily, revealing the doubts and apprehensions which it harbored. Time had been lost and time was of the essence. However, confronted by the implacability of the rebel generals on the one hand and the iron determination of the Spanish masses to defend the Republic on the other, it had been forced to act and it chose to cast its lot with the people. Now the tide was running against the rebels. The next few days would be of critical importance. The generals had not reckoned with such vast and bitter resistance on the part of the people. They had planned a coup d'état; they were now faced with a civil war, a civil war in which the mass of the people, the bulk of Spanish industry, the financial resources of the government, and the legitimate authority of the Spanish State were arrayed against them. Left to their own means, they faced inevitable catastrophe. But beyond Spain were men of great power who stood ready to succor them and to these the generals turned.

The immediate agent of the powerful aid that was soon to reach the insurgent generals from abroad had recently been an obscure clerk for Wilmer Brothers, a German export firm in Spanish Morocco. In the fairy tale the heroine was granted three wishes. Her happiness always retained a magical quality. In the life of

Johannes Bernhardt, the Wilmer Brothers clerk, events unfolded in a more prosaic but not less felicitous manner. A modest prominence brought him first a wife and then a fortune. This character out of Hans Fallada probably rubbed his eyes in wonderment from time to time. Johannes Bernhardt had been among the first of several hundred Germans resident in Spanish Morocco to become a member of the National Socialist German Workers' party. However, he might well have remained forever a simple clerk in a small export firm and continued to have been regarded as something of an eccentric and a crank had not his Führer become the master of the German State on January 30, 1933. For, therewith, Johannes Bernhardt's star began to rise, his political prescience and patriotic faith soon to be fittingly rewarded. As a Nazi party leader in North Africa the little clerk was now a person of some importance. He was thus emboldened to court Fräulein Wilmer. Herr Wilmer, on his part, was pleased to give his consent to the marriage. Her dowry was the managership of the Wilmer Brothers branch at Tetuán. Nazi party leader Bernhardt, with an eye to the future, cultivated the friendship of the Spanish officers stationed in Morocco. On July 19, 1936, he was among those who greeted General Franco when the future Caudillo landed at Tetuán after his flight from the Canary Islands. Bernhardt was to reap a fortune from his role as intermediary between the Spanish rebels and the German authorities.[7]

From the beginning the German government and Nazi party leaders were intensely interested in the rapidly unfolding Spanish situation. In a telegram dated San Sebastián, July 19, 1936, the German chargé d'affaires, Hans Voelckers, reported to the German Foreign Ministry that "beginning yesterday, the expected military revolts have broken out all over Spain." [8] The word "expected" does not necessarily have the sinister connotation that the German government was privy to the plans of the Spanish rebels in specific detail. It probably reflected the general awareness in Berlin that a military insurrection in Spain was in the offing. However, an able journalist, Charles Foltz, Jr., who was in Spain both during and after the Civil War, affirmed that when General Franco landed at Tetuán

he was handed by Johannes Bernhardt a personal letter from Adolf
Hitler in which the Führer expressed sympathy with Franco's
efforts to "save" Spain.[9] This was on July 19, 1936. If what Foltz
reported is true, then the German government was extremely well
informed with respect to both the intentions and the plan of revolt
of the Spanish generals and, in this case, the word "expected"
acquires a deeper meaning.

On July 24, 1936, the counselor of the German Embassy in
Madrid, Dr. Karl Schwendemann, sent a lengthy telegram to the
German Foreign Ministry in which he described recent developments in Spain and evaluated the advantages and disadvantages of
the contending Spanish forces. In conclusion he noted that:

> The consequences of a Government victory would be very grave for
> internal and foreign affairs. Domestically they would insure Marxist
> control of Spain for a long time, with danger of a Spanish Soviet
> regime. As regards foreign policy, Spain, ideologically and materially,
> would become closely allied to the Franco-Russian bloc. The effects
> of such a development on German-Spanish relations and on the Ger-
> mans in Spain would be very serious. An opposite development would
> result in case of a victory of the monarchist-Fascist rebels.[10]

Within a week of the uprising in Morocco, then, the German
Embassy in Madrid had made it clear to Berlin that German interests would be furthered by a rebel victory in Spain. However,
Herr Schwendemann was "carrying coals to Newcastle." When the
Spanish generals, who now found themselves in desperate circumstances, made overtures for assistance to Berlin, the Germans responded with alacrity.

There is irony in the fact that the self-appointed custodians of
"the traditional Spain"—the Spain of consummate pride and independence of spirit—were forced by the fierce resistance of the
Spanish masses to seek, almost from the beginning, foreign aid in
their bid to win mastery over Spain. For, only five days after Lieutenant Colonel Juan Yagüe had begun the revolt in Morocco,
Lieutenant Colonel Beigbeder, in the name of General Franco, requested the immediate dispatch of ten Junkers transport airplanes

from the Germans. The message, asking that the airplanes be flown "with German crews to any airfield in Spanish Morocco," was sent through the German Consulate in Tetuán to General Kühlental, the German military attaché in France who was also accredited to Portugal.[11]

On July 24, 1936, a German Lufthansa airplane, the D-APOK, that ostensibly had been seized by Spanish rebel forces at Las Palmas, arrived at Tempelhof airport in Berlin after a flight from the Canary Islands by way of Spanish Morocco, Sevilla, and Marseilles. Two days before, while at Tetuán in Spanish Morocco, it had received as passengers two Spanish rebel officers and the German citizens Johannes Bernhardt and Adolf Langenheim, both of whom were members of the Auslandsorganisation of the N.S.D.A.P. (the foreign branch of the Nazi party). Bernhardt carried letters from General Franco addressed to Chancellor Hitler and Air Minister Göring. These letters were immediately delivered to the Führer who was at Bayreuth. Hitler thereupon summoned Göring and the minister of war, General Werner von Blomberg. In the late evening of the same day (July 24) support for the Spanish rebels was agreed to in principle.[12]

It is significant that in these early days of the Spanish Civil War contact between the Spanish rebels and the German leaders was first established through the Auslandsorganisation of the N.S.D.A.P. This had come about because, in the first place, Spanish rebel overtures made to the German government through normal diplomatic channels had encountered the cautious conservatism of the German Foreign Ministry under Baron Constantin von Neurath.[13] The Auslandsorganisation provided the Spanish rebels with a means to expedite matters and to negotiate directly with such Nazi stalwarts as Bernhardt, Langenheim, and, ultimately, Göring and the Führer himself. Secondly, the Germans themselves encouraged this informal approach on the part of the Spaniards as a necessary safeguard against any untoward development.[14]

On July 29, 1936, Adolf Langenheim who had meanwhile returned to Tetuán where he was the Ortsgruppenleiter of the local

branch of the N.S.D.A.P., sent by way of the German Consulate
the following telegram to Air Minister Göring:

In accordance with instructions I report the following: I had a conversation with General Franco. The future Nationalist government
of Spain has been organized in the form of a directorate of the three
Generals, Franco, Queipo de Llano, and Mola, with General Franco
presiding. Our view of future German commercial, cultural, and military relations with Spain conforms fully with General Franco's desires
and intentions. Heil Hitler! [15]

By the end of July German aircraft, arms, munitions, and other
supplies began to reach the Spanish rebel forces.[16] Shuttling back
and forth between Morocco and Andalusia, Junkers transport airplanes, complete with Luftwaffe crews, discharged thousands of
fully-armed Legionnaires and Moors at the Sevilla airport. Franco
was thus enabled to surmount the obstacle of the Republican
fleet in the Straits of Gibraltar below.[17]

On August 15 a telegram marked "urgent" reached Admiral
Canaris in Berlin. It had been sent by a German agent in Spain,
Seydel, through the German ambassador in France, Count Johannes
von Welczeck, who until April, 1936, had been the German ambassador in Spain. This document confirms that by the middle
of August General Franco had already received important German
assistance. It reveals, moreover, that the Germans were now contemplating an expansion of their support of the rebel forces to include the northern theater of war. It follows:

1. General Mola has just communicated the following through a
special agent:
    (a) Liaison with Franco is still not satisfactory.
    (b) The northern group is most urgently in need of planes (partic-
ularly fighters), bombs, rifle and machine-gun ammunition, hand
grenades, and side arms. Most of all, ammunition is needed.
    (c) The point of destination for all supplies is La Coruña.
2. In my opinion, supplies for the northern group are especially
urgent at present, since thus far the southern group has been supplied
exclusively.
I am more and more of the impression that it is extremely urgent

to dispatch an expert at once to appraise on the spot the question of supplies for the northern and southern groups. The place for him to report with the northern group: Pamplona, Colonel Solchaga at the Comandancia General, Noain Airport.

3. General Mola's representative is waiting here for decision on points 1 and 2.[18]

Another document, in contrast with Seydel's crisply efficient report, strikes a somewhat comic note. However, it, too, reveals that the Germans had intervened in Spain almost from the beginning of the conflict. On August 14 the German consul at Sevilla, Draeger, sent a dispatch marked "secret" to the German Foreign Ministry in which he lamented that "the Germans who came to Seville in order to deliver certain materials to Spain" were by their "white uniforms and white Olympic caps" immediately recognized as Germans. "It is manifest, therefore, what our people are doing here," Draeger added. He noted, by way of contrast, that the Italian fliers who had arrived in the Andalusian capital were attired in the uniforms of officers of the Spanish Foreign Legion. Draeger ruefully concluded that while he assumed that the matter had already been brought to the attention of the proper authorities in Berlin he wanted "to point out that, because of the way it has been handled, it has long since been impossible to keep the enterprise secret." [19]

Thus, the Germans were playing a double game. While powerful aid was being clandestinely dispatched by the Nazis to the Spanish rebels, the German government continued to proclaim that it was strictly neutral in the Spanish conflict. When, for instance, the French ambassador in Germany, André François-Poncet, called on the German foreign minister the morning of August 4, 1936, and broached the idea of a joint declaration by the interested powers regarding nonintervention in the internal affairs of Spain, Baron von Neurath replied that it would be superfluous for the German government to make such a declaration inasmuch as Germany "naturally did not intervene in Spanish internal political affairs and disputes." [20]

However, the discrepancy between what the German government was saying and what the Nazis were doing reflected no fundamental and permanent clash of ideas within the German leadership.
It was, at most, a fleeting phenomenon occasioned by the need of
the German leadership to assay the situation created by the Spanish
war and to formulate and effectuate a policy with respect to it.
In the final analysis, the Nazis and the German government were
sufficiently one to obviate what slight influence lingering careerists
from the Weimar period might have on German diplomacy. After
only a brief time the Reich's sympathy with the rebel cause was
openly expressed. Indeed, twenty-four hours before Baron von
Neurath reassured Ambassador François-Poncet of the rectitude
of German diplomacy and the "natural" disinclination of the Reich
to interfere in Spanish affairs, the German government's first overt
gesture of sympathy with the Spanish rebels was made in Morocco
and the Mediterranean. On the morning of August 3 a German
squadron commanded by Rear Admiral Rolf Carls and composed
of the pocket battleship *Deutschland* and the torpedo boat *Luchs*
put in at Ceuta. The same day Rear Admiral Carls inspected the
Legionnaires and Moors assembled in his honor and received the
thanks which General Franco gave Germany and the Führer for
the moral support that this visit symbolized.[21] The "Viva España"
of the Teuton was answered by the "Viva Alemania" and the
"Viva Hitler" of the Spaniards.[22] In the afternoon of that same
day Rear Admiral Carls was able to give substance to the "moral
support" for which General Franco had expressed his gratitude by
maneuvering the *Deutschland* between Ceuta and the Republican
battleship *Jaime I* which had come to bombard the city but which
after a time steamed away without having fired a shot.[23]

Meanwhile, the steady flow of German technicians and war
supplies to rebel-held territory continued. On August 9 there arrived in Sevilla, in addition to ten new Italian Savoia tri-motor
bombers accompanied by about twenty Italian pilots, eighteen
German Junkers tri-motor bombers (most of which were new)
accompanied by about thirty German pilots, six German pursuit

planes capable of 450 kilometers an hour, and six German anti-
aircraft guns of the latest model and with an effective range of
700 meters.[24]

The intervention of Fascist Italy in the Spanish conflict occurred
simultaneously with that of Nazi Germany. In the ensuing months
and years, moreover, Italian support of the Spanish rebels continued to grow until it became, in terms of the number of men
involved and the amount of equipment employed, a veritable
Italian invasion of Spain. There can be no doubt that Italian soldiers
and Italian arms were essential factors in General Franco's triumph.

While German and Italian intervention in Spain occurred simultaneously and soon became something of a joint enterprise, there
were important differences between the German and Italian con-
tributions to the rebel victory. Quantitatively, the Italian military
effort in Spain was greater than that of Germany. The Italians
provided masses of infantry, field artillery, light tanks, and fighter
planes as well as some bombers.[25] However, qualitatively, the German military effort was superior to the Italian. While the Germans
provided some infantry, field artillery, light tanks, and fighter
planes, their principal contribution lay in making available to General Franco large quantities of heavy equipment and in organizing,
supplying, and manning those highly technical services without
which a modern war cannot be waged.[26] From Germany came most
of the heavy artillery and trained artillerists, the heavy bombers
and pilots, navigators, and bombardiers, and the antiaircraft guns
and gunners of the rebel army.[27] The Germans were the engineers
who designed and built the field fortifications from behind which
the rebels turned back repeated Republican attacks. They organized and conducted the officer and noncommissioned officer
training schools of the rebel army. Rebel naval operations which
demanded high technical proficiency, such as mine-laying, were
supervised by the Germans. The cartographic headquarters at
Vitoria was staffed by them.[28]

At least as important as the high quality of the German military
effort in Spain was the swift efficiency with which the Germans,

once they had decided to intervene in the conflict, organized and dispatched assistance to the rebel forces. In this respect the decisive importance of German intervention as over against that of Italy admits of no doubt. For in late July and early August, 1936, it was Germany, rather than Italy, which supplied the margin of military superiority that enabled the Spanish generals to escape from the cul de sac in which their own ineptitude and the vast and bitter resistance of the Spanish people had placed them. While Italian aid was not negligible, it was committed to the struggle in a hesitant and piecemeal fashion. Berlin, in contrast, acted with speed and determination. It was the prompt arrival of a sufficient number of German Junkers transport airplanes in Spanish Morocco that enabled General Franco to ferry thousands of troops across the Straits and to begin the advance on Badajoz, whose fall was to prove an unmitigated disaster for the Republic.

It is more than doubtful that Italy, left to its own means, could have rescued the rebels from the ignominious defeat that would have followed from the failure of the generals' coup d'état. Germany's greater strength, superior organization, and, of salient importance, central role in the diplomacy of the 1930s, permitted Hitler to take the long chance of prompt and effective intervention in Spain that if taken by Mussolini—unsupported by Germany and in the face of a Great Britain still smarting from the hurt of the Ethiopian affair and a France ever fearful of Italian designs on the Balearic Islands—might well have ended in fiasco. Thus, the intervention of Germany was one thing, that of Italy alone would have been quite another.

However, given the operational nature of the war in Spain—a war in which the front was long and rambling and thinly-held and in which rifle battalions, machine gun companies, and field batteries constituted the basic combatant elements—Italian infantry played a role of considerable importance. For, with the passage of time and the gradual decimation of the Moorish levies, the Italians were to become the hard core of the rebel army. It can be said, then, that the relationship between Italy and Germany vis-à-vis the war in Spain was sympathetically symbiotic. In the military sphere there came to exist something of a division of labor between them, in the political sphere an increasing cooperation, tempered, to be sure, by the rivalry and jealous bickering which so often mar the relations between allies. It is not entirely coincidental that the formation of the Rome-Berlin Axis and formal recognition of the Franco regime by the fascist powers occurred almost simultaneously (November, 1936). Not only for Spain, then, but for Europe as well, Italian involvement in the Spanish conflict had important consequences.

As early as July 15, 1936, the day the airplane piloted by Captain Bebb and carrying a party of "English tourists" landed at Las Palmas, the pilots and crews of five Savoia bombers belonging to the 55th, 57th, and 58th squadrons of the Royal Italian Air Force were ordered to be ready for duty in Spain.[29] This would seem to suggest that the Italian government was privy to the generals' plan of revolt. However, inasmuch as the designated Italian airmen and aircraft were not ordered to join General Franco until two weeks later, the order of July 15 might have been simply anticipatory and did not necessarily indicate a foreknowledge of events except in a general sense. What seems most probable is that the Italian government, aware of the rebellious intentions of the Spanish generals, believed the projected revolt to be imminent following the assassination of Calvo Sotelo on the night of July 13 and ordered the Italian units to stand by for action. However, the Italian government, awaiting the development of events both in and outside Spain, hesitated to commit Italian airmen and aircraft to the struggle until it had become evident that General Franco could not win without foreign support and that Germany intended to assist the faltering Spanish rebels.

On July 30, 1936, the five Savoia bombers left their base in Sardinia and flying southwest made for Spanish Morocco. Two of the five arrived there without mishap, but the other three were forced to land in French Morocco, one crashing and burning. The French government ordered General Victor Denain, inspector-general of the French air force, to investigate this flagrant violation of its territory. His report established beyond peradventure of doubt the official character of the Italian expedition. Under a recently applied coat of white paint Italian military markings remained discernible on the aircraft. Moreover, the crews carried Italian Army passes and other documents which clearly established their identity and the nature of their mission. While the Italian officers asserted that the delivery of the aircraft was a private transaction between an unnamed private firm and the Spanish rebels, an Italian sergeant admitted under interrogation that their flying orders had come from the commander of the air base in Sardinia.[30]

However, this initial misadventure did not deter Italy from sending further assistance to the Spanish rebels. On August 1, 1936, the *New York Times* correspondent in Oran, Algeria, reported that he had been informed by telephone by a reliable source in Melilla of the arrival of eighteen Italian Savoia-Marchetti airplanes in that Spanish Moroccan city.[31] Two days later, on August 3, an Italian tri-motor monoplane rose from the airfield at Ceuta, flew north over the Straits of Gibraltar, and dropped seven bombs near the Republican cruiser *Libertad* which was engaged in shelling the rebel-held fortress of Tarifa in Spain.[32] And as was noted, ten new Italian Savoia tri-motor bombers accompanied by about twenty Italian pilots arrived in Sevilla on August 9.[33] Italian aid continued to arrive in increasing volume throughout the month of August and, in conjunction with the even greater, better organized, and more effective assistance rendered General Franco by the Germans during this critical phase of the war, was to enable the Spanish rebels to negate the presence of the Republican fleet in the Straits of Gibraltar and to land in force in southern Spain.

On August 14, Badajoz, on the Portuguese frontier, fell to the advancing rebels and soon thereafter junction was made with General Mola's forward units at Cáceres. This was a critically important development and with it the war entered a new phase. For, as long as General Mola was contained in the north and General

Franco isolated in Morocco (save for certain limited areas in southern Spain held by small rebel forces under General Queipo de Llano), the Republican militia, if swiftly concentrated and supplied with sufficient rifles and machine guns, was in a position to turn the aborted coup d'état into a military rout. However, once General Franco had been enabled to cross the Straits of Gibraltar in force and to effect a junction with General Mola, the military position of the Republicans immediately deteriorated to the point where offensive action and a quick end to the war could no longer be seriously contemplated in Madrid. For General Franco's command included the bulk of the best-trained and best-equipped soldiers in Spain. Against unwilling conscripts and a handful of *requetés* the more numerous and enthusiastic Republican militia had a better than even chance. But against the professional soldiers of the Tercio (the Foreign Legion), against the hard-fighting Regulares (the Moorish levies), against German and Italian air power and matériel, the *milicianos* could not hope to advance. They would do well to dig in and hold until such time, perhaps, as the face of things changed and help reached them somehow from somewhere.

The part played by the Portuguese government in these events demands some comment. Lisbon's assistance to the Spanish rebels was not of the same magnitude as that of either Germany or Italy and was in some respects distinctly collateral to the efforts of the fascist powers. However, it was not negligible and during the critical first weeks of the war it exercised an influence on the course of events disproportionate with the very limited resources and power of the Portuguese State. A further significance attaches to the part played by Portugal in the Spanish Civil War. In seeking to meet the exigencies created by the Spanish crisis, the Portuguese government immediately felt the pressures and counter-pressures of the various European powers to whom the Iberian Peninsula represented an area of supreme strategic importance. Therefore, Lisbon, in its own reaction to the crisis, reflected to some extent the interplay of the conflicting ambitions of the great powers.

Portugal under Dr. Antonio Salazar and Austria under Engelbert Dollfuss bore a certain organic resemblance to each other. Both were small states which cherished memories of past greatness but which now were pawns in the game of European power-politics. Their political regimes were much alike and could be described as typical of the "shirtless fascism" in which the absolute power of the politically dominant clique remains festooned with the traditional trappings of authority rather than being freshly bedecked in monochromatic shirts, leader cults, racial myths, and so forth. In both states the Roman Catholic Church enjoyed a pre-eminent position and exercised a pervasive political influence. In both states governmental policies aimed at the preservation of vested interests and vested privileges and at the exorcism of liberal and Marxist influences.

It can be assumed that if Señor Gil Robles, whose CEDA reflected the political philosophy of an important element of the Spanish episcopacy, had been able to establish himself as the Spanish *jefe*, his regime would not have been fundamentally dissimilar from that of Salazar in Portugal or Dollfuss in Austria. It can be assumed, too, that the Portuguese government would have viewed with sympathy such a development in Spain. For it is not without significance that Portugal served as a haven for Spanish Rightist refugees, including Gil Robles himself and, of course, General Sanjurjo, the leader of the August, 1932, uprising against the Republic and the titular head of the July, 1936, military insurrection.

However, for reasons already discussed, it came to pass that not the moderate, semi-constitutional, civilian politician, Gil Robles, not the general of the traditional *pronunciamiento*, Sanjurjo, but an inveterate foe of the Republic and a rigid authoritarian, General Francisco Franco, emerged as the leader of the Spanish Right. And Franco, in pursuance of his ends, was prepared to break the catena of tradition and to venture forth along paths first marked out by Mussolini and Hitler. Perhaps the Portuguese felt some trepidation at this development. The establishment of a militarist, expansionist regime in Madrid could well constitute a threat to the continued independence of Portugal. The sixty years of bond-age to Madrid (1580–1640) had not been forgotten in Lisbon. It was unlikely that they would ever be. For, keeping the memory of them forever fresh, there had been no dearth of Spaniards who, down through the years, continued to bemoan the political division of the Peninsula.[34] The Spanish Republic, on the other hand, pre-sented no menace to Portuguese independence. However, the regime of Dr. Antonio Salazar and the interests it represented seemed prepared to run the risk implicit in the establishment of an expansionist military dictatorship in Madrid (a risk that was, however, contingent on a serious decline of British power and prestige) in order to avoid the social and ideological contagion of a Spain dominated by the Frente Popular.

Having permitted Portugal to be used first as a haven and then as a base of operations by the Spanish conspirators, the Portuguese authorities, with the revolt in Morocco, unreservedly gave their support to the Spanish rebels.[35] The assistance rendered Franco by Portugal falls into three general categories: the use of Portu-guese ports, railroads, and other facilities for the transshipment of German and Italian war materials to the rebels; diplomatic, propa-gandistic, and moral support of the rebel cause; and the dispatch of Portuguese "volunteers" and arms to Franco's armies.

In a letter dated Paris, August 2, 1936, the German ambassador in France, Count Johannes von Welczeck, informed the director of the Political Department of the German Foreign Ministry, Dr. Hans Dieckhoff, that he (Welczeck) had had lunch on July 31, 1936, with Herr Danielson. Danielson, until President Azaña had returned his credentials because of his outspoken criticism of the Spanish government, had been the Swedish ambassador in Madrid as well as in Lisbon. Danielson had informed Welczeck that "Salazar told him [Danielson] confidentially that he planned to support the Spanish Rightists with all available means . . . since the bolshevization of Spain would be a serious danger to Portu-gal." [36]

In a telegram dated Lisbon, August 22, 1936, the German

chargé d'affaires in Portugal, Count Du Moulin-Eckart, reported
to the German Foreign Ministry concerning the arrival in the
port of Lisbon of two German vessels carrying war materials. He
said in part:

After the steamships *Kamerun* and *Wigbert* arrived in Lisbon, the
material was sent on most smoothly through the agency of Herr Bernhardt (Hisma).[37] Prime Minister Salazar removed all difficulties within
a very short time by his personal initiative and *personal* handling of details. He entrusted former Minister of Commerce Ramires with the
project.[38]

The following day, August 23, 1936, Count Du Moulin-Eckart
sent a dispatch marked "confidential" by air courier to the German
Foreign Ministry. This rather lengthy dispatch was concerned with
Portugal's attitude toward the war in Spain. Du Moulin-Eckart
emphasized the staunch anti-communism of the Portuguese Prime
Minister. He reported that Salazar through "his authoritarian in-
fluence" had made the Portuguese press serve the cause of the
Spanish rebels, had facilitated the acquisition of all kinds of war
materials by the rebels, and, on one occasion before the fall of
Badajoz established direct communication between Franco's and
Mola's forces, had permitted a shipment of munitions en route
from Sevilla to Burgos to pass through Portuguese territory.[39]

Du Moulin-Eckart stressed the point that the activities of the
Portuguese government on behalf of the Spanish rebels were the
source of considerable annoyance in London, for the English, as
allies of the Portuguese, did not wish to become embroiled in the
Spanish conflict.[40] Du Moulin-Eckart saw in this situation an opportunity for Germany to win a position of influence in Portugal.
He wrote:

Since Portugal in pursuing this policy is acting in pronounced opposition to her British ally, it is natural that popular sympathy in Portugal
should, as a result of the situation created by the Spanish Civil War,
turn sharply away not only from France but also from England—
whose prestige, moreover, has suffered through the outcome of the
Italo-Abyssinian conflict—and that public opinion is inclined toward

the countries that favor the Spanish revolutionaries [*i.e.*, the Franco forces]. There are thus numerous evidences of admiration for our Führer and respect for the new Germany in Portugal today, and there is no doubt that our reputation here has been greatly enhanced. Under these circumstances the question arises whether one might not take advantage of this favorable sentiment by prompt and generous action with regard to participating in the rearmament program of the Portuguese armed forces, in case the execution of this program should now be accelerated. We should bear in mind that the Italians, who suffered a great deal of damage in this field at the time of the sanctions, have lately been very active here.[41]

The *New York Times* correspondent in London placed a somewhat different construction on Great Britain's position with respect to Portugal and the war in Spain. Reporting that the Portuguese foreign minister, Armindo Monteiro, had asserted while on a visit to London that his country would be endangered if a Red government were established in Madrid, the *New York Times* correspondent went on to note that the British government was anxious to see the Salazar regime maintained in Portugal because, among other reasons, it constituted a bulwark against possible distribution of the Portuguese colonies among the great powers from which England could not profit while Germany had much to gain.[42]

Perhaps there was not as much disagreement between Great Britain and Portugal concerning the assistance that Portugal was giving the Spanish rebels as Count Du Moulin-Eckart believed. In view of Great Britain's desire to retain a position of influence in Portugal, British acquiescence in Portuguese support of Franco was not precluded by the fact that while Great Britain adhered to a policy of strict neutrality in the Spanish conflict Germany was actively assisting the rebels. At the most, it created a fluid situation from which Germany could hope to profit. However, such were the bonds which united the two ancient allies that while Portuguese assistance to the rebels continued throughout the Spanish Civil War,[43] English-Portuguese relations did not deteriorate but remained close and cordial.

The period between July 17 and August 14, 1936, that is, between the initial uprising in Morocco and the fall of Badajoz, was
of critical importance in determining the duration and intensity
and, as it proved, the ultimate outcome of the Spanish conflict.
This period can be divided into three phases. The first, lasting only
a few days, had seen the Spanish generals lead their troops into
the streets of a number of important cities and proclaim the end
of the Republic and the establishment of military rule. At first
blush this had appeared to be but the last in a long series of *pronunciamientos*, an apparently successful coup d'état that would
have seen a military junta established in Madrid to be followed,
in due course, by the reemergence of civilian government in the
form, perhaps, of a restored monarchy. A purely Spanish affair,
it would have had a quite limited effect on the international situation. There had been highly placed persons in the Republican government who had been prepared to accept this turn of events in the
hope of averting a calamitous disintegration of authority and order
and salvaging something, perhaps, from the liberal Republic. However, the successful resistance of the populace in Madrid and Barcelona, coupled with the continued loyalty of most of the Spanish
air force and navy, had resulted in a complete reversal of fortune.
By July 22 it had become evident that the coup d'état had failed.
Thereupon, resolving their doubts and quieting their apprehensions,
the middle-class leaders of the Republic, vigorously supported by
the working classes, had energetically moved to crush the rebellion. Until this time foreign military assistance to either the Republicans or the rebels had been negligible. Toward the end of
July, however, German, Italian, and Portuguese support of the
rebels had begun in earnest. Because of this support Franco had
been enabled to cross the Straits of Gibraltar, to capture Badajoz,
and to join with Mola.

It was now apparent that unless equally prompt and com-
mensurate military assistance reached the Republicans from abroad
their situation was desperate.

IV

The Friendless Neighbor: The Origins of "Nonintervention"

WHAT had been the signs and guideposts of the foreign policy of the Spanish Republic? Who were Spain's friends, her enemies? From what quarter could the Republic expect assistance to come?

Among the "General Propositions" of the constitution of 1931 appeared the statement: "España renuncia a la guerra como instrumento de política nacional." [1] This reflected, of course, the widespread pacifism of the post-First World War years as well as the idealistic sentiments of the Constituent Cortes. The constitution declared that the president of the Republic did not have the power to sign a declaration of war except under the conditions prescribed in the Covenant of the League of Nations and only after exhausting all pacific means and submitting to all the arbitration and conciliation procedures to which Spain had agreed and which were registered with the League of Nations. The president, finally, would have to be authorized to sign such a declaration by a law. [2]

Without detracting from the high idealism that animated the framers of the Republican constitution, it can be said that Spain's constitutional renunciation of war as an instrument of national policy was, to some extent at least, an expression of her poverty and economic backwardness, her limited capacity to wage modern war, and her relative unimportance in the endemic power-struggle of the great European states. Since the Spanish-American

War of 1898—that saw Spain deprived of the last vestiges of her once vast empire—Spain's natural place in international affairs was to be found among the small and peaceful states of Europe, such as Switzerland, Sweden, the Netherlands, Belgium, and Portugal. This comported, moreover, with the needs of Spain as well as with the desires of many Spaniards. It could well have come to pass that, given years of peace and economic development, Spain would have emerged as the leader of the secondary states of Europe. In the halcyon days of the League of Nations, before its prestige and influence were fatally diminished by the successful aggressions against China and Ethiopia, this trend was already discernible.[3]

However, various factors militated against the permanent enrollment of Spain among the small and peaceful states of Europe. To begin with, there was the pride and ambition of many Spaniards who were to be found in all strata of the population but particularly among the aristocracy and the military caste. These Spaniards, as the self-proclaimed custodians of the nation's greatness, demanded that Spain play a role in world affairs in keeping with her imperial traditions.[4] For the fact that Spain had preceded the rest of Europe to the New World and had left her mark on the physical features as well as the habits and sentiments of millions of people below the Río Grande remained fixed in the memory and Weltanschauung of many Spaniards, much as the glory of ancient Rome continued to influence the political thought of many modern Italians. Then, too, the relatively considerable manpower, abundant but undeveloped mineral resources, and strategic geographical position of Spain gave her an inherent importance denied to most of the secondary states of Europe and made her the particular object of the schemes and intrigues of the great powers.

The Gibraltaran irredenta and unsated Spanish ambitions in North Africa, buttressed by the ideological predilections of a large part of the Spanish upper class, served to turn Spain toward Germany and Italy. But the important economic and strategic ties between Spain and Great Britain and France, strengthened by the political and intellectual orientation of Spanish liberals and radicals, strongly influenced Spanish policies in favor of the Western democracies. Thus, if the main thrust of Spanish diplomacy in the period following the First World War aimed at the alignment of Spain beside the small and peaceful states of Europe, it was deflected, first in this direction, then in that, by the dominant historic interests of the Spanish State, by the rival influences of the great powers, and by the discrepant motivations of the Spaniards themselves. With the establishment of the Republic in 1931, Spanish foreign policy exhibited a strengthened desire to align Spain with the small and peaceful states and to uphold the principles of the League of Nations while it reflected a growing tendency to support the two great Western democracies against Germany and Italy.[5] If during the Lerroux–Gil Robles regime these tendencies were considerably less evident than under Azaña, then with the coming of the Popular Front government they were even more marked.

Official relations between the Spanish government and the Russian government, from the establishment of the Bolshevik regime in Russia in 1917 to the outbreak of the Civil War in Spain in 1936, were well-nigh nonexistent. For it was not until 1933 that Madrid and Moscow agreed to extend *de jure* recognition to each other and to exchange diplomatic representatives. However, while the designated Russian ambassador, Anatoli Lunacharski, sought to recover his health on the French Riviera (where he was soon to die) and before the designated Spanish ambassador, J. Álvarez del Vayo, could depart for his new post in the Russian capital, the Spanish Right won the general elections of November, 1933. The Lerroux–Gil Robles government did not withdraw Spain's recognition of Soviet Russia but it showed no interest in an exchange of ambassadors. It was not until August, 1936, that is, after the revolt of the generals, that Marcel Rosenberg, the newly appointed Russian ambassador, was received in Madrid.

Spanish foreign policy following the First World War, particularly as conducted by the liberal-minded foreign ministers of the Republic, must have seemed in Madrid sufficient warrant for the

assumption that with the outbreak of civil war (in which it became immediately evident that many rebel leaders were imbued
with "España Grande" notions and whose cause the expansionist
fascist powers made their own) the Republic would enjoy the support of the small and peaceful states of Europe and of Great Britain
and France.

J. Álvarez del Vayo, who served as foreign minister of the Spanish Republic during the greater part of the Civil War, wrote:

During the most critical period of its existence the Republic remained
steadfast to the high principles which had inspired its international policy since its creation—the loyal observance of commitments, support of
the League of Nations, and a firm determination to serve the cause
of peace. Apart from these general principles, the Republic clearly
realized that it was united to the two great Western democracies by
common interests and geographical situation, and therefore sought a
rapprochement with Great Britain and France by every means in its
power. In spite of the attitude of reserve shown by both those countries, collaboration with Great Britain and France was throughout the
Spanish War the guiding principle and ruling ambition of the Spanish
Republic in so far as its foreign policy was concerned.[6]

In the expectation of support from peaceful and friendly states
in general and from Great Britain and France in particular the
Spanish Republican government must have been confirmed not only
by the course of Spain's diplomacy in recent years but also by the
requirements and practices of international law relative to rebellion. An armed assault on the duly established government of a
state is, by the laws of all nations, an act of treason.[7] However,
when an armed disturbance assumes such proportions that it cannot
be successfully dealt with by the police and must be met by the
military forces of the established government, then a *de facto*
situation of insurgency exists. By opening the arsenals and arming
the workers' militias the Madrid government had tacitly acknowl-
edged that a state of insurgency had come to exist. However,
"throughout the stages of both pre- and post-admission of insurgency, the established government of the distraught state continues to enjoy its normal peacetime personality and status. It may

continue its diplomatic relations with all friendly states and participate in international organizations as if no rupture of its domestic
peace had occurred. Customarily, it has been permitted to purchase
arms and war materials in the private markets of other states for
the suppression of the revolt, a privilege often denied to insurgents
by the domestic laws of foreign states." [8]

When it became evident that the Republic had to contend with
a widespread and formidable military rebellion, the Spanish government sought to purchase arms and munitions from friendly
foreign powers. Given the circumstances in which the Republic
found itself—except for detachments of Civil Guards and Assault
Guards (Guardias de Asalto, a small and purely Republican force
of shock police organized after the Sanjurjo *putsch* of August 10,
1932), most of the small and poorly-equipped air force, and the
virtually autonomous and inadequately armed workers' militias,
it was bereft of military power, the army, almost en masse, having
gone over to the rebels [9]—this move to acquire war materials from
abroad was not only a legitimate exercise of its right under international law but a desperate effort to counterbalance the military
advantage enjoyed by its foes.

There is no doubt that in the first days of the war the Republicans, and the rebels as well, succeeded in obtaining an odd collec-
tion of civilian and obsolete military aircraft and various types of
arms and supplies from the British and the French.[10] This was before the Anglo-French policy of nonintervention had come into
being. Moreover, this early procurement of arms and supplies had
no particular relation to national policies as such, involving people
of several nationalities and diverse backgrounds and being in the
nature of gun-running, private transactions, and sales through
intermediaries, such as the plan of the (American) Vacuum Oil
Company to furnish aviation gasoline to the Franco forces through
third parties and by arrangement with pro-rebel Portuguese authorities.[11] This sort of clandestine, helter-skelter interference in the
factional strife of a nation is an ancient and almost uncontrollable
practice and is in no way comparable to the dispatch by foreign

powers of men and equipment from their regular armed forces. The attempt of Count Galeazzo Ciano, the Italian foreign minister, to equate the two in the conversation he had on July 29, 1936, with Count Louis Charles de Chambrun, the French ambassador in Rome, must be viewed as sheer sophistry.[12]

In these first days of the Civil War Republican Spain received, in addition to such arms and supplies as she was able to procure through devious and secondary channels from Great Britain and France, many expressions of sympathy and moral support and even financial assistance from liberal and radical groups in the Western democracies and from places as distant as Soviet Russia and Latin America. At the end of July, 1936, Léon Jouhaux, secretary general of the French General Confederation of Labor that claimed a membership of 4,000,000, announced that organized labor in France had begun a drive to raise funds to assist the Spanish unions in their struggle against the rebellious generals, warning that a rebel victory in Spain would constitute a "permanent menace against our country and the French Republic."[13] A few days later the British Labor party announced that it, too, was soliciting funds to be sent to the Spanish government, a spokesman for the Labor party declaring that "we do not regard the conflict in Spain as between Communists and Fascists, but between an elected government and its opponents."[14] It is of some interest to note that while French labor planned to give financial support to the Spanish unions directly and pointed to the menace to France and to the "French Republic" implicit in a Franco victory, British labor spoke in terms of defense of an "elected government" and of monetary assistance to the Spanish government. Meanwhile, mass demonstrations of solidarity with the Spanish people were being held in Moscow and scores of other Russian cities and towns. Moreover, hundreds of thousands of rubles were contributed by Russian workers "for the assistance of the fighters."[15] However, the American chargé d'affaires in Moscow, Loy Henderson, observed in a report to the United States Department of State, dated August 4, 1936, that "there is no indication as yet that the Soviet Union is expecting to lend the Spanish Government other than pecuniary assistance." [16] In fact, the wisdom of lending even pecuniary assistance to the Spanish government was questioned by some Soviet officials who argued that Germany and Italy would seize upon it in justification of their intervention in Spain.[17] However, other Soviet officials maintained that the Soviet Union's position as leader of the international proletariat rendered imperative some such gesture of solidarity with the embattled people of Spain.[18]

Yet, not Russia, not even Great Britain, but France was the pivot around which the hopes of the Spanish Republic turned. Geographical propinquity was an important but not the only factor which prompted the Spaniards to look to Paris for help. For it was appreciated in Madrid that France would be the most directly menaced of the great powers by a fascist victory in Spain and might be expected, therefore, to act energetically to forestall this threat to its security. Moreover, France was governed by the Front Populaire which was ideologically analogous to the Frente Popular and which might be expected to harbor strong feelings of friendship and sympathy for the Madrid government. On August 16, 1936, Roger Salengro, the French minister of the interior, made a speech in Lille. He was the mayor of the city and he spoke quite frankly, and in doing so he probably voiced the sentiments of many Frenchmen. He said in part: "I am aware of the responsibility that I assume and I weigh my words: as a Frenchman and as a member of the government of the Republic, I hope that, beyond the Pyrenees, the legal government of a friendly nation gains the victory." [19]

Beyond an odd assortment of obsolete aircraft, First World War rifles and machine guns, beyond eloquent words of encouragement (morally significant as these were), beyond pecuniary support (the Spanish Republic had ample reserves of gold), what Madrid needed and wanted was to be assured of an adequate and continuous supply of first-class war materials for which it was able to pay and to which it was entitled under international law. To this end Madrid had approached the French government within a few days of the uprising in Morocco and when it had become apparent that a hard struggle lay ahead.[20] The Spanish request had produced a sharp division of opinion within the French government. Some French officials, among them Pierre Cot, the minister of aviation, were in favor of permitting the Spanish government to purchase arms and supplies in French markets.[21] They maintained that in so doing France would not be transgressing established convention and would be safeguarding its own interests. Other French officials, including Yvon Delbos, the minister of foreign affairs, and Édouard Daladier, the minister of war, were strongly opposed to such a course, being fearful that it might involve France in grave international complications.[22] Premier Léon Blum had initially supported Cot, then had wavered, and had finally come to stand with Delbos and Daladier.[23] At a meeting of the French Cabinet on July 25, 1936, it was formally decided not to supply arms to the Madrid government.[24]

This decision of the French government, involving an apparent change of heart on the part of Premier Blum, was of salient importance. It came to mean, in the fulness of time, that the Spanish Republic was doomed to defeat and destruction. Meanwhile, it served to create a political milieu both within Spain and as regards the foreign relations of the Spanish Republic extremely favorable to a rapid growth of Communist influence. It should be remembered that the Spanish Communist party had received less than 4 per cent of the total vote cast in the general elections of February 16, 1936 [25] (only five months before the uprising in Morocco) and that normal diplomatic relations did not exist between the Spanish Republic and the Soviet Union until August 1936 (a full month after the uprising in Morocco). At the time of the Franco revolt there was not a single Communist of Cabinet rank in the Frente Popular government and the mass organizations of the Spanish Left were composed of and controlled by either Socialists, who adhered to the Second International, or anarchists, who were as scornful of orthodox Communists as they were of bourgeois Republicans. It should also be remembered that strong

economic and strategic bonds existed between Spain and Great
Britain and France and that the foreign policy of the Spanish Republic had sought to align Spain with the Western democracies
against Germany and Italy. The conclusion is inescapable that
the rapid growth of Communist influence in Spain following the
Franco revolt is in large measure attributable to the inability or
unwillingness of the Western democracies, particularly France,
to afford the Spanish Republic the opportunity to purchase arms
and supplies without which it could not cope with the military
rebellion. For the default of the Western democracies created a
vacuum that Soviet Russia swiftly and at least partially came to
fill. The growth of Communist influence within Republican Spain
was an inevitable concomitant of the emergence of Soviet Russia
as the principal source of war materials of the Spanish Republic.
Thus, there was not a little irony in the fact that many Western
officials, in opposing the sale of arms to Republican Spain, decried
the inordinate influence of communism in Madrid.[26] It proved a
vicious circle: the initial refusal of the Western democracies to
permit Spain to purchase arms and supplies from them (and thus
to strengthen the already firm ties which existed between Spain
and the Western powers) forced the Republic to turn to and receive support from Soviet Russia, which led inevitably to the
growth of Soviet (and Communist) influence in Spanish affairs.
This in turn further alienated Anglo-French opinion from the
Republican cause, driving the isolated Spanish Republic into an
ever greater dependence on Soviet Russia. Apparently, what Germany and Italy, and the Soviet Union, knew so well did not occur
to the Western democracies; to wit, that he who pays the piper
calls the tune.

What were the decisive factors in the determination of French
policy with respect to the Civil War in Spain? If the coup d'état
had been successful and by July 21, or 22, or 23, 1936, the Spanish
Republic had been overthrown and there had been established
in Madrid a military junta under General Sanjurjo, or General
Mola, or General Franco, events in Spain could have been con-

strued in Paris as simply another revolt of the Spanish generals
that, as a purely Spanish affair, could not have any appreciable
affect on Spanish foreign policy in general and on Spanish-French
relations in particular. However, with the failure of the coup d'état
and the transformation of the civil strife in Spain into a civil war
in which the rebellious generals were being actively supported by
Germany and Italy, it was seen in Paris that a situation had developed in Spain that was fraught with peril for the peace and
stability of Europe. In a dispatch to the *New York Times* dated
Paris, July 26, 1936, Jules Sauerwein, the foreign editor of the
Paris-Soir, observed:

> At least four countries are already taking active interest in the battle
> —France, which is supporting the Madrid Government, and Britain,
> Germany and Italy, each of which is giving discreet but nevertheless
> effective assistance to one group or another among the insurgents.
> If this civil war lasts several more weeks it is to be feared that a
> serious quarrel will come out of it, involving these four countries, and
> Russia might also play a dominant role.[27]

The threat of a general European war aroused considerable
anxiety in France where, as an aftermath of the bloodshed and
destruction of the First World War, an abiding pacifism had entered the hearts and minds of millions throughout the land. Moreover, important conservative and Catholic groups in France viewed
the Popular Front government of Spain, and that of France of
course, with open hostility, an attitude that was considerably
strengthened by reports of revolutionary seizures of property,
massacres of Rightists, looting and burning of churches, and other
outrages perpetrated in Republican Spain in the first days of the
war. It must be remembered that since the French Revolution
there were two Frances, two traditions vying with each other for
the sympathy and support of the broad masses of the French
people: the one aristocratic, militarist, conservative, and Catholic;
the other republican, democratic, radical, and anti-clerical. While
such a cleavage of thought and sentiment exists in many of the
nations of modern Europe, it is, perhaps, deeper-going and more

embittered in France than elsewhere.[28] The famous case of Captain Alfred Dreyfus at the turn of the century had momentarily revealed the profound division that existed in the political and intellectual life of France.[29] The war in Spain produced a similar open antagonism between the two Frances, an antagonism that lacked the overtones of personal drama of the Dreyfus affair and did not end with the vindication of the hapless Captain and a renewal of democratic faith but one that was more far-reaching and fatally corrosive of the national spirit, resulting in a paralysis of French initiative during a most critical period of history.

Yet, it is well-nigh inexplicable that this paralysis of French initiative came at the full tide of democratic enthusiasm. Léon Blum, leader of the victorious Front Populaire coalition, had assumed the premiership on June 4, 1936, only some six weeks before the outbreak of the Spanish Civil War. Probably at no time since the Dreyfus affair was the French Left as solidly united as in the summer of 1936. The menace to France of a rearmed and aggressive Germany, the danger to the French Republic of fascist groups such as the Croix de Feu and the Jeunesses Patriotes, the belated but nonetheless heavy impact of the Great Depression on the French economy had combined to produce a reawakening of the French democratic spirit. When Blum took office the nation was in the grip of widespread and extremely effective "sit-down" strikes. The demands for social reforms, for the "forty-hour week," expressed the temper of the French people and were in marked contrast to the "cannon and not butter" of the Germans and the "discipline, order, and hierarchy" of the Italians.

To assist the Spanish Republic with arms and supplies would have comported not only with established practice under international law as well as with the ideological sentiments of the French Left but would have served to insure the tranquillity of the Pyrenean frontier and to safeguard the legitimate interests of France in the Mediterranean and North Africa. It challenges credence that out of the context of French political life in the summer of 1936, that from a Popular Front government fresh with

victory at the polls, should come the first official suggestion of a
nonintervention agreement with respect to the war in Spain. The
profound pacifism of the French people, the open hostility of
French conservative and Catholic circles to support of the Spanish
Republic, the preoccupation of the French masses with domestic
problems, the weakness and vacillation of men like Blum and
Daladier, while contingently of considerable importance, do not
suffice in themselves to explain the decision of the French Cabinet
on July 25, 1936, not to permit the Spaniards to acquire war materials in France. Too much has been made of the popular dread
in France of a general European war. After all, in centuries and
decades past it had not been the practice of the French government, nor of any other government for that matter, to conduct a
popular referendum on the question of war or peace. And on September 3, 1939—only a year after the Munich Conference and
some five months after the last shot had been fired in the Spanish
war—the French government (at whose head was Daladier as
he had been at the time of Munich) did not allow itself to be
deterred by the pacifist sentiments of the French people from declaring war against Germany. Dread of war is a constant with
the European masses. Governments must always reckon with it.
But it is a factor that acquires particular significance only in conjunction with a complex of circumstances that will determine
when, where, with whom, against whom, and for what objectives
a war shall be fought.

It is important to remember that the first impulse of the French
government, of Premier Blum himself, had been to allow the
Spaniards their rights under international law.[30] Then, on July 25,
almost abruptly, the decision not to supply war materials to Spain
was announced in Paris. What had transpired between July 21 and
25 to bring about this change of heart in the French capital? The
added weight that tipped the scales against Spain came from England.[31] Learning that on July 21 the French government, with
Pierre Cot playing a leading role and with Premier Blum giving
his tacit approval, had decided to accede to the Spanish request for

war materials, Charles Corbin, the French ambassador in London, telephoned Premier Blum and brought to his attention the grave concern felt by the British government that France might become embroiled in Spain.[32] Corbin urged Blum to proceed at once to London and to discuss the matter with Prime Minister Stanley Baldwin and Foreign Secretary Anthony Eden.[33] Blum flew to London where he met with the British leaders. Eden stressed the great danger to the peace of Europe that, in view of the German and Italian attitude regarding the war in Spain, might result from French support of the Madrid government.[34] When Blum returned to Paris on July 25, he immediately called a meeting of the French Cabinet. The question of aid to Spain was debated at length, with much of the discussion turning on the meaning and import of the British point of view. Finally, when Premier Blum shifted his support from Cot to Daladier and Delbos, the neutralists prevailed over the interventionists.[35]

Elizabeth R. Cameron writes that it was Alexis Saint-Léger Léger, secretary general of the French Foreign Ministry, who persuaded Premier Blum to go to London (and shortly thereafter to propose a nonintervention agreement) out of fear that unless France remained strictly neutral England would openly support Franco!

When war broke out in the peninsula in the summer of 1936, once more Léger's first concern was with the state of opinion in Britain. He saw with alarm that the new socialist government in France, the turmoil of French strikes and workers' agitation, had raised a red scare across the Channel. Accordingly, he persuaded Blum to accompany him to the diplomatic conferences scheduled for London [to discuss the Locarno Pact in the light of Germany's violation of it in the Rhineland]. Léger's *cauchemar* was nothing short of a British alignment with White Spain, Germany, and Italy "in a new Holy Alliance in the style of Metternich." And however right or wrong his judgment, he was convinced that British neutrality could not be assured unless the French government agreed to forego the shipment of arms and volunteers to the legal government of Spain. Therefore, against all Blum's sympathies, he got him to propose nonintervention as the best available insurance against the spread of conflict.[36]

However, whether Léger's influence with Blum was as great as Cameron suggests is not as significant as the fact that important members of the French government and Diplomatic Corps were strongly opposed to an independent French policy toward Spain and that, in the final analysis, Blum himself was not prepared to alienate British opinion. Blum, moreover, did not wish to exacerbate the deep split in French opinion occasioned by the war in Spain.[37]

Within a week after the Blum government had rejected the Spanish request for arms and supplies, it proposed that the principal Mediterranean powers, Great Britain, France, and Italy, formally agree not to intervene in the Spanish Civil War. Thus, on August 1, 1936, the first step was taken that was to lead to the establishment of the International Committee for the Application of the Agreement regarding Non-Intervention in Spain. Inasmuch as the effects of the establishment of the "Non-Intervention Committee" proved of decisive importance in determining the outcome of the Spanish Civil War, it would be well to consider why, how, and under what circumstances this committee came into being.

It is reasonable to assume that if the Front Populaire government were prepared to relinquish its rights under international law to supply the legitimate government of Spain with war materials and thus to offend the political sensibilities of millions of its supporters and to incur grave risks with respect to the military and strategic position of France, it must have expected that the other powers would likewise refrain from any interference in the Spanish struggle. While Paris was prepared to initiate an agreement, this was not to be a matter of unilateral abnegation. In its official communiqué of August 8, 1936, the French government announced that in suspending all shipments of war materials to Spain it "confidently" expected that its initiative would serve to facilitate general agreement regarding nonintervention in Spain "in the interests of international peace." [38] The desire to localize the war in Spain, then, constituted the principal motivation of the French government in first broaching to the other powers the idea of a formal nonintervention agreement. It cannot be gainsaid that the main-

tenance of the fragile peace of Europe comported with the sentiments and interests of France. In late July and early August, 1936,
moreover, it was not possible for the French government to fore-
see fully the course that the war in Spain would take.

However, a number of circumstances suggest that other factors
beside the extremely plausible desire to localize the war in Spain
influenced the policy-makers at the Quai d'Orsay. Four things in
particular point to the conclusion that the French attitude was
not simply a matter of pacifism and humanitarian idealism or of
political and strategical myopia. To begin with, the French government was aware that the Italians had intervened in Spain from
the beginning and that Italian support of General Franco was con-
tinuously being expanded.[39] Then, too, the pattern of recent international events must have suggested to the Quai d'Orsay that Italian
intervention in Spain was not an act of Mussolinian whimsy but a
logical development in the permanent crisis in diplomacy that extended back to the Japanese conquest of Manchuria, saw the reemergence of an armed and aggressive Germany as well as the
expansion of Italian power in Africa and the Mediterranean, and
threatened, ultimately, to encompass the destruction of French
military hegemony in Europe. Third, even if Paris had been completely sanguine concerning the efficacy of the nonintervention
agreement to prevent large-scale interference in Spain and thus
to localize and to limit the Spanish conflict, the French government must have been disabused of this expectation before many
weeks had elapsed. Yet, despite incontrovertible evidence of continuous violations of the nonintervention agreement by Germany
as well as by Italy on behalf of the Spanish rebels, France, unlike
Soviet Russia, made no serious effort to regain its freedom of action. Notwithstanding its communiqué of August 8 and repeated
declarations that France would not countenance violations of the
nonintervention agreement, the French government remained committed to what, in effect, amounted to a self-denial of its prerogatives under international law and, more important, of its vital
interests in the Iberian Peninsula. Lastly, and perhaps of greatest

significance, the deference that the Quai d'Orsay had shown for
the opinions and suggestions of No. 10 Downing Street during the
critical first days of the Spanish conflict revealed that French
policy was only in part a response to internal factors. It was, at
least as much, a reflection of the military and diplomatic depend-
ency of the Third Republic on the British Empire. Just as British
importunities had strengthened the hand of the neutralists against
the interventionists in the Blum government and had greatly influenced the decision of the French Cabinet on July 25 not to accede to the request of the Spanish Republic for arms, so in the fortnight between July 25 and August 8, 1936, it was the diplomatic
pressure of London that underlay the French initiative toward a
formal nonintervention agreement [40] and that, during subsequent
weeks and months and despite flagrant violations of the nonintervention agreement by others, sought to keep the French Republic
steadfast to its pledge.[41]

The Spaniards, like the Germans,[42] appreciated the sway of
London over Paris. The Spanish premier, José Giral, remarked
when he learned of the French decision to ban shipments of arms
to Spain:

Nothing is more mistaken than the view, so firmly held in Spain, that
the British Foreign Office never makes mistakes and always acts with
wisdom. By forcing the hand of Paris they have committed more than
a crime, they have committed an enormous ineptitude for which sooner
or later they will have to pay. It was sufficient for the City of London
to fear a Republican victory—they are blind enough to suppose that
the Republican emblem is the hammer and sickle—and to go scuttling
to the Foreign Office like a lot of frightened old maids. The latter
promptly made common cause with them, and accepted the responsibility before history of more or less threatening the French Popular
Front Government with a cancellation of the Locarno Pact if they
allowed the export of arms to Spain. But the Spanish people will defend the Republic with their own bodies, and we shall defeat the rebel
generals in spite of the disgraceful selfishness of London and the traitors
in our own midst.[43]

British foreign policy during the 1930s is not susceptible of simple analysis, for, unlike the diplomacy of a small and weak state

which is decisively conditioned by its geographical position, its limited resources and manpower, and its strategic immobility, the diplomacy of a great world power reflects a barometric change-ability and is the particular resultant of a multiplicity of sentiments and interests. Yet, the British position on the Spanish question, despite the appearance of doubt and vacillation, of "muddling through," was rather well defined from the beginning, was consistently maintained throughout the months and years of the Spanish conflict, and was consonant with the basic aims of British diplomacy in the decade preceding the Second World War.

The premises, speculations, and hypotheses which underlay the formation of British foreign policy in the 1930s reflected, of course, the social background and experience, the moral and intellectual predilections of the statesmen, officials, businessmen, publicists, and others who in a kind of diosmotic relationship with what is called public opinion determined the imperatives of this policy. Out of the rich variety of British life emerged a pattern of values, beliefs, and aims that amounted to a prevailing philosophy of life. Thus, while there were many loose ends in the tangled skein of British diplomacy in the 1930s, a certain consistency of purpose wound through the whole of it.

The most critical mistake made by British statesmen in the years immediately following the First World War was to assume that the military strength of France as against the military weakness of Germany reflected a fundamental, rather than an apparent and ephemeral relation of power between these states. On this mistaken assumption and on the fear that a defeated and disgruntled Germany might succumb to the blandishments of Soviet Russia and Communist propaganda, the British Foreign Office had sought to thwart the consolidation of the French "security system," *i.e.*, French military hegemony on the continent. There was in the British attitude, probably as a result of the terrible costs and spent emotions of the First World War, something of a return to the "splendid isolation" of England's Victorian heyday and to her classical policy of the balance of power.

The onset of the Great Depression, with its attendant political and social unrest and international disorders, was soon to confront British statesmanship with new and more strenuous tasks. Beginning with the Japanese conquest of Manchuria in 1931, and continuing with the Italian attack on Ethiopia and the reëmergence of an armed and aggressive Germany, British statesmen were beset by problems of increasing complexity, beside which the French occupation of the Ruhr and the Italian bombardment of Corfu had been relatively simple matters. The maintenance of general peace comported with the sentiments and interests of Great Britain. As in France, strong pacifist sentiments existed among the broad mass of the people. A British diplomacy that aimed at the preservation of peace would be certain to find general support among the people. The maintenance of the established values of the English way of life and, by extension, of those of Western civilization, probably reflected the hopes and desires of most Englishmen. The British masses were neither socially dissatisfied nor politically turbulent. The British Labor party was led by moderate, responsible men steeped in the traditions of Fabianism. Communism was virtually nonexistent. If France reflected in its political and intellectual life so profound a cleavage that one could properly speak of two Frances, then England, in marked contrast, revealed a homogeneity of thought and political ideals that was almost unique among modern nations. A British diplomacy that sought to preserve the status quo against revolutionary change would meet with widespread approval not only among the English upper and middle classes but probably among the lower classes as well.

To preserve the peace, to safeguard vital British interests, and to maintain the established values of Western civilization in a world where armed adventurers and avowed revolutionaries stood ready to profit from any lack of vigilance, any error of judgment, any untoward development, were problems to which British statesmen sought solutions. They sought them not in terms of the League of Nations and collective security, but amongst old formulae which harked back to the 1920s, to the balance of power between France and Germany, and to the Russian question.

Support of the principles of collective security embodied in the League of Nations had never been the guiding star of British diplomacy, notwithstanding the preeminent position that Great Britain enjoyed at Geneva. The attitude of the British government during the Italo-Ethiopian War does not contradict but rather substantiates this statement.[44] It must not be supposed that it was fear of Italian military might that led the British to acquiesce in the Italian conquest of Ethiopia with no more than the emasculated protest contained in the League's partial economic sanctions. Appeasement as a policy did not derive as much from pacifist sentiment, military unpreparedness, fear of war, or sheer ineptitude, as from the desire and aim of the British government, supported by powerful and influential circles in France and elsewhere, to deflect the main thrust of resurgent rival imperialisms toward the dynamic center and most powerful base of the modern revolutionary movement, thereby at one and the same time forestalling the projected despoilment of the imperial patrimony of the Western powers and safeguarding the established social order from the contagion of revolutionary innovations.[45]

As early as November 28, 1934, Lloyd George, prime minister of Great Britain during the First World War, had declared before the House of Commons:

. . . in a very short time, perhaps in a year, perhaps in two, the Conservative elements in this country will be looking to Germany as the bulwark against Communism in Europe. . . . Do not let us be in a hurry to condemn Germany. We shall be welcoming Germany as our friend.[46]

The crux of the matter was that while French military hegemony on the continent—predicated on a weak Germany whose freedom of action was effectually circumscribed by the French system of alliances in central and eastern Europe—endured, an economically riven and politically turbulent Germany might seek, in the spirit of Rapallo, an accommodation with Soviet Russia, thereby placing in the greatest peril the security of the Western democracies. The advent to power of Adolf Hitler on January 30, 1933, had somewhat mitigated but had not entirely negated this possibility. A Nazi Germany that was not also an expansionist Germany was a contradiction in terms. If the Führer spoke of a renewed *Drang nach Osten,* he did so in the expectation of a neutralized France at his back, a France that had forsaken its allies in the east. Thus, while the maintenance of French military power was the *sine qua non* of British security, the perpetuation of French military preponderance was another matter, for it constituted the single greatest impediment to the fulfillment of the fundamental purposes of the policy of appeasement.

There can be little doubt that the British position on the Spanish question reflected the larger purposes of British diplomacy. In a speech delivered at the Cutlers' Feast at Sheffield on October 14, 1936, Anthony Eden, the British foreign secretary, reaffirmed England's position concerning the war in Spain. He said in part:

Events in Spain have not only brought suffering to that distressed country, but, owing to the exceptional circumstances of the conflict, they might have had consequences scarcely less serious over a much wider area of Europe. The fighting that broke out in this comparatively isolated corner of Western Europe threatened at a moment's notice to scatter strife far beyond the borders of Spain.

Faced with this situation His Majesty's Government welcomed and supported with all their influence the initiative of the French Government. That initiative was taken in a sincere attempt to circumscribe, by international agreement, the dangerous situation which had arisen in Spain. The French Prime Minister's action was a courageous one, and that of a good European. . . .

I am well aware of the criticisms which are being directed against the agreement. It is even being suggested that the time has now come to give up this effort. His Majesty's Government do not share that view. . . . They support non-intervention. That view is strongly held and has never wavered. We are for our part determined to carry out loyally our own undertaking and to promote in every way possible the execution of the terms of the agreement. We consider this is the best, if not the only, way to avert the dangerous developments which are inherent in the Spanish situation. However tragic the civil strife in Spain may be, it in no way absolves us from our duty to make every effort to confine that tragedy within the boundaries of the country wherein it is being enacted.[47]

The alarm felt by the British government that the fighting in Spain "threatened at a moment's notice" to spread "far beyond" the borders of Spain would seem to have been, like the premature reports of Mark Twain's death, "greatly exaggerated," particularly in view of what had actually occurred in Spain during the first days of the military revolt and given the relation of power that existed then and for a considerable time thereafter between General Franco's foreign supporters and the Western democracies. It must not be forgotten that the generals' coup d'état had failed and that by July 22, 1936, theirs had become a hopeless cause unless they received immediate and powerful assistance from abroad and the government did not. On July 26, 1936, Dr. Karl Schwende-mann, counselor of the German Embassy in Madrid, sent a telegram to the German Foreign Ministry in which he briefly outlined the military situation in Spain. He concluded:

The development of the situation since the beginning of the revolt consequently shows distinctly increasing strength and progress on the part of the government and standstill and retrogression on the part of the rebels. . . . Unless something unforeseen happens, it is hardly to be expected that in view of all this the military revolt can succeed, but the fighting will probably continue for some time. I have the impression that the real situation is not generally recognized in Germany.[48]

Herr Schwendemann's "something unforeseen" soon materialized in the form of powerful support given the rebels by Germany and Italy coupled with Anglo-French "nonintervention."

Among the few staff officers of the Spanish Army who remained loyal to the Republic was José Martín Blázquez. Major Martín Blázquez, from his post in the War Ministry, helped transform the raw workers' militia into an efficient fighting force. While a sincere republican, Major Martín Blázquez was not an extremist. In the spring of 1937, filled with the horror of the fratricidal struggle, he left Spain for France, where, with the guns still booming beyond the Pyrenees, he wrote his memoirs. His testimony is that of an expert and a former participant and it is not marred by the blind partisanship that characterizes so many other personal accounts of the Civil War. At the beginning of the conflict Major Martín Blázquez believed a Republican victory to be inevitable. He wrote:

The fact that the gold of the Bank of Spain was in our hands made us confident of ultimate victory. It never for a moment entered our heads that a legitimate democratic government might be deprived of its right to buy war material abroad.[49]

However, not only did "nonintervention" come into being, but it soon proved to be a quite one-sided affair. Major Martín Blázquez wrote:

All our calculations were upset by foreign intervention, German and Italian, the possibility of which had never occurred to us. Without German and Italian aid the rebels would never have been able to mobilise their civil population. Without German and Italian aid, in men and, above all, in *matériel*, they would have succumbed, perhaps before three months were out, to the reckless heroism of our militia-men.[50]

But for a few hundred bombers and tanks, a few thousand rifles and machine guns, moderate quantities of ammunition and supplies which Madrid did not receive in the fortnight following the Moroccan uprising, the generals' unsuccessful coup d'état was transformed first into a civil war and then into an Italo-German invasion of the Peninsula. In London and in Paris it was announced that the refusal to supply these war materials to Madrid was in the interests of general peace. In view of the fact that the war in Spain was to continue for nearly three years and to cost hundreds of thousands of lives—whereas, with sufficient arms Madrid might well have suppressed the revolt within a few weeks or months and without such terrible carnage—the British and French governments must have accepted as a certainty that Hitler and Mussolini, in pursuance of their aims in Spain, would have themselves incurred the risk of general war in order to thwart Anglo-French support of Madrid. Perhaps the British and French leaders truly believed that in the summer of 1936 Germany and Italy were ready to assume the burdens and risks of general war. Men often ignore fact and summon reason to the support of purpose.

The real beginning of German-Italian amity, that was in time to be embodied in the Rome-Berlin Axis and the Pact of Steel, dates from the collaboration in Spain. It must be remembered that during the Italo-Ethiopian War the German government, while it did not join with the League powers in imposing sanctions on Italy, declared its neutrality and placed an embargo on the sale of arms, oil, textiles, iron and steel, and other items to both belligerents. At this time, too, the Austrian question remained unsettled and continued to vex relations between Germany and Italy. It was only toward the end of the Italo-Ethiopian conflict, when an Italian triumph appeared certain, that Germany and Italy began to draw together. This tendency was strengthened by the Austro-German Accord of July 11, 1936, which declared that while Austria was a "German" state it was also an independent state. With the Moroccan uprising and subsequent German and Italian intervention in the Spanish conflict, the two fascist powers evinced a growing friendship and intimacy.[51] However, to have assumed in the summer of 1936 that there already existed between Germany and Italy such a close identity of interests that the two powers would have stood together in the face of any contingency that might have arisen out of an Anglo-French determination to succor the Spanish Republic was to ascribe to German-Italian relations an amity and unity of purpose which only the months and years of their comradeship in arms in Spain was ultimately to produce. It is important to recall, too, that sanctions were formally lifted from Italy on July 15, 1936, only 48 hours before the Moroccan uprising. While partial economic sanctions had not been able to prevent the Italian conquest of Ethiopia, they had imposed a rather severe strain on the intrinsically weak Italian economy.[52] Thus, to have expected that Italy, without the assurance of German support, would have seized on the dispatch of French war materials to the Madrid government as the occasion to unleash a major war in Europe was to credit the Duce's most fatuous boasts with the substance of reality.

But what of Germany? Were not the Germans capable of striking across the Rhine if France sent aid to the embattled Spanish Republic? Notwithstanding the clandestine activities of the leaders of the *Reichswehr* in promoting German rearmament in defiance of the Treaty of Versailles, in which, following Rapallo, they were aided and abetted by the Soviet Union, the existing military strength of the Weimar Republic remained negligible in comparison with that of France. With the advent to power of Adolf Hitler German secret rearmament was considerably accelerated. However, it was not until March 16, 1935, that Hitler openly denounced the military clauses of the Treaty of Versailles and that the small, long-service, professional army imposed on Germany at Versailles was transformed into a mass, short-service, conscript army. The sixteen months which elapsed between Hitler's promulgation of the "Law for the Reconstruction of the National Defense Forces" and the Moroccan uprising constituted an insufficient period of time in which to draft, train, and organize a mass army that could compare in quality with the French Army whose organization had remained intact since the end of the First World War. This was particularly true with respect to such vitally important matters as the training of an efficient corps of officers and noncommissioned officers and the building of an adequate reserve. Moreover, it was not until March 7, 1936, only four months before the Moroccan uprising, that Hitler marched his troops into the Rhineland. Despite the feverish haste of the German military engineers an adequate system of fortifications had not been erected in the Rhineland by the summer of 1936.[53] Without strong fortifications in the West and adequate trained reserves, Hitler sought to augment his military strength in being by raising the period of active military service from one to two years. But this occurred on August 24, 1936, a month after the French government had formally refused the request of the Spanish Republic for arms and supplies.

Clearly, then, for the British and French leaders to have feared that if they had permitted the Spanish Republic to purchase war materials in their markets, they would have been immediately threatened with the military power of Italy, or Germany, or both, was to have been frightened by hobgoblins out of their own imaginations. Given the power of the British navy, of the French army, given the active support of the Czechoslovakian and, quite conceivably, of the Russian armies, given the vast resources, the gold reserves, and the merchant fleets of the Western democracies, and given the moral support of most of civilized mankind, London and Paris had little to fear and much to gain by permitting the Madrid government to buy the war materials necessary to put down the military revolt.

However, it was not a matter of fear. It has already been suggested that British diplomacy, in seeking to solve the vexatious problems attendant upon the international lawlessness of the 1930s, was not guided by the principles of collective security embodied in the League of Nations but rather by old formulae which harked back to the 1920s, to the balance of power between France and Germany, and to the Russian question. It was this virtual abandonment of League principles by London (and Paris), coupled with the absence of concerted independent Anglo-French resistance to acts of aggression by Tokyo, Rome, and Berlin, that resulted in what came to be known as the "policy of appeasement," the motivations of which ran the gamut from honest pacifist sentiment to anti-communist, pro-fascist Machiavellianism.

With respect to appeasement of the fascist powers in Spain it is important to remember that Paris, out of fear of alienating London, was content to follow the British lead from the outset.[54] The position of Great Britain vis-à-vis the war in Spain was determined by several important factors. To begin with, there was the desire of the British government to localize the Spanish conflict and thus to nullify any possibility that it might develop into a general war. In view of the pacifist sentiments of many Englishmen and the state of British rearmament, it is not surprising that the British government's support of "nonintervention" received wide approval at home, at least until "nonintervention" was seen to be almost entirely a one-sided affair. But the British also had important economic, political, and diplomatic reasons for pursuing their Spanish policy. Englishmen had vast holdings in Spain, their mining investments there, for example, being among the most lucrative British mining investments in the entire Hispanic world, *i.e.*, Spain, Portugal, and Latin America.[55] The British, moreover, were confident that despite General Franco's present reliance on Italo-German military support, he inevitably would be forced to turn to Great Britain for financial and economic assistance when he faced the task of reconstruction.[56] Because of Spain's ultimate dependence on Great Britain, then, a Franco victory would not present politico-military problems which London did not have the means to solve. In this connection the remarks made by Sir Henry Chilton, the last British ambassador to Spain, on May 31, 1938, are particularly significant. According to Herschel V. Johnson, the counselor of the American Embassy in London, Chilton "expressed the conviction that a Franco victory was necessary for peace in Spain; that there was not the slightest chance that Italy and/or Germany would dominate Spain; and that even if it were possible for the Spanish government to win (which he did not believe) he was convinced that a victory for Franco would be better for Great Britain." [57]

On the other hand, the Popular Front movement, whether seen as a manifestation of the French (and the Spanish) democratic spirit or as a tactical maneuver on the part of the Kremlin, or both, raised up serious problems in London, no less than in Berlin and Rome. Implicit in Popular Frontism, with respect to international politics, was the strengthening and broadening of the system of collective security. Popular Frontism, then, was the antithesis of appeasement and was basically discordant with the British aim of avoiding extensive commitments in Eastern Europe. The victory of the Frente Popular in Spain, coupled with the consolidation of the Front Populaire in France, could have important repercussions in the realm of international affairs; whereas, the collapse of the Popular Front movement would facilitate an understanding between London and Paris on the one hand and Berlin and Rome on the other. On June 1, 1937, British Foreign Secretary Anthony Eden said to the American ambassador in London, Bingham, that it appeared that the Soviet government wanted the British to pull its chestnuts out of the fire. As Eden saw it, Moscow would not be displeased if war between the Anglo-French and the Germans left the Russians a free hand in the East. Eden was hopeful that his government, with the support of the French government, could gain time and find a way out of the difficult situation.[58]

The position of France was pivotal. In significant measure the matter of collective security as against a regional understanding turned on what the French did or failed to do concerning Spain. But France, as noted, was content to follow the British lead. It was only for the brief time Joseph Paul-Boncour was French foreign minister in the Cabinet headed by Léon Blum from March 13 to April 10, 1938, that it appeared that France might pursue an independent policy with respect to Spain. While he did not formally abandon nonintervention as a policy, Paul-Boncour was prepared to permit a steady flow of war materials to cross the Pyrenees into Spain.[59] What might have come to pass if Paul-Boncour had continued as foreign minister and had persisted in his attitude is, of course, a matter of conjecture. As a matter of fact, Paul-Boncour's bold approach was a thing of little time and substance and produced no real change in the relationship between the Quai d'Orsay and No. 10 Downing Street during these critical years. In this connection the report of the American chargé d'affaires in France, Wilson, to his government on April 13, 1938, is of considerable interest. It follows:

I am reliably informed that considerable pressure, particularly from members of the Left friendly to the Spanish Government cause, was brought to bear on Daladier [appointed Premier on April 10, 1938] to maintain Paul-Boncour at the Foreign Office.

Daladier's refusal to agree to this and his appointment of Bonnet throw a light on the foreign policy which the Government may be expected to follow.

Bonnet will certainly avoid adventure in Spain and he may be

counted upon to deal in a realistic manner with the question of protecting French interests in that country in the expectation of a Franco
victory. It may be assumed that he will try to work closely with the
British, that he will endeavor to put French relations with Italy on a
sensible basis as soon as possible and that he will welcome any opportunity—if opportunity exists—to come to a reasonable understanding
with Germany.[60]

Despite fleeting instances of French recalcitrance, then, Paris
sought to act in concert with London vis-à-vis the war in Spain,
while British policy remained singularly consistent throughout the
course of the conflict. Needless to say, perhaps, there were certain
dangers inherent in London's Spanish policy. For one thing, a
Franco victory might result in a fascist Spain allied to Germany
and Italy. If British influence in Spain did suffer serious diminution
and the "New Spain" did become an active partner of the fascist
powers, then the military position of France would be dangerously
undermined. Confronted by hostile forces on three frontiers and
bereft of eastern allies, France would find her military hegemony
a thing of the past. London could not be certain that once French
military power had been undermined the fascist powers would not
elect to strike westward rather than eastward, that is, toward Paris
and the Channel ports rather than toward Prague, Warsaw, and
Moscow. For another, the defeat of Republican Spain might serve
to discredit the Left in France. London could not be certain that,
with the collapse of the Front Populaire, elements traditionally hostile to Great Britain might not come to power in France and make
common cause with the fascist dictators. However, some risks had
to be taken and these, possibly, were preferable to others.

Gaetano Salvemini, in discussing British foreign policy during
this period of history, observed:

From the summer of 1936 on, it was clear that Russia, if attacked by
Germany, could not count on any help from England, and that Mussolini had gone over to Hitler's camp. The Four-Power Pact which
the French Government had scotched in 1933 had become a reality.
The English Conservatives, who had disannexed the Far East and East

Africa from the League of Nations, had now cut off Eastern Europe as well.[61]

That England conceived of her fundamental obligations as limited to the defense of the Empire and to certain areas in Western Europe was made evident by Foreign Secretary Eden in a speech to his constituents at Leamington on November 20, 1936. Mr. Eden, of course, employed the circuitous and guarded language of an experienced diplomat—in contrast to the pithy, forthright style of the Italian historian—but the import of his remarks could not be mistaken. In discussing the purpose of British rearmament, Mr. Eden said in part:

But, it may be asked, for what purpose will these arms be used? Let me once again make the position in this respect perfectly clear. These arms will never be used in a war of aggression. They will never be used for a purpose inconsistent with the Covenant of the League or the Pact of Paris. They may, and if the occasion arose they would, be used in our own defence and in defence of the territories of the British Commonwealth of Nations. They may, and if the occasion arose they would, be used in the defence of France and Belgium against unprovoked aggression in accordance with our existing obligations. They may, and, if a new Western European settlement can be reached, they would, be used in defence of Germany were she the victim of unprovoked aggression by any of the other signatories of such a settlement. Those, together with our Treaty of Alliance with Iraq and our projected treaty with Egypt, are our definite obligations. In addition our armaments *may* be used in bringing help to a victim of aggression in any case where, in our judgement, it would be proper under the provisions of the Covenant to do so. I use the word "may" deliberately, since in such an instance there is no automatic obligation to take military action. It is, moreover, right that this should be so, for nations cannot be expected to incur automatic military obligations save for areas where their vital interests are concerned.

Such are the bases of our policy.[62]

V

The Nonintervention Agreement:
Intervention and
Counter-Intervention

THE month of August, 1936, saw twenty-seven European
nations formally adhere to the nonintervention agreement.[1] However, this did not mean that by the end of that eventful summer
foreign interference in the Spanish conflict had ceased, or even
had appreciably diminished. On the contrary, the evidence is incontrovertible that foreign intervention in Spain was considerably
greater and more open following the general agreement not to intervene than it had been before. If the flow of war supplies from
France to Republican Spain was reduced to a mere trickle, then
that from Germany, Italy, and Portugal to the Spanish rebels became a torrent. Moreover, before the cold winds of winter blew
out of the Sierra de Guadarrama across the Castilian plain, thousands of volunteers from all parts of the earth had flocked to Madrid
to form the International Brigades. Meanwhile, from places as
distant as Mexico and Soviet Russia came arms, munitions, and
supplies for the embattled Republic. The help that Soviet Russia
sent was to grow both in volume and importance. This sequence of
events had been adumbrated in the exchange of notes, in the proposals and counter-proposals, in the procrastination and legalistic
artifices which marked the diplomacy that had resulted in the formal adherence of the European powers to the nonintervention
agreement.

Following initial overtures to Great Britain and Italy concerning an agreement not to intervene in the Spanish conflict, the French government addressed similar appeals to Germany, Portugal, and Soviet Russia. On August 4, 1936, the British government replied that it agreed in principle with a policy of nonintervention in Spanish affairs. However, on August 6, the Italian foreign minister, Count Galeazzo Ciano, informed both the French Ambassador and the British Chargé d'Affaires in Rome, who, in support of his French colleague, had handed Ciano an *aide-mémoire* relating to the French proposal for a nonintervention agreement and indicating Great Britain's acceptance in principle, that while Italy also agreed in principle with a policy of nonintervention the Italian government was greatly concerned with "ideological and spiritual" intervention in Spain which "must be prevented at the same time as, and concurrently with, the supply of arms." [2] Ciano's reference to "ideological and spiritual" intervention was, of course, a reference to the activities in support of the Spanish Republic by private organizations and private individuals in England, France, and Soviet Russia (in this last instance the "private" character of such activity was open to legitimate doubt). The Ciano-Chambrun talks floundered on this reef for the next few days. Then, on August 14, the French Ambassador informed the Italian Foreign Minister that the French government agreed in principle with the Italian proposal to prevent the subscription of funds and the recruitment of volunteers for Spain. However, Chambrun expressed the concern of the French government that the Italian proposal might result in further delay in the conclusion of a general agreement and suggested that in order to expedite the matter the French conception of the nonintervention agreement be submitted to the other powers but with the Italian suggestions duly noted. Ciano replied that this "appeared absolutely unacceptable" but that he would discuss the Ambassador's proposal with the Duce.[3] There the matter stood for the next few days.

Meanwhile, the French ambassador in Berlin, André François-Poncet, was experiencing the same frustration with the German

foreign minister, Baron Constantin von Neurath. As was noted, the
French Ambassador first broached the idea of a nonintervention
agreement to the German Foreign Minister on August 4, 1936, only
to be informed that Germany "naturally did not intervene in Spanish internal political affairs and disputes." [4] However, Baron von
Neurath indicated that Germany was prepared "to participate in
a discussion aimed at preventing the extension of the Spanish Civil
War to Europe" but only if all the interested powers, particularly
Soviet Russia, adhered to the nonintervention agreement that might
result from such a discussion.[5] On August 7 François-Poncet again
called on Baron von Neurath and handed him a draft of the French
declaration of nonintervention in Spain. The German Foreign Minister promised to study the draft "thoroughly" but forthwith noted
the great difficulties which would attend the enforcement of the
French scheme. Baron von Neurath stressed that these would be
particularly onerous with respect to the activities of the Comintern
which, the official attitude of the Soviet government notwithstanding (François-Poncet had informed Baron von Neurath that Moscow had agreed in principle to a policy of nonintervention), would
not be bound by it. François-Poncet conceded that the difficulties
attendant upon the enforcement of the nonintervention agreement
would be great but insisted that agreement by the principal states of
Europe on an arms embargo would constitute an excellent beginning.[6]

The following day, August 8, the British ambassador in Berlin,
Sir Eric Phipps, called at the German Foreign Ministry and expressed his "warmest support" of the French proposal concerning
nonintervention in Spain. Baron von Neurath assured his British
visitor that the German government was "carefully examining" its
reply. Then the Baron called the attention of Sir Eric Phipps, as
he had that of M. François-Poncet, to the practical difficulties of
such a plan and suggested that in order to be truly efficacious it
would have to include all countries with "a large arms and munitions industry of their own" and, therefore, the United States,

Sweden, and Switzerland. The Baron, moreover, expressed his doubts concerning the sincerity of the Russians.[7]

To insist that all countries with "a large arms and munitions industry of their own" be included in the nonintervention scheme was patently dilatory on the part of the German government. To specifically mention the United States, Sweden, and Switzerland was particularly gauche on the part of Baron von Neurath. For Sir Eric Phipps must have been aware that Berlin was not unaware that the American Republic, which had refused to join the League of Nations and in which isolationist sentiment continued widely manifest, could hardly be expected to adhere formally to the nonintervention agreement and that Sweden and Switzerland were "traditionally neutral states."

The misadventure of a German pilot provided the German government with further occasion to continue its dilatory tactics. On August 9, 1936, the pilot of a German tri-motor Junkers 52, the D-AMIM, landed at the Madrid airport but, perceiving that he had made a mistake, immediately took off again to come down later at Badajoz. However, on August 9 Badajoz was still held by Republican forces. The German aircraft was impounded and its crew interned. When the German government learned of the incident, it instructed its chargé d'affaires in Madrid, Hans Voelckers, to demand that the Spanish government order the immediate release of the airplane and its crew. The Spanish government refused to comply on the ground that inasmuch as the airplane had been flown over Spanish territory without proper authorization it was necessary for the Spanish government to make a thorough investigation of the incident. Acting on instructions from Baron von Neurath, Dr. Karl Dumont, head of Political Division III of the German Foreign Ministry, telephoned the French ambassador in Berlin on August 12 and informed him that the German government was prepared to agree in principle to a policy of nonintervention in Spain but could not do so as long as the Spanish government continued to hold the German aircraft and its crew.[8] On August 13,

the German chargé d'affaires in Madrid handed the Spanish foreign minister, Señor Augusto Barcia, a note in which the German
government again demanded the immediate release of the D-AMIM
and its crew and which warned that "should the government of
the Spanish Republic fail to comply with this justified demand, the
German government would feel obliged to resort to the most serious measures." [9] In its quarrel with Madrid, Berlin found support in Paris. On August 15 the French government, hoping
to remove the last obstacle to German adherence to the nonintervention plan, urged the Spanish government to comply with the
German demand.[10] But Madrid, possibly out of a desire not to see
the nonintervention agreement consummated, proved obstinate. It
consented to release the crew of the D-AMIM but continued to
hold the aircraft itself. There the matter stood for the next few
days.

Meanwhile, on August 7, both the British and French governments had invited Portugal to adhere to the nonintervention plan.
The Portuguese foreign minister, Dr. Armindo Monteiro, while
promising to give "careful consideration to this invitation," had noted
the "special dangers for Portugal arising from the present situation in
Spain" and had intimated that Portugal in its own defense might find
it necessary to recognize and assist the Burgos government, *i.e.*, the
Spanish rebels.[11] On August 13, however, Lisbon had informed
London and Paris that the Portuguese government agreed in principle with a policy of nonintervention in Spain but that it reserved
"liberty of action in case an emergency arises involving the security
of Portuguese frontiers or the internal peace and security of Portugal itself." [12]

It can be assumed that this *volte-face* on the part of the Portuguese government resulted, in large measure at least, from British
diplomatic pressure. However, Lisbon's agreement in principle to
nonintervention in Spain was little more than a gesture, for Portugal continued to abet materially the rebel cause and Portuguese
newspapers, including those of a semiofficial character, greeted the

fall of Badajoz with headlines to the effect that "Portugal has now ceased to have any frontier with robbers and assassins." [13]

As was noted above, the Soviet government had agreed in principle to a policy of nonintervention in Spain as early as August 5. However, Moscow made its participation in the scheme contingent upon the fulfillment of three conditions. These were, according to *Pravda* of August 6, 1936, that Portugal adhere to the nonintervention plan, that "aid being rendered by several states to the rebels against the Spanish Government" cease immediately, and that the Soviet government not be considered responsible for the activities of international proletarian organizations whose headquarters were in Moscow.[14] The Soviet government's refusal to accept responsibility for the activities of Moscow-centered "international proletarian organizations" and its insistence that it had no more control over the private activities of its own citizens (such as demonstrations and fund-raising drives on behalf of the Spanish Republic) than had the French and British governments over their own nationals engaged in similar activities [15] not only provided Rome, Berlin, and Lisbon with pretexts to defer their adherence to the nonintervention plan but at the same time revealed the profound reluctance with which the Soviet government had responded to the French initiative.

The political situation in Moscow in 1936 was extremely fluid. In August of that year occurred the first of the "treason trials," involving, among others, Zinoviev and Kamenev who, along with Stalin, had formed the triumvirate that had ruled Russia following the death of Lenin; in December the Stalin Constitution, which "registered the achievements of the Revolution as claimed by the Bolshevik leaders," [16] was formally adopted. The bitter struggle between "Trotskyists" and "Stalinists" impinged importantly on the dual role of Moscow as the capital of the Russian national state and the center of a world-wide revolutionary movement, and amid accusations of "the revolution betrayed" and counter-accusations of "traitors and wreckers" the relationship between the "capital" and the "center" was redefined.[17] The domestic situation in Russia, the crisis in the international Communist movement, and the rapidly changing situation abroad greatly affected, of course, Soviet foreign policy.

In the period between 1933 and 1935 something of a "diplomatic revolution" had occurred.[18] With the coming to power of Adolf Hitler in Germany, Soviet-German friendship, that dated from Rapallo, quickly cooled. Moscow sought security in amity with the Western democracies. In November, 1933, Moscow and Washington exchanged ambassadors. In September, 1934, Soviet Russia became a member of the League of Nations. France and Soviet Russia and Soviet Russia and Czechoslovakia, on May 2 and May 16, 1935, respectively, signed mutual assistance pacts. In August, 1935, the Seventh World Congress of the Third International formally endorsed the Popular Front movement. By the summer of 1936, then, the Soviet Union had left the "revisionist" camp and had come to urge the collaboration of Communists with Socialists and liberals in the struggle against "war and fascism" and to champion the principles of collective security. This rather abrupt change of direction on the part of the Soviet government was indubitably motivated by concern with its own interests. It was not achieved, however, without a sharp clash of opinion within the Soviet leadership and serious repercussions throughout the international communist movement. The Moscow Trials and the May Days in Barcelona were not totally unrelated phenomena.

The Soviet government's contention in August, 1936, that it could no better control the private activities of its citizens with respect to Spain than could either the French or British government, was patently sophistical. Its contention that it could not be held responsible for the activities of international proletarian organizations with headquarters in Moscow was possibly less so in that it might have reflected, in part at least, the growing crisis within the Russian government and within the Communist movement.[19] However, be that as it may, the Soviet position on these matters was, objectively, as obstructive of general agreement on nonintervention as was Berlin's insistence on the release of the D-AMIM or Rome's demand that French trade unions end their fund-raising activities on behalf of the Spanish Republic. Yet, aside from the fact that in August, 1936, Soviet Russia had not yet intervened in the Spanish struggle while Germany and Italy were already Franco's active allies, there was this important difference between the position taken by Moscow with respect to the nonintervention plan and that taken by Berlin and Rome. Moscow did not believe in either the legality or the efficacy of the nonintervention scheme but, in order not to jeopardize its newly established relations with the West, it responded favorably to the French initiative and adhered faithfully to the plan until, in October, 1936, in the face of continued Italo-German support of the Spanish rebels, it openly declared that it would not be bound to a greater extent than the fascist powers. An editorial that appeared in *Izvestia* on August 26, 1936, made the Soviet position with respect to the nonintervention agreement abundantly clear. It said in part:

It must be stated frankly that a declaration of neutrality in connection with events which are taking place in Spain is not our idea, but a special type of innovation in international theory and practice. Up to the present time there has been no precedent whereby the government of any country elected in accordance with its laws and recognized by all powers is put on a level both judicially and in practice with rebels fighting it. There has never been a case wherein the fulfillment of orders of such a government and the supplying of it has been considered as intervention in internal affairs.[20]

Neither Rome nor Berlin, on the other hand, raised serious legal or moral questions concerning the nonintervention agreement. They were content to adhere expediently to it and at the same time expediently to violate it, as will be shown in the pages which follow. They were soon to find that the existence of the agreement constituted a positive advantage in the pursuit of their purposes in Spain. They then defended it even as they continued to violate it.

On August 15, 1936, the French government, without waiting for general agreement on the matter but hoping thus to expedite it, issued a formal declaration of nonintervention in the Spanish struggle. This declaration was in the form of a note addressed by the French foreign minister, Yvon Delbos, to the British ambassador in Paris, Sir George Clerk. It was to become the prototype of similar declarations by the majority of the other powers which ultimately adhered to the nonintervention agreement, including those of both Great Britain and Soviet Russia. The French declaration follows:

Paris, August 15, 1936

Mr. Ambassador,

The negotiations pursued between the Government of the French Republic and the Government of His Majesty in Great Britain having given proof of their accord on a common attitude to be observed in regard to the situation in Spain, I have the honor in conformity with the proposal laid before the other European Governments, and mindful of the initiatives already taken unilaterally by the Government of France, to make to your Excellency the following declaration:

The Government of the French Republic,

Deploring the tragic events of which Spain is the theatre;

Resolved to abstain rigorously from all interference, direct or indirect, in the internal affairs of that country;

Animated by the desire to avoid every complication which might prejudice maintenance of good relations between nations,

Declares the following:

1. The French Government, in so far as it is concerned, prohibits direct or indirect exportation, re-exportation and transit, to a destination in Spain, the Spanish possessions or the Spanish zone of Morocco, of all arms, munitions and materials of war as well as all aircraft, assembled or dismantled, and all vessels of war;

2. This prohibition applies to contracts in process of execution;

3. The French Government will keep the other governments participating in this entente informed of all measures taken by it to give effect to the present declarations.

The French Government, in so far as it is concerned, will put this declaration into effect as soon as the Government of His Britannic Majesty, the German Government, the Italian Government, the Government of the U.S.S.R., and the Portuguese Government shall likewise have adhered to it.

As soon as the adhesions of the other governments concerned reach it, the French Government will take care to communicate them to the British Government as well as to the other interested Governments.

I have the honor, Mr. Ambassador, etc.

(Signed) Delbos.[21]

That same day, August 15, the British government, through its Ambassador in Paris, addressed a note to the French Foreign Minister that both in form and content was virtually identical with the original French declaration. This exchange of notes between Yvon Delbos and Sir George Clerk gave considerable impetus to the conclusion of a general agreement. Within a fortnight after the exchange, Germany, Italy, Soviet Russia, and Portugal, as well as most of the other interested powers, formally adhered to the nonintervention agreement.

On August 17 the German government, in a note to the French ambassador in Berlin, M. François-Poncet, indicated that it was prepared to adhere to the plan. However, the German note, omitting the preambulatory reasons for making the declaration but repeating the three basic statements of policy of the French note, declared that the German government could not put this policy into effect until the Spanish government agreed to release the D-AMIM and "Governments of the other States which possess, in appreciable quantity, industries capable of producing the articles cited by the prohibition . . . likewise contract the same engagement and this engagement . . . be applied to delivery by individuals or by private societies." [22] The note, moreover, inquired as to what measures would be taken by the interested powers to prevent the departure of volunteers for Spain. However, a week later, on August 24, the German government in another note to the French Ambassador in Berlin formally adhered to the nonintervention agreement, basing its adhesion on its note of August 17 but waiving the condition with respect to the D-AMIM.

Meanwhile, on August 21, the Italian government, in a note to the French ambassador in Rome, Count de Chambrun, had announced its adhesion to the nonintervention agreement. However, the Italian note, like the German note of August 17, did not contain the preambulatory reasons for the declaration. Moreover, the Italian note interpreted the phrase "indirect interference" of the original French declaration to mean the prohibition of subscription of funds and recruitment of volunteers for Spain. Yet, it declared that "the Italian Government, in accepting adherence to 'direct' non-intervention, has the honor, in consequence, to maintain its observations concerning 'indirect' non-intervention." [23] The Italian note concluded with the statement that the Italian government deemed it essential that all important European states which produced arms join in the nonintervention plan.

The Portuguese government had also announced its formal adherence to the nonintervention agreement on August 21. However, the Portuguese note, somewhat anomalously in a declaration of neutrality and noninterference, stated that "the Portuguese Government deplores the events which are taking place in Spain and it formally censures the barbarous treatment of people by the communist and anarchist troops in areas which they control." [24] The Portuguese government, moreover, made its adhesion to the agreement subject to a number of conditions and reservations. These included, beside the prohibition of subscription of funds and the recruitment of volunteers for Spain on the part of all the interested powers, the right of Portugal to act in its own defense "against all régimes of social subversion which might be established in Spain, if the necessity of safeguarding western civilization requires such a defense," [25] and the right of Portugal to maintain "relations with central or local authorities which control, in fact, the government or administration in Spanish territory." [26]

On August 23 the Soviet government formally adhered to the nonintervention agreement. The Soviet note was virtually identical with those of the French and British governments, repeating verbatim, *mutatis mutandis*, the preambulatory reasons for making the declaration and the three basic statements of policy of the original French declaration.

Having reached general agreement with respect to a policy of nonintervention in Spain, the next step to be taken by the interested powers was to establish some sort of central committee which could deal with the various problems which might arise under the plan. The suggestion to establish adequate supervision of the agreement first came from the Italian government.[27] It was made by Foreign Minister Ciano in a conversation with the French ambassador in Rome, Count de Chambrun, as early as August 10, but Ciano's purpose in making it might well have been dilatory and, therefore, was not necessarily constructive. However, by the end of the month and with general agreement achieved, the French government, supported by the British government, earnestly sought the establishment of a supervisory committee. Berlin, however, was reluctant to accede to the idea, fearing that "the committee suggested by the French government might gradually develop into an agency of extended competence with control functions." [28]

However, just as German Foreign Minister Constantin von Neurath had been able to prevail upon the Führer to permit the German government to announce its formal adherence to the nonintervention agreement on August 24 (the very day that the German government announced the extension of the period of military service from one to two years) and thus not to have it appear that Berlin was "sabotaging the whole matter," [29] so the German Foreign Ministry, assured by the British chargé d'affaires in Berlin, Mr. Basil Newton, that "the work of the committee would not expand in an undesirable manner," [30] was able to persuade Hitler to accede to the establishment of a supervisory committee in London. It appears that it was Dr. Hans Dieckhoff, at the time acting state secretary in the German Foreign Ministry, who supplied the initiative in this matter. In a letter dated August 29, 1936, to Baron von Neurath, Dieckhoff wrote that not only were the French and British governments in favor of the establishment of a supervisory committee but the Italian government was as well, provided that this committee were located in London and not in Paris. "Thus we would probably be quite alone in our negative attitude," said Dieckhoff.[31] But he added:

I hardly believe that the plan could really entail any serious danger for us. The word "control" does not appear in the French note; according to François-Poncet's explanation, too, what was involved was primarily an exchange of information and a coordination. We ourselves, after all, can play a part in seeing that this London arrangement does not develop into a permanent political agency which might make trouble for us; and in this we can secure Italian and British support, too.

Naturally, we have to count on complaints of all kinds being brought up in London regarding failure to observe the obligation not to intervene, but we cannot avoid such complaints in any case. It can, in fact, only be agreeable to us if the center of gravity, which after all has thus far been in Paris because of the French initiative, is transferred to London.[32]

On September 9, 1936, the first meeting of the International Committee for the Application of the Agreement Regarding Non-Intervention in Spain was held at the British Foreign Office in London. Mr. W. S. Morrison of England was elected chairman of the committee, but he was soon succeeded by Lord Plymouth (Ivor Miles Windsor-Clive). Mr. Francis Hemming, also of England, was named secretary to the committee. At the second meeting of the committee, on September 14, a sub-committee to assist the chairman was created. It was composed of the representatives of Belgium, Czechoslovakia, France, Germany, Great Britain, Italy, Soviet Russia, Sweden, and, by September 28, Portugal. To this steering committee fell most of the real work of the London Non-Intervention Committee.

From the foregoing account of the conclusion of a general agreement and the establishment of a supervisory committee in London the inference is plain that the interested powers, particularly Germany, Italy, and Portugal, did not conceive of the nonintervention plan as a legal and moral instrument that would seriously limit the part they might seek to play in the Spanish drama nor of the London committee as other than an innocuous gathering of fainéant diplomats. In a report dated August 28, 1936, to the German Foreign Ministry, the German chargé d'affaires in Rome, Baron Johann von

Plessen, wrote that Italian adherence to the nonintervention scheme came "sooner than was to be expected." [33] The Baron believed that even the French Embassy was surprised by the Italian decision. The German added that he inferred from a remark made to him by the Italian under secretary of state, Giuseppe Bastianini, that the Italian government had come to believe that further delay in concluding the nonintervention agreement might benefit the Madrid government more than General Franco. Baron von Plessen then noted:

That the Italian government has attempted, by the way its reply has been formulated, to reserve far-reaching freedom of action for all contingencies is just as obvious as that it does not intend to abide by the declaration anyway.[34]

The Italian note of adherence to the nonintervention agreement was, indeed, Machiavellian. It did not contain the preambulatory resolution of the original French note to refrain from all interference, direct or indirect, in Spanish internal affairs. The Italian note, moreover, interpreted the phrase "indirect interference" to mean such activities as the subscription of funds and the recruitment of volunteers for Spain. Thus, in adhering to "direct nonintervention" but maintaining its "observations" regarding "indirect non-intervention," the Italian government sought to limit the freedom of action with respect to both "direct" and "indirect" interference of those nations which in their notes of adherence embodied the aforementioned preambulatory resolution (ultimately, the majority of the twenty-seven participating states, including France, Great Britain, and Soviet Russia) while binding Italy only with respect to "direct intervention." [35]

However, so little disturbed by this Italian maneuver was the French ambassador in Rome, Count de Chambrun, to whom the Italian note had been addressed, that he stated in a conversation with Mr. Kirk, the American chargé d'affaires in Rome, that he was "well satisfied" with the Italian note.[36] Chambrun appeared particularly pleased that the Italian government maintained only "observations" and not "reservations" concerning "indirect non-intervention." [37] British circles in Rome shared Chambrun's satisfaction.[38]

As was indicated above, the German government in its note of adherence to the nonintervention agreement did not include the preambulatory reasons for making the declaration of the original French note, so that its position with respect to "indirect intervention" was not unlike that of Italy. While the Portuguese note of August 21 declared that the Portuguese government would refrain from all interference, direct or indirect, in Spanish affairs, it contained enough important reservations not only to obviate the validity of this particular declaration but to render Portuguese participation itself virtually an empty gesture.

The attitude of the German government concerning the proper role and function of the London Non-Intervention Committee has already been discussed. On this matter, Rome was in substantial agreement with Berlin. Count Dino Grandi, the Italian ambassador in London and Italy's representative on the London Committee, received secret instructions "to do his best to give the committee's entire activity a purely platonic character." [39] At the same time, Prince Otto Christian von Bismarck, the counselor of the German Embassy in London and Germany's representative on the London Committee, was instructed by Berlin to work closely with Count Grandi.[40]

A close study of the documents pertaining to the nonintervention plan reveals that not only was sincere adherence to it not contemplated by at least some of the participating powers and that, objectively, it failed to prevent large-scale intervention in the Spanish conflict even after it had been strengthened by more stringent arrangements but that it intrinsically was not, and never really became, a legally binding obligation such as would have been the case if the nonintervention plan had been embodied in a formal treaty. It remained, therefore, little more than a moral commitment on the part of each of the participating powers. In discussing the status of the nonintervention agreement in international law, Norman J. Padelford noted:

It must be emphasized that the accord was not a formal international agreement or treaty in the sense that the participating states subscribed by signature and ratification to one written instrument. It was an "accord" only in a very loose form, a series of *unilateral declarations of intention* of the national policy which would be pursued. Departures from the accord cannot be condemned as violations of international law or of treaties. They constituted only deviations from a line of policy which each state suggested its readiness to follow for the time being. The fulfillment of the accord, or its enforcement in any particular state depended entirely upon the good-will and coöperation of the authorities of that state, and upon the enaction and/or enforcement of such legislative, executive or administrative measures as were deemed to be desirable.[41]

Certainly the continued and increasingly expanded intervention of Germany and Italy in the Spanish conflict constituted a violation of the spirit of the nonintervention agreement. Yet, those statesmen, publicists, and journalists in the Western democracies who raised a hue and cry about Italo-German violation of the nonintervention agreement were either victims of a terrible self-deception or parties to a huge hoax.[42] For they successfully created the impression in the public mind that a hard and fast nonintervention agreement did exist and that while England and France faithfully adhered to it the fascist powers did not. Moreover, they successfully established the idea in the public mind that the task at hand was somehow to force the Germans and Italians to abide by the agreement. Thus, an emphasis was placed where it did not belong, for it was foolish, if not worse, to insist that an agreement that was little more than a moral commitment be regarded as a legally binding instrument. The real task at hand was either to establish an effective, legally binding instrument of nonintervention, and this forthwith, or to regain the freedom of action that had been unilaterally surrendered by the Western powers.

The conclusion is inescapable that the nonintervention scheme

was cut from the same cloth as the partial economic sanctions imposed on Italy during the Italo-Ethiopian War, the inefficacy of the
one matching the inadequacy of the other. It is not without significance that, with the warm approval of both Berlin and Rome,
the Non-Intervention Committee came to sit in London and that
its Chairman was an Englishman. With respect to the nonintervention agreement, it was the Quai d'Orsay which proposed but No.
10 Downing Street which disposed.

VI

The Nonintervention Agreement:
Intervention and
Counter-Intervention (*continued*)

IN the light of the nugacity, or "platonic character," of the nonintervention agreement, it should occasion no real surprise to discover that Germany, not only throughout the period of diplomatic discussion concerning nonintervention but also after a general agreement had been concluded, continued to assist the Spanish rebels.[1] On August 12, the German cargo ship *Schleswig*, escorted by the German destroyer *Leopard*, put in at Palma, the rebel-held capital of Majorca, and unloaded quantities of arms and munitions, including modern anti-aircraft machine guns.[2] Additional German war materials arrived at Vigo, in Galicia, on August 28, again shipped in German bottoms.[3] On September 7, 1936, thirteen days after Berlin's formal adherence to the agreement and two days before the first meeting of the Non-Intervention Committee in London, Dr. Friedrich Gaus, director of the Legal Department of the German Foreign Ministry, sent a telegram to the German Legation in Portugal in which he inquired about a possible change in the attitude of the Portuguese authorities with respect to the transshipment of German war materials to the Spanish rebels. Dr. Gaus' telegram had a certain "business as usual" quality. It read:

At the request of the Portuguese government, the German ship *Usaramo* was unable to discharge a "certain" cargo in the port of Lisbon and must return to the northern coast of Spain. According to information received by the Navy [very likely by the office of Admiral Wilhelm Canaris, head of the German Intelligence Service], the Portuguese government acted under British pressure. I request a telegraphic report as to whether, in your judgment, we must count on a change in the Portuguese attitude under British influence.[4]

Dr. Gaus was unnecessarily anxious. The case of the *Usaramo* proved to be exceptional and not at all indicative of a change of heart in Lisbon. British diplomatic pressure on the Portuguese government must not have been unduly severe, for Portugal continued to assist the rebel cause in Spain in every way within her means.[5]

The days between August 27 and September 8, 1936, must have been a little hectic for Herr Eberhard Messerschmidt, the representative in Spain of the Ausfuhrgemeinschaft für Kriegsgerät (Export Cartel for War Matériel). During that time he had traveled from Lisbon to Sevilla, then north to Cáceres, where he had an interview lasting nearly an hour with General Francisco Franco and his chief of aviation, General Alfredo Kindelan, and back again to Lisbon. On September 8, he wrote a lengthy report on his trip for the German Foreign Ministry. It was forwarded to its destination by Baron von Huene, the German minister in Portugal. In his report Herr Messerschmidt observed that the delivery of German war materials to the Spanish rebels was in the hands of the Hisma organization headed by Herr Johannes Bernhardt. Messerschmidt noted, too, that there was some disagreement between General Kindelan, the chief of the rebel aviation, and General von Scheele, the military adviser of the Hisma organization, over the proper employment of German aircraft and pilots. From his interview with General Franco, Herr Messerschmidt concluded that the rebel leader's political ideas were quite sound. What the future of the Falange would be, Messerschmidt continued, remained to be seen. At the present time, he noted, the Spanish fascists appeared to be without real aims and ideas, contenting themselves with rounding up communists and socialists. "For the rest, they rely on our efforts and the courage of the Moroccans, who fight at the front." [6] Messerschmidt was particularly critical of Bernhardt. While he conceded that Bernhardt had shown "great energy and zeal in getting the implementation of the aid program under way,"[7] he maintained that Bernhardt, largely for personal reasons and with an eye to the future, had not demanded from Franco *quid pro quo*. This, indeed, was the crux of Messerschmidt's criticism of Bernhardt's policies. Messerschmidt concluded:

we must look ahead to our future interests, and I believe that now, while Franco is still under a certain pressure, is the moment for getting pledges from him with respect to our future economic and perhaps even political influence. For otherwise there is no doubt but that England or Italy, with an eye to preserving their influence, will turn up at the last moment and pose as the real moving spirits.

Thus, for instance, now would be the moment to assure ourselves of a basic treaty, as contemplated earlier, which would lay down for a number of years to come what raw materials Spain is to deliver to us and to what extent Spain must buy manufactured goods from us. I am sure that Franco would be willing in every respect to conclude such an agreement, provided that Herr Bernhardt is now prepared to give up his role of Santa Claus and demand value in return for our gifts.[8]

What is the significance of the Messerschmidt report? First, it reflects the importance of German assistance to the Spanish rebels. Moreover, it reveals that, Germany's formal adherence to the nonintervention agreement notwithstanding, Berlin was continuing to support the rebel cause and was not contemplating a cessation of its aid. Then, too, it throws light on the economic aims and aspirations of the Reich in Spain.

Herr Messerschmidt was something of a jackdaw in peacock's feathers. His attack on the policies of Herr Bernhardt was most ill-considered, for it appears that Bernhardt and the Hisma organization enjoyed the powerful support of Marshal Hermann Göring.[9] Moreover, Messerschmidt's concern to attain in Spain immediately and directly what others were securing more slowly and quietly betrayed a certain lack of coordination among the departments of the German government as well as Messerschmidt's meddling self-importance. At any rate, the very candor of the Messerschmidt report compelled the Intelligence Department of the German War Ministry to call in all copies of the report on September 21, 1936.[10] Then, on October 3, 1936, the German Foreign Ministry requested that all correspondence relating to the Messerschmidt report be placed in "an especially secret category." [11]

Meanwhile, on September 29, 1936, in the rebel-held city of Burgos, the Junta de Defensa Nacional [12] had formally invested General Francisco Franco with the titles and offices of Head of the Government and of the Spanish State and Generalissimo of the Nationalist Armies. One of General Franco's first acts as Jefe had been to send a telegram to Adolf Hitler, informing the Führer of his assumption of the leadership of the Spanish State and expressing his "warmest wishes" for the well-being of the Führer and the prosperity of the German nation "with which we are united by so many bonds of sincere friendship and deep gratitude." [13] On October 3, the German government dispatched Count Du Moulin-Eckart, counselor of the German Legation in Portugal, to Spain to convey the Führer's "most sincere congratulations" to Franco and his "best wishes for the further success of the work of liberation." [14] Du Moulin-Eckart was instructed to explain to Franco "that the Führer refrained from giving a telegraphic or written reply to the telegram because the world might have considered this to mean recognition of the Nationalist government . . . recognition at the present moment would compromise our work in Spain and therefore serve neither Franco nor Germany's interest." [15] On his return from Spain to his post in Lisbon Count Du Moulin-Eckart reported that he was the first diplomatic representative to call on General Franco since the General had been designated chief of state. Du Moulin-Eckart added that Franco understood perfectly the reasons why the Reich had not yet recognized his government, agreeing that it was much easier for Germany "to furnish aid to the extent done heretofore as long as the possibilities of support were not hampered by international complications." [16]

However, while much was said of the mutual regard and esteem between Berlin and Burgos, the Germans were not really satisfied with the Spaniards' conduct of the war. On October 30, the German government sought to induce General Franco to agree to the virtual autonomy of the German air force units fighting in Spain, thus assuring that they would be commanded by German officers who would be responsible only to General Franco himself.[17] (Such an arrangement, of course, would leave General Alfredo Kindelan, the nominal chief of the rebel aviation, with no authority over the German air units fighting in Spain and, therefore, with considerable leisure.) General Franco was informed that if he accepted this arrangement "a further activation of German aid is envisaged" that would include one bomber group, one fighter group, one long-range reconnaissance squadron, one flight of short-range reconnaissance planes, two signal companies, two operating companies, three heavy antiaircraft batteries, and two searchlight platoons.[18]

It would seem that aircraft and interests are more substantial things than pride and moral agreements, for neither General Kindelan's sensibilities nor the notes and protestations of strict neutrality which issued regularly from Berlin served to diminish the flow of German war materials, officers, and soldiers to rebel Spain. The Condor Legion—the term applied to regular formations of German forces, including infantry, fighting on Spanish soil—came into existence on November 7, 1936.[19] The rebel-held port of Cádiz was a beehive of activity in November, 1936, "owing to visits of numerous German vessels."[20] Fully equipped contingents of artillery and infantry as well as aviation units, involving thousands of men, were disembarked.[21] On November 17, some 1200 Germans, "some in khaki and boots," arrived in Sevilla, their equipment including "small touring cars of foreign design" and "field kitchens."[22] Following the recognition of the Franco government on November 18, 1936, by the fascist powers, the flow of German men and equipment to rebel Spain was considerably accelerated. On December 1, 5000 Germans landed at Cádiz.[23] At about the same time, 2500 Germans landed at Vigo.[24] According to information received by the American ambassador to Spain, Claude G. Bowers, from American correspondents who had been with the rebel forces, Salamanca, where General Franco made his headquarters, resembled "a German military camp, German officers predominating." [25] By the first week of January, 1937, the number of Germans fighting with the rebels was estimated at about 12,000, and approximately 80 per cent of the rebel air force was said to be German.[26]

The Italians, like the Germans, continued unabatedly to assist the Spanish rebels both while the discussions which led to the non-intervention agreement were in progress [27] and after a general agreement was concluded. On August 28, one week after Italy's formal adherence to the nonintervention agreement and on the very day Rome placed a ban on the exportation of war materials to Spain, twelve Italian pilots and airplanes arrived at Vigo, proceeding at once to Burgos.[28] On September 3, Madrid protested to the non-intervention powers against the arrival of additional Italian aircraft at Vigo.[29]

A particularly flagrant violation of the Italian pledge not to interfere in Spanish internal affairs was the occupation of Majorca, the largest of the Balearic Islands, by Italian forces in early September, 1936.[30] Majorca had been in the possession of rebel forces since the beginning of the insurrection, the military commander of the Balearic Islands with headquarters at Palma having been General Manuel Goded, the insurgent leader who was later captured and executed in Barcelona. The Catalans, upon suppressing the revolt in Catalonia, had dispatched an expedition to recover Majorca, but the effort had floundered against Italian air power. One of Francisco Largo Caballero's first acts upon becoming premier of the Spanish Republic on September 4, 1936, was to recall the Catalans fighting on the island. Majorca remained in the hands of the rebels throughout the war. However, with the arrival of thousands of Italian soldiers, sailors, and airmen, it became, in fact, an Italian military base. In a conversation with Herr Hans Frank, German minister without portfolio, at the Palazzo Venezia in Rome on September 23, 1936, Mussolini declared that much Italian blood had been shed in Spain and that "the Balearics were saved only by Italian men and Italian material." [31]

From Majorca the Italians were able to harass the Catalonian and Valencian coasts of Republican Spain, attacking shipping making for Barcelona, Valencia, Alicante, and Cartagena and subjecting these cities to fierce aerial assaults. In the event of a general war, moreover, the Italians on Majorca could pose a serious threat to French communications with North Africa. However, it remains a most curious fact that while in November, 1936, the Italians proceeded to occupy Iviza, one of the smaller islands of the archipelago, they never made a serious attempt to seize Minorca which is second in size to Majorca and which boasted an excellent harbor and base in Port Mahón. Minorca was to remain in Republican hands until almost the end of the war. This military anomaly can hardly be explained by allusions to the skill and bravery of the Republican defenders. Italian mastery of the air over these islands was practically undisputed. Against a determined Italian effort to reduce Minorca, it is difficult to see what the Republicans could have done to stave off defeat. But the point is that the Italians never made such an effort. Perhaps Italian forbearance in this matter was in the nature of a gesture toward London, an earnest of Italy's good faith, as it were, regarding her repeated assurances that she did not seek to alter the *status quo* in the Mediterranean by her course of action in Spain, assurances which were embodied in the Anglo-Italian Gentlemen's Agreement of January 2, 1937. As long as the Balearic Islands were only partially occupied by the Italians their presence there could be construed to be only a military measure devoid of permanent political significance. If this interpretation is correct it is not without significance that in September, 1938, when the Czechoslovakian crisis produced a threat of general war, Italian and German aircraft, based on Majorca, bombed Minorca for the first time in a year, an action not dictated by Spanish military developments.[32]

Upon being named chief of state and generalissimo of the Nationalist armies, General Franco had sent a message of greetings to Benito Mussolini, as he had Adolf Hitler. However, the Duce, like the Führer, had demurred at extending immediate recognition to the Franco government, deeming the fall of Madrid, which was expected momentarily, to be a more suitable occasion.[33] Meanwhile, in Berlin, on October 21, 1936, the Italian foreign minister, Count Ciano, informed the German foreign minister, Baron von Neurath, that he (Ciano) had been instructed by the Duce to tell the Führer that he "intends to make a decisive military effort to bring about the collapse of the Madrid Government." [34] Ciano, in the name of the Duce, then asked if the Führer "is ready to associate himself with this operation." [35] Neurath replied that he believed that the Führer would certainly do so but that the question would have to be dealt with by the Führer himself. Ciano and Neurath then agreed to the following: an immediate joint military effort in Spain; recognition of the Franco government after the occupation of Madrid; and, joint action, "to be defined in due course," to prevent the emergence of a Catalan State.[36]

The military failure of the rebels before Madrid did not prevent the fascist powers from extending *de jure* recognition to the Franco government. And the Italians, like the Germans, redoubled their efforts on behalf of the rebels after November 18, 1936. By the end of the month an expeditionary force of some 10,000 Blackshirts was being prepared for service in Spain.[37] On December 18, 3000 Blackshirts with full equipment sailed from the Italian port of Gaeta for Cádiz.[38] Moreover, by this time seven Italian submarines were active in Spanish waters.[39] Between December 23 and 29, another 3000 Blackshirts embarked for Spain.[40] On December 29, an Italian Red Cross unit of 24 trucks arrived in Sevilla.[41] Moreover, Rome had already dispatched some 1500 military specialists to Spain and another 1500 specialists with technical equipment were expected to embark shortly.[42] By the first week of January, 1937, the number of Italians with Franco's forces was estimated at about 14,000 and approximately fifteen per cent of the rebel air arm was said to be Italian.[43]

Not only had timely German and Italian support of the Spanish rebels in late July and early August, 1936, prevented the aborted coup d'état from becoming a military rout, but the steady flow of German and Italian soldiers and war materials to rebel Spain through August, September, and October had given General Franco an important advantage in capable officers, trained soldiers, motorized transport, air power, artillery, and technical services and had enabled him to take Badajoz and effect a junction with General Mola, to capture Toledo and relieve the Alcázar, and, finally, to invest and attempt to storm Madrid. By the end of October, Frank L. Kluckhohn, *New York Times* correspondent with the rebel forces, could write that the "backbone" of the rebel army was Italian, German, and Moorish.[44] Following recognition of the Franco government by Rome and Berlin on November 18, 1936, Italian and German soldiers and supplies reached rebel Spain in such numbers and in such quantities that by the end of the year not only was the "backbone" of the "nationalist" army non-Spanish but much of the rest of the skeleton as well as most of the flesh and blood of the "rebel monster" had come from the laboratories of the Frankensteins in Rome and Berlin. In the important realm of air power this was most apparent. On the eve of the Civil War the Spanish air force had been pitiably weak, its aircraft few and, in large part, obsolescent. Moreover, when the generals revolted, much of the air force remained loyal to the Republic. The rebels, then, possessed precious little strength in the air in mid-July 1936. Yet by the end of the year the rebel air arm boasted hundreds of swift, modern aircraft, including long-range, heavy bombers. But, as was noted above, approximately eighty per cent of the rebel air force was German and another fifteen per cent Italian, leaving General Alfredo Kindelan very little to do, indeed.

Both the Italians and the Germans were aware, of course, of the almost complete dependence of General Franco on their support. On November 25, one week after the fascist powers had recognized the Franco government, the American ambassador in Paris, William Bullitt, reported to his government that the French government was extremely apprehensive that continued foreign support of the warring factions in Spain might result in a general European conflagration. Bullitt went on to note, relevant to this contingency, that "the Italian Ambassador this evening expressed to me his conviction that it would be impossible for the Italian Government at this time to cease to support Franco even if the Soviet Government should cease to support the Madrid and Barcelona Governments, Franco's effectives being clearly insufficient to enable him to conquer the whole of Spain."[45] Two days later, from another conversation with Signor Vittorio Cerruti, the Italian ambassador in France, Bullitt inferred that Mussolini had decided to give the faltering Franco all aid necessary to insure his victory but that he (Mussolini) was waiting before committing it to make certain that Great Britain would remain passive.[46]

The Germans were as cognizant as the Italians of the real situation in Spain. On December 13, 1936, Captain Ronald Strunk, a personal agent of Adolf Hitler in Spain, returned to Sevilla from the Madrid front. In a conversation with the American consul in Sevilla, the German stated that were it not for German men and matériel Franco's armies would collapse and that "the successful conclusion of the struggle depends on German and Italian support."[47] Strunk added that he was recommending to Hitler the dispatch to Spain of more material, particularly aircraft, as well as more men.[48] Having said "a" the Italians and Germans were going on to "b."[49]

What with the steady flow of German and Italian soldiers and supplies to rebel Spain as well as the arrival of Portuguese and even of Irish volunteers in Franco's camp,[50] what with the open hostility of the Portuguese government toward Republican Spain, culminating in the severance of diplomatic relations between Lisbon and Madrid on October 23, 1936, and the formal recognition of the Franco government by Germany and Italy on November 18, 1936 (in itself a premature and therefore a hostile act of the fascist powers vis-à-vis the Spanish Republic),[51] it could be concluded that the nonintervention agreement was without significant deterrent effect. However, such a conclusion would not be entirely warranted. For it might be argued, as British Foreign Secretary Eden did in a speech delivered at Liverpool on April 12, 1937,[52] that, whatever the shortcomings and abuses of the nonintervention agreement, it did serve to limit foreign interference in the Spanish conflict and thus to reduce the risks of general war. With respect to foreign interference in general and not German interference, Italian interference, or French interference in particular, it is beyond cavil that Mr. Eden and those who believed as he did were right in holding that the nonintervention agreement had proved in some measure efficacious. For, in the case of France—the one nation whose vital interests, political sympathies, geographical position, and arms-producing capacity made her the natural arsenal of the embattled Spanish Republic—the nonintervention agreement all but ended the flow of French war materials to Republican Spain. Having toured the French-Spanish frontier in almost its entirety, the American consul in Bordeaux, Mr. Finley, reported to his government on August 29, 1936, that while doubtful at Hendaye the rest of the border seemed to be effectively closed.[53] Mr. Finley added that if supplies seeped through at some points this occurred in spite of the sincere efforts of the French government to prevent it.[54] And the land route, because of the activities of Italian aircraft and submarines,[55] provided safer ingress to Republican Spain than did the sea. With respect to this matter, it is important to recall that owing to the visits of numerous German vessels the rebel-held port of Cádiz was bustling during the month of November, 1936. However Barcelona, the greatest port of Republican Spain, was "almost bare of shipping" at approximately the same time.[56]

While it can be affirmed that France, in the main, sought sincerely to abide by the nonintervention agreement, enough evidence exists to establish that French support of Republican Spain continued beyond August, 1936,[57] and that it was not entirely unimportant. French aid to Spain must be divided into two general categories, to wit, direct aid, under which would come the dispatch of aircraft, guns, munitions, supplies, and soldiers by the French government to the Republican forces, and indirect aid, under which would be included the use of French port, rail, and other facilities for the transshipment of war materials coming from abroad and destined for Republican Spain, the private subscription of funds on behalf of Madrid as well as the enlistment of French volunteers to fight in Spain, and, for a time, the movement of Republican troops and equipment from Catalonia to the Basque front by way of southern France. At no time during the Civil War did the French government dispatch regular French forces, pseudo-volunteers, or bona fide volunteers to fight in Spain. And, it might be observed, at no time during the course of the conflict did either Rome or Berlin lodge official protests on this score with either the London Non-Intervention Committee or Paris itself. The closest approach to such a protest was made by Italy when Count Dino Grandi, the Italian ambassador in England and the Italian representative on the London committee, in a conversation with Prime Minister Chamberlain and Foreign Secretary Eden on February 18, 1938,[58] sought to equate the French and other foreign volunteers serving in the International Brigades with Italian soldiers forming part of the rebel army. This was, of course, patent nonsense, for the totalitarian nature of the fascist regime gave an official character to the movement of Italian soldiers to Spain. With respect to the dispatch of French war materials to Republican Spain it should be noted that Pierre Cot, the minister of aviation in the Blum government, played an important role in the delivery of some seventy French aircraft, including thirty-five new pursuit planes, to the Republican forces during 1936.[59] However, seventy aircraft in more than five months of war, as against the hundreds of German and Italian aircraft (with their pilots and crews) which were dispatched to rebel Spain during this same period, reflects both the divided counsels which prevailed in Paris and the relatively limited amount of direct aid sent by France to Spain. For the available evidence indicates that the delivery of other types of equipment was on the same modest scale.[60]

French direct aid to Republican Spain, however minimal, was supplemented by indirect assistance of various kinds. During the early months of the war, for example, a number of young Spaniards were trained as pilots in French training schools.[61] Then, too, until the collapse of the Basque front, the French authorities occasionally

permitted Catalan reinforcements and supplies to reach the Bis-
cayan region by way of southern France.[62] Moreover, local French
officials, sometimes on their own initiative, sometimes in connivance
with Paris, occasionally allowed war materials and volunteers to
cross the Pyrenees into Catalonia. Yet, this intermittent flow of illicit traffic notwithstanding, the Pyrenean frontier was, for most of
its length and for most of the time, effectively closed. The difficulties experienced by Steve Nelson and his companions, American
volunteers in the International Brigades, in seeking to enter Spain
by way of France attest to the vigilance of the French authorities.[63]
It was, of course, well-nigh impossible to prevent small groups of
determined men, traveling by night and risking the hazards of un-
frequented, snow-filled, wind-swept paths through the forests and
mountains, from crossing the Pyrenees. By the same token, it was
almost impossible to prevent a certain amount of smuggling and
gun-running. Nevertheless, except for brief periods when Paris
sought either to placate public opinion in France or to put pressure
on the fascist powers, the French did their utmost to prevent illicit
traffic from crossing the Pyrenees. When, after March 8, 1937,
the efforts of the French border guards were buttressed by observation officers of the London Non-Intervention Committee stationed
along the French-Spanish frontier, the border can be said to have
been, for all practical purposes, hermetically sealed. General Franco
himself, in the summer of 1938, expressed his satisfaction to the
British government that the Pyrenean frontier was effectively
closed.[64]

   In the light of the available evidence, then, it is apparent that
French aid to Spain, both direct and indirect, was quite meager,
however important this little was to the struggling Republicans.
Moreover, if French aid to Republican Spain was slight in an
absolute sense, it can be said to have been, relative to the great
numbers of men and the vast amounts of equipment sent to rebel
Spain by Germany and Italy, virtually nonexistent. As far as
Madrid was concerned, this disparity was the tolling bell, the open
sepulcher, the very end of mortal striving. To bring about a change

of attitude in the Quai d'Orsay, to reopen the Pyrenean frontier became the fundamental aims of Republican diplomacy.[65] Even after Soviet Russia sent bombers and fighter planes, tanks and artillery, machine guns and rifles, munitions and supplies, and military technicians and instructors to Spain, the fundamental aims of Republican diplomacy did not change. Nor did they change when it became quite apparent that they were but *ignes fatui*. For France was the one nation which could have given the Spanish Republic really effective assistance.

When an important measure of foreign aid did reach Republican Spain it came not from her European neighbor to the north but from far distant lands, first from her former colony of New Spain and then from Soviet Russia. Mexican support of the Spanish Republic was distinguished by two qualities, its disinterestedness and its inevitable insufficiency. The Republic of Mexico, under the leadership of President Lázaro Cárdenas, was engaged in a program of social reform which, while essentially reflective of Mexican social conditions and problems, derived its inspiration, in part at least, from the political philosophy upon which the Frente Popular in Spain was predicated. There was, then, between Mexico City and Madrid, besides the ties of blood, language, culture, and sentiment, the bond of a common progressivism. This last must have been the compelling factor in Mexican policy toward Spain because Mexico, almost alone among the nations of Latin America, was openly pro-Republican during the Civil War. Furthermore, there was little, if anything, that Mexico could have hoped to gain, either in political influence or strategic position or economic advantage, by her pro-Loyalist course. Thus, Mexico was not motivated by ulterior purposes but solely by sympathy with the Madrid regime.

Holding the nonintervention agreement to be a wrongful denial of the legitimate rights of the Spanish Republic,[66] the Mexicans did what they could to succor the embattled Republicans. In late August, 1936, a Spanish ship that had put in at Vera Cruz was loaded with Mexican arms and munitions.[67] In early September some twenty thousand Mexican rifles were landed at the Republican port of Alicante in southwestern Spain.[68] However, owing to her limited productive capacity, her distance from Spain, her lack of shipping, her "gentlemen's agreement" with Washington not to deliver to Spain war materials purchased by Mexico in the United States,[69] and, by the end of 1936, her reluctance to risk the hazards of rebel, *i.e.*, Italo-German, control of Spanish waters, the help that Mexico could send Spain amounted to little more than a gesture of moral solidarity. The large, qualitatively important, and sustained shipments of war materials which reached Republican Spain in the autumn of 1936 came not from Vera Cruz but from Odessa and other Russian ports.

Russian aid to Republican Spain passed through two main phases and took a variety of forms. During the first three months of the Spanish Civil War the Soviet Union adhered reluctantly but more or less faithfully to the nonintervention agreement. On October 7, 1936, the Soviet government in a note to the London committee threatened to withdraw from the nonintervention agreement unless violations of it ceased immediately.[70] Thereupon events moved swiftly and by the end of the month, the Soviet Union, refusing to be bound by the nonintervention agreement "in any greater measure than any of the other participants in this agreement," [71] dispatched Russian war materials and military specialists to Spain.[72]

Before direct Russian aid was forthcoming in late October, 1936, the Soviet Union had sought to assist Republican Spain in other ways. To begin with, Moscow made no effort to conceal her sympathy for Madrid. From the first days of the conflict the Soviet government gave its moral support to the Republican cause, and, when it became apparent that General Franco was receiving important German and Italian aid, the Soviet press launched a bitter attack against the "fascist aggressors." On August 29, 1936, on instructions from his government, the German ambassador in Moscow, Count Friedrich von Schulenburg, protested to the Soviet foreign minister, Maxim Litvinov, against the vilification of Germany and German leaders in the Soviet press.[73] During September,

1936, moreover, relations between Soviet Russia and Italy became strained and trade negotiations then in progress between the two countries were broken off. In Rome on September 14, 1936, Count Ciano observed in a conversation with Guido Schmidt, the Austrian foreign minister, that the Spanish situation and the subsequent Soviet press campaign against the fascist powers had contributed to the deterioration of Italo-Soviet relations.[74]

It has already been noted that by the first week in August, 1936, funds "for the assistance of the [Spanish Republican] fighters" were being collected in Soviet factories and on Soviet farms. On September 19, 1936, the first Russian ship, the *Neva,* with a cargo of 2000 tons of foodstuffs, left Odessa for the Republican port of Alicante.[75] According to the German chargé d'affaires in Moscow, who quoted from an article in *Pravda* of September 22, 1936, the *Neva* was carrying 30,000 pood (one pood = 36.113 pounds) of butter, 95,000 pood of sugar, 17,000 pood of canned goods, 18,000 pood of margarine, and 12,000 pood of confections.[76] The German concluded his report (dated Moscow, September 28, 1936) by observing that while "the wide expanse of the Soviet Union" and "the well-known Soviet system of surveillance" made the gathering of accurate information very difficult, thus far "it has been impossible to obtain reliable proof of violation of the arms embargo by the Soviet government." [77] It is of interest to note that Major José Martín Blázquez, who was sent by Madrid to Alicante to welcome the *Neva* and to make certain that its cargo was forwarded to the capital, substantially confirmed what the German chargé d'affaires had reported to his government, thus strengthening the validity of the German's conclusion that Russian arms had probably not been sent to Spain as of the end of September, 1936. Major Martín Blázquez said:

Next day the *Neva,* from Odessa, drew into the harbour with two thousand tons of provisions, raised by subscription among the Russian people. Reactionary newspapers all over the world announced the landing at Alicante of a Russian ship laden to the brim with armaments. The cargo of the *Neva* consisted of butter, milk, flour, sugar, and salted cod.[78]

In the wake of the *Neva* other Russian ships carrying cargoes of foodstuffs, medical supplies, and other noncombatant goods began to arrive in Republican ports. However, Russian assistance in noncombatant goods was soon supplemented by the clandestine activities of Russian and Comintern agents who organized the purchase and delivery to Republican Spain of war materials obtained in Western markets and transported to their destination by Western facilities. According to W. G. Krivitsky, at that time chief of the Soviet Intelligence Service in Western Europe, the Soviet government, although it was fully informed as to the extent of German and Italian aid to General Franco, did nothing to help the Spanish Republic until toward the end of August or not until some six weeks had elapsed since Lieutenant Colonel Juan Yagüe had raised the standard of revolt in Morocco.[79] But in late August, 1936, Joseph Stalin called a special meeting of the Politbureau, at which time the Russian leaders agreed to embark upon a cautious and limited intervention in the Spanish conflict.[80] On August 30 a special courier, flying from Moscow, arrived in The Hague, where Krivitsky had his headquarters. The courier brought the following instructions: "Extend your operations immediately to cover Spanish Civil War. Mobilize all available agents and facilities for prompt creation of a system to purchase and transport arms to Spain. A special agent is being dispatched to Paris to aid you in this work. He will report to you there and work under your supervision." [81]

By the middle of September, 1936, the Russian plan to give clandestine military aid to Republican Spain was completed. General Uritsky, a member of the general staff of the Red army, was made responsible for the technical military problems which would naturally arise, such as determining the types and quantities of war materials to be sent to Spain and assigning various military technicians to their proper tasks.[82] Captain Oulansky of the Secret Police (the OGPU) was placed in charge of a "private firm" that was to deal with Spanish Republican representatives who had arrived in Odessa in late August to purchase arms. Oulansky was instructed to be extremely circumspect and to arrange that the war materials bought from his "private firm" be delivered to Spain in Spanish or neutral bottoms.[83] The Soviet government was concerned not to reveal its hand in the affair. The foreign branch of the enterprise was to be directed by Krivitsky, as was noted above.

From Paris, on September 21, 1936, Krivitsky launched his operations.[84] From behind the façade of ostensibly private export-import firms established in Paris, London, and other large European cities, his agents purchased a huge quantity of arms from Skoda in Czechoslovakia and from other firms in France, the Netherlands, Poland, and even Nazi Germany.[85] Krivitsky had originally planned to use France as an entrepôt. However, inasmuch as the French Foreign Ministry refused to grant clearance papers for arms shipments to Spain, Krivitsky found it necessary to have his agents falsely consign these arms to ports in Latin America and Asia. Once at sea, however, the ships which Krivitsky's agents had engaged to transport the arms, mostly of Scandinavian registry, would proceed directly to Spain.[86]

José Martín Blázquez wrote that the day following the departure of the *Neva* from Alicante an English vessel carrying a cargo of twenty thousand rifles, twenty million rounds of ammunition, and a number of machine guns put in at the Republican port.[87] Part of the arms were packed in cases bearing German inscriptions indicating that they had come from Hamburg. Major Martín Blázquez remarked: "I never found out where they really came from, but I should not be surprised if they were really German." [88] In view of the fact that Krivitsky's agents had managed to purchase a quantity of rifles and machine guns from a German firm in Hamburg,[89] it might well have been that Major Martín Blázquez was receiving the first shipment of Russian-procured Western arms to reach Republican Spain. This notion gains credence when it is learned that the English vessel was engaged in somewhat irregular business and that Major Martín Blázquez found it necessary to bestow a "gift" of three thousand pesetas on the ship's captain because he had put in at Alicante and thereby to induce him to do so again.[90]

From the available evidence it must be concluded, then, that until the end of August, 1936, the main support Soviet Russia gave Republican Spain was of a moral nature, consisting largely of a press campaign in which the rights of the Spanish Republic under international law were stoutly defended and German, Italian, and Portuguese aid to the rebels was vigorously attacked. During this period, too, many public demonstrations occurred in various Russian cities and millions of rubles were collected among the Russian people "for the assistance of the fighters." At the end of August the decision was made by the Kremlin to bring material succor, including arms, to the embattled Republic. But this decision was to be implemented in the greatest secrecy. By late September the first Russian ships carrying foodstuffs and other noncombatant goods arrived in Republican ports. By the middle of October Russian-procured Western arms reached Spain. And by late October and early November Soviet war materials, including airplanes and tanks accompanied by pilots, crews, military technicians, and instructors, reached the Loyalist forces.

Aside from pilots, tankists, artillerists, and other specialists, and staff officers and instructors—their total number variously estimated from 500 to 5000 [91]—the Russians did not send to Spain, either at this time or later, large bodies of fighting men, as did the Italians and, on a more limited scale, the Germans. However, this statement should be qualified in two respects, one of considerable importance. The Russians, through the Comintern, played a principal role in the formation, the recruitment, and the leadership of the International Brigades.[92] Then, too, some 600 political refugees in Russia were encouraged by the Soviet authorities to go to Spain and to fight in the International Brigades.[93] Yet, it would not be correct to assume that the Kremlin, in order to avoid the involvement of its own troops in the Spanish conflict, created the International Brigades *ad arbitrium*. The part played by the Russians in the organization of the International Brigades was one of adroit manipulation and utilization of the enthusiasm that the Republican cause evoked throughout the world, particularly in the Western democracies. In this regard it would be well to remember that while as early as the second week in August, 1936, a limited number of foreign volunteers, including the well-known French author, André Malraux, had entered Spain to fight for the Republic,[94] the International Brigades did not go into action until November 8, 1936, at the height of the battle for Madrid.[95]

The International Brigades were composed of bona fide volunteers and included Frenchmen, Englishmen, Americans, anti-Nazi Germans, anti-Fascist Italians, Belgians, Poles, Bulgars, Canadians, Latin Americans, and others. Among them were some mere adventurers and many Communists, but the greatest number appear to have been young men of liberal sentiments to whom the ideological battle-cry of the 1930s, "Down with War and Fascism," had particular meaning and appeal.[96] The Great Depression, the march of fascism, Hitlerian anti-Semitism, the Anglo-French policy of appeasement, first in Manchuria, then in Ethiopia, now in Spain, Russia's role at Geneva and her part in the Spanish conflict, and, above all, the epic struggle of the Spanish people in defense of the Republic had produced a new social awareness, a sobriety of thought and manner that was in marked contrast with the disillusionment and frivolous apathy of the "Lost Generation" which had fought the First World War. The Popular Front and the International Brigades were cut from the same cloth. The Kremlin, through the Comintern, sought to tailor both the one and the other to its purposes. And in significant measure, it succeeded. In many respects the purposes of the Kremlin and the aims and hopes of liberal democrats in the 1930s were not antithetical. While it is true, as persons with an intimate knowledge of the International Brigades such as W. G. Krivitsky and Louis Fischer report,[97] that the Kremlin successfully sought to make of the International Brigades "the army of the Comintern," [98] it is also true that this was possible only because of the kinship of purpose between Communists and liberal democrats in the 1930s in general and during the Spanish Civil War in particular, and because Western democrats were bereft of important governmental and organizational support.

Probably some 40,000 men passed through the muster rolls of

the International Brigades.[99] According to a statement in the Introduction to *The Volunteer for Liberty*, a volume containing the complete file of a publication of that same title that had served as the official organ of the English-speaking battalions of the International Brigades (Ralph Bates, the English novelist, was its first editor and its first issue was published in Madrid on May 24, 1937, its sixty-third and last in Barcelona on November 7, 1938), the Internationals never numbered more than 25,000 men, with never more than 6000 in action at a given time.[100] When it is remembered that the Internationals were used most intensely during the earlier phases of the war while Franco's forces were still relatively small and the Republican *milicianos* were being made into a regular army, this statement appears accurate. It gains further credence from a remark made by General Franco himself to the German ambassador in rebel Spain, Dr. Eberhard von Stohrer, after the battle of Teruel, a particularly severe engagement which saw the Republicans capture the city on December 22, 1937, and the rebels recapture it on February 22, 1938. Franco declared to Stohrer that since the end of December his forces had taken 14,500 prisoners at Teruel but that "there were only a very few foreigners among them." [101] Franco asked that "this latter fact be treated as strictly confidential." [102]

For reasons of geography and previous military experience, as well as political conviction, the single largest national group in the International Brigades was French.[103] The Americans, organized in the Lincoln and Washington Battalions, numbered some 3000 men.[104] Inasmuch as the Internationals were used as shock troops they suffered heavy casualties. About half of the Americans, for example, were either killed in action or died from wounds received in battle.[105] When the International Brigades were disbanded at the end of 1938 they numbered but 7000 effectives.[106]

Russian intervention in the Spanish conflict was prompted not by a desire for economic aggrandizement, nor for strategic advantage, nor even, basically, for ideological reasons, all of which, in one measure or another, can be said to have accounted for the presence of both the Germans and the Italians in Spain. What with their own vast lands and abundant resources and pressing problems of internal development there was little in Spain to tempt the economic appetites of the Russians. Then, too, while a Spain allied to the fascist powers could enable the Italians, from bases on the Balearics, to challenge Anglo-French supremacy in the western Mediterranean and the Germans, from bases on the Canaries, to menace the sea routes which lead to Casablanca and the west coast of Africa, a Spain friendly to Moscow, if only for reasons of geography, could do little, if anything, to enhance the military power or strategic position of the Soviet Union. And the notion that a Communist regime could be established in Madrid, given the contextual reality of the 1930s, the sheer physical distance between Soviet Russia and Spain, the historical traditions of the Spaniards, the strength of Spanish anarchism, the threat that such a development would present not only to Rome and Berlin but to London and Paris as well, was patently preposterous.[107] The Kremlin could, and did, seek to gain a position of preponderant influence in Republican Spain. And, by and large, it succeeded. The prestige and authority of the Communists in Spain increased in direct proportion with the amount and relative importance of Soviet aid to Spain. In seeking to occupy key positions in the government and army and thus to influence the war policy of the Republic, the Communists used a number of techniques, including the setting of an example of industry, discipline, and efficiency, incessant propaganda, and terroristic tactics, the latter directed mainly against the anarchists, the Trotskyist Poum, and some Left Socialists. Major José Martín Blázquez, who was often critical of the Communists, observed:

The Communist Party must be granted the credit of having set the example in accepting discipline. By so doing it enormously increased not only its prestige, but its numbers. Innumerable men who wished to enlist and fight for their country joined the Communist Party.[108]

However, the Communists did not attempt to use their influence to transform the civil war into a social revolution and to supplant the Republic with a Communist dictatorship.[109] On the contrary, the Communists in Spain, whether Russian, Comintern, or Spanish, along with middle-class liberals and Right Socialists, championed policies which aimed at a minimum of social change in the rear and a maximum of military discipline and unity at the front. Felix Morrow, an American Trotskyist, declared:

The Spanish Stalinists . . . joined Prieto and Azaña in appeals to the workers not to seize property. The Stalinists were the first to submit their press to the censorship. They were the first to demand liquidation of the workers' militias, and the first to hand their militiamen over to Azaña's officers. The civil war was not two months old when they began—what the government did not dare until nearly a year later—a murderous campaign against the POUM and the Anarchist Youth. The Stalinists demanded subordination to the bourgeoisie, not merely for the period of the civil war, but afterward as well.[110]

Morrow's accusations amounted to a condemnation of the Spanish Communist party as a counter-revolutionary force, a condemnation whose validity could only be determined in terms of the ultimate objectives of communism in Spain. Inasmuch as the Spanish Communist Party was pretty much the tail to the Soviet kite, the ultimate objectives of communism in Spain must be sought in Soviet policy.

Perhaps the key to an understanding of why the Russians intervened in Spain is to be found in the manner and course which their intervention took. It is important to remember that for the first six weeks of the Civil War Moscow did virtually nothing to help Madrid beyond giving the Republic moral support. Prompt and sufficient deliveries of arms at this time might well have enabled the Republicans to quell the revolt. That the Russians did nothing to succor the Spanish Republicans at this critical juncture strongly suggests that the Kremlin had not, in terms of the rapidly unfolding situation, formulated a Spanish policy of its own and that it was prepared, however reluctantly, to support the French initiative with respect to a policy of nonintervention in Spain.

Russian readiness to cooperate with the French can be explained

by the fact that following the advent to power of Adolf Hitler in
Germany Moscow had begun to quit the revisionist camp and to
move toward a rapprochement with Paris. There had been many
Frenchmen, in turn, who, prompted by the fear of a rearmed and
aggressive Germany, had advocated the reestablishment of firm
ties with Russia. Not the least important of these Frenchmen,
whose political affiliations reflected every color of the spectrum,
had been Foreign Minister Louis Barthou. With the entry of the
Soviet Union into the League of Nations in September, 1934, and
the signing of the Soviet-French and Soviet-Czechoslovakian
mutual assistance pacts in May, 1935, the cordon sanitaire had been
breached. As in the past, so at this time, French security and Russian security against the menace of an expansionist Germany lay
in friendship and alliance between Paris and Moscow.

With the coming to power of the Front Populaire in France
in June, 1936, it was expected that the cement of friendship between Paris and Moscow would quickly harden. The revolt of the
Spanish generals the following month, however, confronted Paris
and Moscow with a severe test of their friendship and mutuality
of interests. When the Blum government, with strong support from
London, embarked on a policy of nonintervention in Spain, Moscow found it necessary to acquiesce, lest it alienate Paris. That
the nonintervention agreement was viewed with suspicion and distrust by Moscow has already been noted. It would appear, moreover, that to the extent that public opinion in the Soviet Union
can be said to have had independent expression it was genuinely
sympathetic with the Republican cause in Spain.[111] It would appear,
too, that to the extent that the Comintern can be said to have had
an independent existence, it was also strongly in favor of the
Spanish Republic.[112]

When the Kremlin decided to give material support, including
arms, to the Spanish Republic, it implemented its decision in a
manner that suggested that its main objective was not the defense
of the Republic as such. What the Kremlin sought in Spain was
to stave off, for as long a time as possible, a fascist victory, and

thus to prevent Anglo-French acceptance of a *fait accompli* which could serve as a basis for the tranquilization of relations between the Western democracies and the fascist powers in the spirit of Locarno, a development which would find the Soviet Union once again isolated and gravely menaced by the growing power of Germany and Japan. Russian intervention in Spain was not an all-out effort. Such an effort was not feasible. Soviet Russia could not hope to aid the Spanish Republicans more effectively than Germany and Italy could assist the rebels. Soviet Russia could not accept the risk of completely alienating the West. For the Russians might then have found themselves in a war against the fascist powers (and Japan) in which the latter might well have enjoyed the tacit support of the Western democracies. Russian intervention in Spain, like the Popular Front movement itself, was principally designed to counter and check the policy of appeasement, to gain time and possibly allies for the Soviet Union. Thus, Georgi Dimitrov, the secretary-general and titular head for the Third International, wrote:

If we are briefly to formulate the most important, immediate tasks which the whole situation today [November 7, 1936] places before the world proletariat, they may be reduced to the following:

To exert every effort to help the Spanish people to crush the fascist rebels; Not to allow the People's Front in France to be discredited or disrupted; To hasten by every means the establishment of a world People's Front of struggle against fascism and war.

All these tasks are closely linked up. The most urgent, though, of these tasks, the very first at the present moment, is that of organizing international aid to the Spanish people for their victory over fascism.[113]

In a telegram dated Moscow, October 17, 1936, the American chargé d'affaires in the Soviet Union, Loy Henderson, reported to his government that the Soviet press campaign with respect to the Spanish situation was aimed at maintaining Soviet prestige with the world revolutionary movement and at prodding England and France into taking action against German and Italian violations of the nonintervention agreement. Henderson noted, too, that there was "a distinct possibility" that the Soviet government would send "a limited amount of military equipment to Spain even though it realizes that it is not in a position to compete with Germany and Italy in the matter of furnishing such equipment." [114]

A few days before, the French foreign minister, Yvon Delbos, in a conversation with the American ambassador in Paris, William Bullitt, had arrived at conclusions similar to Mr. Henderson's concerning the motives which underlay Moscow's Spanish policy.[115]

In the light of the Soviet desire to use Spain as an anvil upon which to hammer into being a firm, anti-fascist West-Soviet alliance the reasons why Moscow did not denounce the nonintervention agreement outright but stated only that it was not going to be bound by the agreement "in any greater measure than any of the other participants in this agreement" [116] become clear. Moscow could not risk offending Paris by a forthright denunciation of the agreement, yet it could not permit, by withholding its aid, the Spanish Republic to be quickly overthrown. Unlike the Germans and Italians who publicly proclaimed their adherence to the agreement but who openly violated it, the Russians were equivocal in their adherence to the agreement while they strenuously sought to camouflage their support of the Spanish Republicans. However, the Russians (and the Germans and Italians, for that matter) cannot be accused of illegal violations of the nonintervention agreement because the accord was not a legally binding instrument under international law. Yet both Soviet Russia and the fascist powers were morally guilty of violating it. With respect to Soviet intervention, however, there were these extenuating circumstances; first, Soviet intervention followed Italo-German intervention by some three months, and, secondly, the sale of war materials to an established government engaged in suppressing a rebellion is a legal act while to support with men and arms rebels against an established government is not.

Not only did Soviet Russia sell,[117] rather than give, lend, or barter for economic concessions,[118] arms to Spain, not only did Soviet Russia refrain from sending her own forces, aside from military specialists and technicians, to Spain, but the total amount of Soviet war materials sent to Republican Spain was considerably less than the total amount of war materials sent by Germany and Italy to rebel Spain.[119] This was true, in part, for reasons of geography, but it also reflected the fundamental purpose which underlay Soviet intervention. The Russians were fighting a delaying action. In part, they were quite successful. Without Russian aid, it is inconceivable that the Republic could have held out against the rebel forces, strongly supported by the fascist powers, for more than a few months.[120]

However, Russian policy did not attain its primary objective. The war in Spain did not produce an anti-fascist West-Soviet alliance. Indeed, as early as November, 1936, the French government, according to American Ambassador William Bullitt, harbored fears that Moscow's Spanish policy aimed at bringing about war between the Western democracies and the fascist powers, with the bolshevization of Europe the result.[121] England, too, was not well-disposed toward Soviet intentions in Spain. In replying to a question in the House of Commons as to how the British government proposed "to meet this new aggression" (the recognition of the Franco government by Germany and Italy on November 18, 1936), Foreign Secretary Anthony Eden had occasion to observe: "So far as breaches [of the nonintervention agreement] are concerned, I wish to state categorically that I think there are other Governments more to blame than those of Germany and Italy." [122] It would seem, moreover, if the report (dated Alicante, October 16, 1936) of the German chargé d'affaires in Spain, Hans Voelckers, to his government can be credited, that the British had been supplying the Spanish rebels with munitions and the Germans with information concerning Russian arms deliveries to Spain! Voelckers said in part:

As for England, we have made the interesting observation that she is supplying the Whites [*i.e.*, the rebels] with ammunition via Gibraltar and that the British cruiser commander here has recently been supplying us with information on Russian arms deliveries to the Red government [*i.e.*, the Loyalists], which he certainly would not do without instructions.[123]

The lack of success of Russian policy in forging an anti-fascist West-Soviet coalition ultimately proved disastrous for the Republic. Toward the end of 1936, for the first time since the suppression of the Barbary corsairs more than a century before, "pirates" began to infest the Mediterranean. On December 14, 1936, the Russian freighter, *Komsomol*, was sunk off the African coast. In 1937 acts of "piracy" became increasingly frequent. And Russian arms shipments through the Mediterranean practically ceased.[124] Moreover, in 1937, when hostilities were resumed on the Chinese mainland, the Russians began to supply Chiang Kai-shek with war materials and technicians.[125] Their role and purpose in China were somewhat analogous to their role and purpose in Spain. At any rate, in the measure that Russian war materials were sent to China, to that extent they were not available for Spain.[126] When, at Munich in September, 1938, it became apparent that the Western democracies were not prepared to make a stand against fascist aggression,[127] the Kremlin sought to formulate and to implement other policies. With the end of 1938 Soviet Russia ceased to send arms and supplies to Spain.[128] In March, 1939, the Germans occupied Prague while the Spanish Republicans fought in their last redoubt. On May 3, 1939, Vyacheslav Molotov replaced Maxim Litvinov in the Soviet Foreign Ministry. Litvinov had been the champion and the symbol of Soviet policies which aimed at friendship with the West and a system of collective security. And Molotov? On August 23, 1939, the Reich-Soviet Non-Aggression and Mutual Friendship Pact was signed. The Spanish Civil War had ended less than five months before and, with the last shot, the Popular Front movement had been consigned to the limbo of lost causes.

VII

The United States and the
Spanish Civil War

ON July 14, 1936, the American ambassador in Spain, Claude
G. Bowers, who was at San Sebastián, the Spanish "summer capital," reported to Secretary of State Cordell Hull that a military uprising appeared imminent.[1] Following the outbreak of hostilities
in Morocco, the United States Department of State was kept informed of developments by a steady flow of reports from its representatives in Spain. These reports made clear that before the Civil
War was two weeks old German and Italian men and equipment
had entered the struggle on the rebel side. They revealed, too, the
efforts of Paris, supported by London, to localize the conflict
through a general nonintervention agreement.[2]

American interests in Spain, whether economic, strategic, or
political, were not great. But given the strong ties between Spain
and the Latin American nations and the important relations between the latter and the United States, Washington could not view
with indifference the rapidly unfolding situation in Spain. Then,
too, it was soon apparent that the conflict in Spain was potentially
of vast significance in the endemic power struggle of the great
states of Europe.

While it is not mandatory under international law for other
governments to allow an established, friendly government seeking
to suppress a rebellion to purchase arms and supplies in their markets, it is generally acceded to in practice.[3] Furthermore, the succoring of rebels has long been viewed as a distinctly unfriendly

act, justifying retaliatory action on the part of the constituted government.[4] In the light of these well-established attitudes as well as the fact that since 1912 the only established government denied the privilege of importing war materials from the United States with which to quell a revolt was that of Mexico and then only until the Huerta regime was overthrown in 1914,[5] it might well have been expected that Washington would permit the Spanish government to purchase arms and supplies in United States markets. While there were important advocates of such a course, both in and outside the government, Washington never seriously contemplated taking it. Given the isolationist sentiments of the American people, the refusal of the United States to join the League of Nations, and the continued reluctance of the United States government to enter into international organizations and agreements outside of the Western Hemisphere, it was not surprising that Washington did not formally associate itself with the Anglo-French effort to conclude a general nonintervention agreement or that it did not formally adhere to the agreement after it had been concluded. The position of the United States government was appreciated in Paris and London and there was no substance to the current rumors which had it that the Quai d'Orsay had sought to induce Washington to give formal adherence to the nonintervention agreement.[6] Throughout the war the United States government continued to maintain relations with the legally constituted Spanish government. Washington had ignored the communication it received on July 29, 1936, from General Miguel Cabanellas, president of the rebel Junta de Defensa Nacional, in which Cabanellas proclaimed the establishment of a new government in Spain.[7] Except for informal contacts between American diplomatic representatives and rebel officials concerning the protection of American nationals and property in rebel-held territory—a practice for which precedents existed in American experience during Latin American revolts [8]—Washington officially continued to ignore the existence of the rebel government until the end of hostilities. However, on August 7, 1936, Washington embarked on a policy that served, in effect, to equate the legitimate Spanish government with the insurgents. On that date Acting Secretary of State William Phillips sent a circular telegram to all American diplomatic representatives in Spain in which he stressed that while the Neutrality Law (Joint Resolution of Congress, approved August 31, 1935) did not apply to the situation in Spain American policy regarding the civil strife had been and would continue to be one of complete impartiality and noninterference.[9]

The need for Washington to make public its position soon developed. On August 10 Mr. Hartson of the Glenn L. Martin (Aircraft) Company of Baltimore, Maryland, inquired of the government as to what its attitude would be in the event of the sale of eight bombers by his company to the Spanish Republic.[10] Hartson explained that an agreement to manufacture these airplanes had been made with the Spanish government in February but, owing to certain difficulties pertaining to payment, the matter had been left in abeyance.[11] However, for obvious reasons, the Spanish government was now most anxious to consummate the matter on almost any terms. Hartson believed that delivery could not be made before November and he hoped that by then "the situation in Spain would have quieted down and there would be no possible objection to the export."[12]

The same day, following telephone conversations with President Roosevelt and Secretary of State Hull, Phillips drafted a reply to the Glenn L. Martin Company. Enclosing a copy of his August 7 circular telegram, Phillips explained that while American neutrality laws did not apply to the Spanish situation the contemplated manufacture of aircraft by the Glenn L. Martin Company for the Spanish Republic "would not follow the spirit of the Government's policy."[13]

Meanwhile, on August 8, Ambassador Bowers, whose sympathies were with the Spanish Republicans, had sent a telegram to the American Secretary of State in which he averred that American diplomatic personnel in Spain had acted in conformity with the spirit of the Department of State's circular telegram of the previous

day. Bowers had gone on to note that Indalecio Prieto, the Right
Socialist Spanish leader, had decried the use of the word *neutrality*
by various European states in defining their policies with respect
to the Spanish conflict as an affront to the legitimacy of the
established government which only four months before had won
popular approval in the general elections and which at this time
was certainly not overthrown. Bowers had added: "Since we are
not here involved you may wish to consider the wisdom of refraining publicly from the use of the word 'neutrality' at this juncture
of events and confining ourselves to the protection of the lives of
Americans." [14]

Ambassador Bowers' suggestion notwithstanding, the Department of State formally announced on August 11 that it was the
policy of the United States government not to interfere in the
internal affairs of other countries, thus imposing a "moral embargo" on arms to Spain.[15] There can be no doubt that American
policy with respect to the Spanish conflict served as an important
adjunct of Anglo-French policy embodied in the nonintervention
plan. Regarding the relationship between the action of the United
States government and those of the British and French governments, Norman J. Padelford wrote:

Admitting the traditional policy toward the internal politics of European states, the issuance of the announcement [by the Department of
State on August 11, 1936] at the moment negotiations were in progress
between the French and British Governments for the Non-Intervention Accord, and four days before that accord took the form of the
exchange of notes upon which the entire structure of non-intervention
was based, is an interesting coincidence. Combined with the fact that
measures similar to those adopted first by Britain and France, and
then by all of the non-intervention parties, to stop the passage of
volunteers to Spain, were taken at the time these two Powers were
negotiating with the other states in Europe, substance would seem to
be lent to the argument that the policy of the United States was one
of support of Britain and France and of their policies toward Spain,
albeit by separate and parallel rather than by collective action.[16]

The Madrid government now made an oblique attempt to circumvent the American "moral embargo." On September 14, 1936,

the Mexican ambassador in the United States, Señor Castillo Nájera, on instructions from President Lázaro Cárdenas who, in turn, had been approached on the matter by the Spanish ambassador in Mexico, inquired of the United States government as to what its attitude would be with respect to the reshipment by Mexico to Spain of war materials purchased in the United States.[17] The following day Castillo Nájera received a telephone call from Mr. Edward L. Reed, the chief of the Division of Mexican Affairs in the Department of State. Reed informed him that while the United States government entertained "the most friendly feelings toward the Mexican Government" and was "always more than willing to listen to any suggestions or requests which it may desire to make," Washington's policy with respect to the shipment of war materials to Spain had been established some time before, that it had been publicly proclaimed, and that Washington "had no intention of departing from it." [18]

Fernando de los Ríos, the newly appointed Spanish ambassador in the United States, paid his first visit to Cordell Hull on October 10, 1936. In the course of their conversation Señor de los Ríos depicted the conflict in Spain as one between two theories of government, involving the survival of democracy in Spain or its destruction and replacement by a totalitarian state. The Spanish conflict, he averred, was a phase of a larger struggle. Léon Blum understood this but "other factors" were involved.[19] In view of the nature of the Spanish conflict, Señor de los Ríos inquired "whether the United States would not find it possible to extend facilities to the Spanish Government which would be of practical aid in assisting it out of its present complications." [20] Mr. Hull replied that the American policy of noninterference was based on two important considerations. One was the fact that the nations of Europe which were most directly concerned with the Spanish situation had formally agreed not to intervene in Spain. The other was the matter of the Montevideo Convention (a Pan-American agreement signed in 1933 forbidding interference in each other's internal affairs) that established a moral precedent which the United States, if only for the sake of consistency, would have to follow with respect to the Spanish situation. When Señor de los Ríos declared that the nonintervention agreement had, in fact, worked to the detriment of the legitimate government and that, concerning the Montevideo Convention, the collapse of democracy in Spain could have, in view of the close ties which existed between Spain and Latin America, serious repercussions in that region, Mr. Hull was content to reiterate the reasons which had prompted American policy toward Spain. By way of pointing up the moral inadvisability as well as the impracticality of interference in distant Spain by the United States, Mr. Hull inquired of Señor de los Ríos "why the French Government, the neighbor and special friend of the Spanish Government, had taken the lead in the intervention [sic] movement." [21]

The Spaniard was turning the wrong key in the wrong lock. Washington could not be expected to do what Paris and London would not do.

From August to the end of December, 1936, American arms exporters who might have sought to profit from the situation in Spain were dissuaded by the Department of State from asking for export licenses.[22] However, the close of the year saw the collapse of the government's "moral embargo." On December 28 the Department of State was obliged to issue two licenses for the exportation to the Loyalist port of Bilbao of a shipment of airplanes and aircraft engines valued at $2,777,000.[23] The licencee was Mr. Robert Cuse, a naturalized American and the president of the Vimalert Company of Jersey City, New Jersey. Mr. Cuse had ignored the moral arguments and patriotic appeals of State Department officials and had insisted on his legal rights. There was fear in Washington that others might seek to emulate the intractable Mr. Cuse.[24] On December 29 the then acting secretary of state, R. Walton Moore, sent a telegram to the American ambassador in France, William Bullitt, in which Bullitt was informed of the Cuse case and was authorized "in your discretion to bring the facts with regard to the issuance of these licenses orally to the attention of the Government to which you are accredited." [25] Moore then instructed Bullitt: "Please transmit a copy of this telegram to Embassies at London, Berlin, and Rome for their appropriate action. Repeat to Moscow without preceding paragraph [quoted above] stating that it is for Embassy's information only and for background in the event of receiving any inquiries on the subject from the Government or any of the other diplomatic missions." [26]

That same day President Roosevelt, at a press conference, denounced Mr. Cuse's activities as unpatriotic even though legal.[27] He then said that he had given his approval to plans of congressional leaders to amend the Neutrality Act to cover the Spanish situation.[28] The following day, December 30, the President conferred with Acting Secretary of State Moore, Senator Key Pittman (Democrat from Nevada), chairman of the Senate Committee on Foreign Relations, and Representative Sam D. McReynolds (Democrat from Tennessee), chairman of the House Committee on Foreign Affairs, on proposed measures to bring the Spanish Civil War within the compass of the Neutrality Act.[29]

The quick, angry reaction of the United States government to the flouting of its "moral embargo" by Mr. Cuse prompted the Spanish Ambassador to call on Acting Secretary of State Moore on December 31 and to express his regret at the attitude taken by the United States government.[30] Señor de los Ríos went on to state that he considered American policy toward Spain to be most unfortunate, holding that the Spanish government ought to have the support of the great democracies in its struggle against fascism. Mr. Moore explained that American policy was based on the "desire and determination" to avoid involvement in a situation which could develop into a general war.[31] The Acting Secretary added that his government was preparing to buttress this policy with appropriate legislation.[32] The Spanish Ambassador then noted that during the past week some 12,000 German and Italian soldiers, with full equipment had arrived in Spain.[33]

But Señor de los Ríos, like Don Quixote, had tilted his lance in vain. For on January 5, 1937, President Roosevelt again conferred with Moore, Pittman, and McReynolds and authorized the two legislators to introduce resolutions in the Senate and House banning shipments of war materials to Spain.[34]

The following day the President, in his annual Message to Congress, declared that "circumstances of the moment compel me to ask your immediate consideration of . . . an addition to the existing Neutrality Act to cover specific points raised by the unfortunate civil strife in Spain." [35] That same day Pittman in the Senate and McReynolds in the House introduced resolutions banning shipments of war materials to Spain. In the course of the brief debate on the resolution in the Senate, Senator Gerald Nye (Republican from North Dakota) deplored what he considered the influence of certain European governments, particularly that of Great Britain, in the determination of American policy with respect to Spain.[36] Senator Nye's allegation provoked a vehement denial of any such influence from Senator Pittman.[37] The North Dakotan went on to raise other objections, observing that during the Italo-Ethiopian War an embargo on oil was not given "serious consideration" by Congress because it would have been deemed an act of unneutrality toward Italy which was in great need of oil.[38] During the First World War, Nye continued, a similar attitude had prevailed in Congress, to wit, that to institute an embargo while a war was in progress was to commit an act of unneutrality against one side or the other. Thus a precedent had been established which was invoked at the time of the Italo-Ethiopian War.[39] The North Dakotan then noted:

Now we find ourselves this afternoon moving, as we will do unanimously, I assume, to write an embargo even though a state of war exists, writing an embargo which under the present situation is going to be a greater hardship upon the one side than the other engaged in Spain's trial. . . . Mr. President, if this action this afternoon is to be conceived, as I am going to conceive it, in the light of an effort to keep the hands of the United States clean and removed from the danger of being drawn quickly into that war or strife in Europe, I am quite willing that it shall be done; but I hope it is not going to be done in the name of neutrality, for, strictly speaking, neutrality it is not.[40]

Whatever the individual conception of each senator of the meaning and purpose of the resolution, it was unanimously adopted by the Senate that same afternoon.

In the House, meanwhile, debate on the resolution proved equally brief but no less searching. Representative Maury Maverick (Democrat from Texas) declared that in seeking the adoption of this resolution the United States government was reversing a policy that it had pursued for 150 years.[41] He decried, too, the need for the great haste which the administration attached to the matter, saying, "we talk for hours, days, and weeks on matters which are unimportant, and we rush through matters of such grave importance as this." [42]

Representative McReynolds observed that, in view of impending arms shipments to Spain, an emergency existed which demanded prompt adoption of the resolution.[43] But Representative Maverick was not to be easily persuaded. He returned to the attack, pointing up what he thought to be the unfairness and ineffectiveness of an arms embargo that was not general in application but limited to a single nation.[44] As Nye had done in the Senate, Maverick recalled on the floor of the House the unwillingness of Congress to consider embargo measures in the midst of the Italo-Ethiopian War.[45] He went on to say:

Let us be frank. Suppose there was a revolution in England. Suppose that England wanted some munitions to stop a rebellion against the British Crown. Nearly every man on this floor would say, "My God, are you taking sides against the ancient Crown of England?" Of course not. We would sell England all the munitions she wanted—and that is the reason this resolution only applies to Spain. They are selling munitions now to England, to Germany, and many different countries. So we sell munitions to Germany, but refuse to sell munitions to Spain. Is this not a fine diplomatic pickle? What we ought to do is to prohibit the shipment of arms to all the countries of the world. . . . There are several things about this bill that are objectionable: First, it is unneutral, ill-advised legislation. It is sought to be accomplished in too much of a hurry. Second, it is not fair, not comprehensive enough, does not make a general policy, but only a bad precedent. Third, it does not effectually meet the situation of the munitions business at all. Let us consider Spain. The Government of Spain is the duly authorized, elected parliamentary government. . . . We are now reversing a policy of 150 years by not being neutral, by refraining from sending munitions to the duly authorized Government of Spain.[46]

Maverick's strictures against the sheer improvisation, and worse, of the embargo on arms to Spain prompted considerable applause from the members of the House. Other Representatives, moreover, spoke in a similar vein, with Johnson (Democrat from Minnesota) suggesting that proper control of the traffic in arms could only be achieved through nationalization of the munitions industry,[47] and Amlie (Democrat from Wisconsin) denouncing certain elements in the House, and the Senate as well, whose interest in neutrality legislation appeared confined to denying the Spanish government the right to purchase arms, as being pro-fascist.[48] However, Representative McReynolds' repeated assurances that the administration would soon bring before Congress a bill which would provide appropriate neutrality legislation to cover "any condition of civil warfare in any country"[49] did much to allay the limited but vociferous opposition to the resolution. That same day, January 6, the resolution was passed by the House virtually unanimously. The vote was yeas 406, nays 1, and not voting 22.[50] The single negative vote was cast by Representative John Bernard (Farmer-Laborite from Minnesota).[51] Apparently, isolationist sentiment and party discipline had prevailed over the doubts of the doubters.

Because of a legal technicality the joint resolution of Congress banning shipments of war materials to Spain was not signed into law by President Roosevelt until January 8, 1937.[52] Meanwhile, the Spanish vessel, *Mar Cantábrico*, had been loaded with a portion of the war materials which had been licensed for export and had sailed from New York for Bilbao on January 7.[53] However, luck was run out for the Loyalists both in Washington and at sea. For on January 8 the United States government revoked the licenses for the remainder, and the greater part, of the purchase,[54] and on

March 8 the rebel cruiser *Canarias* shelled and captured the *Mar Cantábrico* in the Bay of Biscay, the latter's long, circuitous voyage having been closely observed by rebel agents.[55]

The virtual unanimity with which Congress had approved it notwithstanding, the Arms Embargo Act was viewed with misgivings by many Americans. Down to the end of the war in Spain, various individuals and groups, both in the United States and abroad, sought to have the embargo lifted or modified. Their efforts were prompted by partisan zeal for the Loyalist cause, by the desire to support democracy and to halt the march of fascism, by a decent regard for the perquisites due the Spanish government under international law, and by alarm and disgust at the manifest unfairness of allowing the fascist powers to extend decisive support to the Spanish rebels while the democracies refrained from assisting the legal government. However, American policy remained unchanged.

Two questions naturally arise. Why did the United States government assume the attitude it did toward the conflict in Spain? Why did Washington persist in this attitude even after it had become abundantly clear that its position was far more detrimental to the Loyalist than to the rebel cause and was thus, in effect, an act of unneutrality?

Isolationist sentiment was widespread in the mid-thirties, powerfully influencing American foreign policy and ultimately achieving legislative expression in the various neutrality acts. Isolationism had its roots deep in the American past. It was reaffirmed with the disenchantment that followed the Great Crusade. Eschewing permanent, world-wide commitments, Americans stood fascinated before an emergent mass culture, the motorized Coney Island that was the Roaring Twenties, as later they faced grimly the hard problems of the Great Depression. The hearings of the Nye Committee (established by the Senate in 1934 to investigate the manufacture and sale of war materials) strengthened the isolationist propensities of many Americans. In Cordell Hull's view the activities of the Nye Committee proved fatal to the possibility of effective American participation in a program of collective security in the mid-thirties.[56]

While its overarching importance must be admitted, isolationism was but one of many factors which helped to determine American policy toward Spain. It is of interest that Nye, remaining a convinced isolationist, saw fit to denounce the arms embargo as an act of unneutrality against the Spanish government, while Hull, continuing to hold to what he described as an "international viewpoint," was a warm advocate of the arms embargo.[57] It can be argued that Hull was the captive of a situation that Nye and his committee had done so much to create. However, while not without an element of truth, this is too facile an explanation of the apparent contradiction in Hull's actions in that it ignores several important matters. Particularly significant is the celerity with which the Department of State announced the complete impartiality of the United States with respect to the civil strife in Spain. In view of President Roosevelt's expressed misgivings concerning the efficacy of the Neutrality Act of August 31, 1935,[58] and Secretary of State Hull's frank opposition to neutrality legislation, per se,[59] it would seem that Washington could have followed a course of "watchful waiting" with respect to Spain that would better have comported with the internationalist orientation of the administration, as well as with established practice under international law, than the "moral embargo" that was so speedily imposed.

On July 23, 1936, a week after Lieutenant Colonel Juan Yagüe had begun the revolt in Morocco, Hull sent a wireless message to Roosevelt, who was cruising off the New England coast, apprizing the President of developments in Spain:

The reports which we are receiving indicate that the situation is, if anything, becoming much worse and it seems like a fifty-fifty chance as to which side may come out on top, and, furthermore, with an equal chance that a completely chaotic condition may arise in Spain which may continue for some time. One of the most serious factors in this situation lies in the fact that the [Spanish] Government has distributed large quantities of arms and ammunition into the hands of irresponsible members of left-wing political organizations.[60]

Hull's anxiety concerning the arming of the Left is not without significance. Four days later, on July 27, he received from the American ambassador in France, Jesse Straus, a report of the London conversations of July 23 and 24 between British Prime Minister Stanley Baldwin and Foreign Secretary Anthony Eden and French Premier Léon Blum and Foreign Minister Yvon Delbos—conversations which led directly to the French government's decision of July 25 to refuse the request of the Spanish government for material assistance.[61] On August 4 the French chargé d'affaires in Washington, Jules Henry, called on Hull to inform him of the French initiative for a general nonintervention agreement.[62] The following day Hull conferred at length with a number of State Department officials, including William Phillips, R. Walton Moore, and Sumner Welles. The decision to adopt "a completely impartial attitude" with respect to the conflict in Spain was reached at this time.[63] The next day Hull left for Hot Springs, Virginia, for a rest.

Exactly what occurred during the conference in the Secretary of State's office on August 5, Hull does not reveal in his *Memoirs*. He reports only that there was "considerable" conversation and that it was decided that the position of the United States government with respect to the Spanish situation be rendered explicit.[64] Whether any one argued the extremely plausible thesis that the United States government was not compelled to act at all in the Spanish situation beyond protecting the lives and property of its nationals is not known. What is clear is the desire of American policymakers to maintain close relations with the European democracies, particularly Great Britain. To this end they were prepared to support British policy toward Spain. Hull, who warmly approved, if he did not conceive, the "moral embargo," appears to have followed the course of British diplomacy toward Spain with close attention. "Within a week after the outbreak of war," he noted, "it was strongly evident that the peaceful nations of Europe, particularly Britain and France, would make a great effort to limit the conflict to Spain." [65] But Hull somewhat misrepresents matters. For he was quite aware of the division of opinion within the French government and of the pressure Baldwin and Eden exerted on Léon Blum to abandon the thought of succoring the Spanish Republic.[66] Yet Hull, following the visit of M. Jules Henry, moved swiftly to define American policy toward Spain as completely impartial, thereby aligning Washington with London. What doubts Paris harbored concerning the equity and wisdom of nonintervention perforce had to be stilled. Such was the celerity with which the Department of State had acted that the "moral embargo" was promulgated four days before France and Great Britain formally exchanged notes relative to the nonintervention agreement. Hull believed his actions enjoyed wide support:

The American public accepted the policy at first virtually without question. For once, our position seemed acceptable to both the apparently irreconcilable isolationists and the internationalists. Isolationists approved because we were keeping aloof from the conflict. Internationalists approved because we were cooperating with Britain and France.[67]

The isolationist climate of opinion that Senator Nye and others had done so much to create enabled Secretary of State Hull to establish a policy toward Spain which otherwise might have proved immediately unpopular. In view of this, there is not a little irony in the spectacle of Hull using the platform of his *Memoirs* to castigate the Nye Committee for plunging the country "into deepest isolationism at the very moment when our influence was so vitally needed to help ward off the approaching threats of war abroad." [68] Hull saw Anglo-American cooperation as prerequisite to the achievement of collective security. He did not see that, in closely cooperating with Great Britain during the Spanish crisis, he was pursuing not a policy of collective security but its very negation. That England's Spanish policy reflected concern for vast British holdings in Spain does not appear to have influenced Hull's thinking.

During late July and early August, 1936, President Roosevelt was on an extended trip that was in part a vacation and in part

an official tour.[69] Starting from Rockland, Maine, aboard the yacht
Sewanna, he had leisurely sailed to Shelburne, Nova Scotia, and
then to Campobello Island, New Britain, where the Roosevelts
had a summer house. On July 31 the President was in Quebec
where he delivered an address on American-Canadian friendship, at
the conclusion of which he invited the Canadian Prime Minister,
Mackenzie King, to visit him at the White House.[70] August 1
found the President in Vermont where he began a tour of the
New England States, then swung west to Ohio, and back again
to upper New York State. The President was, then, away from
Washington during the time that American policy with respect to
the civil strife in Spain was being fashioned. While he was kept
informed of developments relative to Spain by the State Department and his approval of important decisions was sought and received, his part in these matters was relatively passive. Being away
from Washington, he was not in immediate touch with persons
and events that could have influenced his thinking on Spain. He had
to rely on official sources of information and, quite naturally, had
to repose confidence in his secretary of state. Then, too, the full
significance of the Spanish struggle had yet to be revealed. That
Hull played the major role in the shaping of American policy
toward Spain is beyond cavil. But his claim that his Spanish policy
enjoyed the approval and support of the President is no less true.[71]
While there was a considerable difference in temperament and
political philosophy between the liberal Roosevelt and the conservative Hull, this difference was less evident in the realm of international affairs than in the arena of domestic politics.

On August 14, 1936, at Chautauqua, New York, less than a
month after the outbreak of the Spanish war, President Roosevelt
made an important speech on foreign policy in which he spoke
feelingly of the horrors of war and of the need for a lasting peace.[72]
He told his audience that the maintenance of American neutrality
depended on the wisdom and determination of the President and
the Secretary of State. But it did not depend on them alone. He
said:

With that wise and experienced man who is our Secretary of State, whose statesmanship has met with such wide approval, I have thought and worked long and hard on the problem of keeping the United States at peace. But all the wisdom of America is not to be found in the White House or in the Department of State; we need the meditation, the prayer, and the positive support of the people of America who go along with us in seeking peace.

No matter how well we are supported by neutrality legislation, we must remember that no laws can be provided to cover every contingency, for it is impossible to imagine how every future event may shape itself. In spite of every possible forethought, international relations involve of necessity a vast uncharted area. In that area safe sailing will depend on the knowledge and the experience and the wisdom of those who direct our foreign policy. Peace will depend on their day-to-day decisions.[73]

In the context of events Roosevelt's Chautauqua address seemed to press the seal of the President's approval on Mr. Hull's Spanish policy.

Why did American policy toward the Spanish conflict remain unchanged, the deepening implications of the struggle notwithstanding? For one thing, the fundamental considerations of American foreign policy which had originally prompted Washington to take a position of complete impartiality concerning the Spanish war had not changed. Indeed, close relations with Great Britain and the other European democracies were deemed to be increasingly imperative as the armed might and aggressive intentions of the fascist powers became more and more evident. For another, isolationism continued to reflect the feelings of millions of Americans. For a third, once American policy had been determined, first in the more or less plastic form of the "moral embargo" and then in the hard legality of the Arms Embargo Act, it acquired the force of a *fait accompli*. Just as the logic of the "moral embargo" argued for the passage of the Arms Embargo Act so the logic of the Arms Embargo Act argued for the continuance of the established policy toward Spain. And, for a fourth, important conservative opinion in the United States was openly sympathetic with the Franco cause. This matter of conservative opinion, while of limited significance during the first weeks of the war, acquired increasing importance as the war lengthened into months and years.

The Hearst newspapers were quick to label the Spanish Republicans the "Reds" and to dub the rebels the "Nationalists." This grotesque misrepresentation of the real situation in Spain, or some variant of it, came to be widely employed in the American press. It is not devoid of interest to find Hitler stealing a leaf from Mr. Hearst's notebook and ordering, on November 23, 1936, that in the German press Franco's side be designated the "Spanish Nationalist government" and the Republicans the "Spanish Bolshevists." [74]

The direct investments of United States citizens in Spain amounted to more than eighty million dollars in 1936 and were located, in the main, in rebel-held territory.[75] The direct investments of United States citizens in Latin America amounted to nearly three billion dollars in 1936 and political developments in Spain exerted an important influence south of the Río Grande.[76] A government in Madrid in which Socialists, Communists, and anarchists sat was not without menace to American business interests both in Spain and in Latin America.

Many Catholics, both in the United States and abroad, including such eminent persons as George N. Shuster, then managing editor of *The Commonweal*, Edmund L. Taylor, then president of the Anglo-American Press Association and the *Chicago Tribune* correspondent with the rebel forces, Luigi Sturzo, Italian theologian and organizer of the *Popolari* party, José Bergamin, then editor of the leading Spanish Catholic journal, *Cruz y Raya,* and Michael O'Flanagan, popular Dublin priest, were sympathetic with the Republican cause in Spain.[77] However, other Catholics, including important leaders of the Church, were ardent champions of the Spanish rebels. When the Bishops of Spain published a Joint Letter (July 1, 1937) describing the Franco uprising as a "national movement of defense of the fundamental principles of every civilized society," [78] the general of the Society of Jesus, Father Vladimir Ledochowski, sent the following communication to the editors of the principal Jesuit periodicals:

The collective letter addressed by the Spanish Episcopate to the Bishops of the whole world in connection with the Spanish War and the profound commotion that is shaking Spain, has just been published. In that letter, of which a copy will be sent to you, the principal facts, diligently collected and faithfully stated, are set forth in a clear light by witnesses whose evidence is unquestionable.

The main issues in the Spanish War are the salvation or utter ruin of the Christian Faith and the foundations of all social order. The enemies of the Church and, unfortunately, some misguided Catholics in certain countries have spread unfounded statements about that war, statements that are not only at variance with the truth but are very injurious to Catholic interests. I have therefore thought it would be an act of service to God to instruct you to inform yourself of that Collective Letter and have a knowledge of it spread as widely as possible. For that letter, by reason both of the excellent assurance its authors furnish and weight of their authority, will provide all well meaning men with a sure means of learning the truth and of forming a just opinion on a matter of such great importance.[79]

The conviction of many Catholics that the Franco cause was just was undoubtedly strengthened when the Vatican recognized the Franco government *de facto* on August 28, 1937, and *de jure* on May 3, 1938. These same Catholics must have believed themselves vindicated in their conception of the struggle when Pope Pius XII declared in a radio broadcast on April 16, 1939, with the last shot of the Civil War still faintly reverberating through the Guadarramas: "Peace and victory have been willed by God to Spain . . . which has now given to proselytes of the materialistic atheism of our age the highest proof that above all things stands the eternal value of religion and of the Spirit." [80]

However, many Americans began to experience a sense of disquiet as the Spanish war drew to a close. Henry L. Stimson, former secretary of state under President Hoover and future secretary of war under President Roosevelt, wrote a letter to the *New York Times* on January 23, 1939, in which he said:

In such a case [the outbreak of armed rebellion] the duty which the neighbor States owe to the member of the family whose authority has been challenged is perfectly well settled. It is that such a nation has the exclusive right to the friendly assistance of its neighbors by being permitted to purchase in their markets the necessary supplies and munitions for the purpose of putting down the rebellion; and further that no similar assistance shall be given to the rebels who have challenged its authority. . . .

If this Loyalist Government is overthrown, it is evident now that its defeat will be solely due to the fact that it has been deprived of its right to buy from us and other friendly nations the munitions necessary for its defense. I cannot believe that our government or our country would wish to assume such a responsibility.[81]

Claude G. Bowers, who as American ambassador in Spain had been and remained critical of nonintervention in all its manifestations, reports that when he returned to the United States in March, 1939, ostensibly for consultation but actually to clear the way for American recognition of the Franco government, he went to see President Roosevelt. The first words the President spoke to Mr. Bowers were: "We have made a mistake; you have been right all along." [82] Later that same day Mr. Bowers called at the home of Senator Key Pittman, an old friend. Pittman, as chairman of the Foreign Relations Committee, had seen the Arms Embargo Act through the Senate on January 6, 1937. Now he shook hands with Bowers and, moving toward a table for a cigarette, remarked over his shoulder: "I am afraid we made a mistake in Spain." [83]

Writing in 1944, Sumner Welles, under secretary of state from 1937 to 1943 and one of the State Department officials who met with Mr. Hull on August 5, 1936, when American policy toward Spain was defined, observed: "In the long history of the foreign policy of the Roosevelt Administration, there has been, I think, no more cardinal error than the policy adopted during the civil war in Spain." [84]

From what he writes in his *Memoirs* it would seem that of the leading figures in the American act of the Spanish drama only Mr. Hull continued to believe that he had read his lines correctly the first time.

VIII

False Hopes and Bitter Truths:
The Civil War Ends

THE weeks and months between January, 1937, and April, 1939, produced no fundamental changes in the respective policies adopted by the great powers toward the Spanish conflict during the summer and autumn of 1936. Great Britain, France, and the United States continued to be "neutral," with the French less rigidly so than the Anglo-Saxons. However, Great Britain, perhaps because of her vast properties in rebel-held territory,[1] was rather anxious to establish at least quasi-official relations with the rebel authorities. The British and Franco governments exchanged "agents" as early as November, 1937, Sir Robert Hodgson going to Burgos and the Duke of Alba (who was also the Duke of Berwick) to London. But the British government did not extend *de jure* recognition to the Franco government until February 27, 1939, about a month before the cessation of hostilities. Neither Paris nor Washington exchanged "agents" with Burgos, but Paris extended *de jure* recognition to the Franco government at the same time that London did while Washington did not do so until April 1, 1939.

Having formally recognized the Franco government on November 18, 1936, Germany and Italy redoubled their efforts on behalf of the rebels, the matter of prestige being added now to the factors which had originally prompted their intervention. Throughout 1937, 1938, and the spring of 1939 enough German and Italian soldiers, technicians, weapons, and supplies were committed to Spain

by the fascist dictators to secure victory for Franco who, left to
his own resources, could not have remained in the field for more
than a few months.

Soviet Russia, on the other hand, supplied the Republican forces
—which were overwhelmingly Spanish, in striking contrast to the
so-called Nationalist Army [2]—with war materials, supplies, and
technicians sufficient to enable the Republicans to maintain a moderately successful defense, thereby forcing Germany and Italy to
become ever more enmeshed in Spain, but inadequate for the development of a military force capable of powerful and sustained offensive action. While Italo-German support of the rebels amounted
to a veritable invasion of Spain by the fascist powers, Russian support of the Loyalists, albeit of importance militarily and significant
in the political life of the Republic, did not alter the essentially Spanish character of the Republic's military effort. Thus, while the Republicans fought Germans, Italians, Moors, and the *Tercio*, with
formations of the small, conscripted Spanish Army and other Spanish contingents, principally the Navarrese *requetés*, interspersed
among them, the rebels fought Spaniards who, for a time, enjoyed
the support of the numerically weak but hard-fighting International
Brigades.

Rebel successes in Andalusia and Extremadura in the summer of
1936 had deprived the Loyalists of important wheat-growing and
cattle-raising regions. Thus, to the other problems which beset the
Republic was added a serious shortage of foodstuffs that was, in
time, to become desperate. The capture of Badajoz on August 14,
1936, had enabled the rebel forces in the south and in the north to
join and had given them control of the Spanish-Portuguese frontier
over which they received a steady supply of war materials. The
fall of Irún on September 4, 1936, deprived the Republicans in the
isolated Basque and Asturian regions of their only land connection
with France. This was to have far-reaching consequences inasmuch
as these northwestern provinces of Spain were rich in coal and iron,
Bilbao being the center of the Spanish steel industry.

The capture of Málaga on February 8, 1937, heralded the arrival of a fully panoplied Italian Army in Spain, for that Mediterranean city fell to a purely Italian force. An eyewitness to the event, Sir Peter Chalmers Mitchell, has written:

Then came the rhythmic tramp of marching men, and what seemed one or two regiments tramped down my lane in perfect order. I know nothing about the fighting qualities of Italian soldiers, but these were as fine men as one could wish to see. Sturdy, bronzed, perfectly uniformed and booted, every third man or so carrying what seemed to be a Lewis gun, all with metal helmets, an officer marching by the side every few yards. At the foot of the lane they crossed the *arroyo* and streamed across to take possession of the Calenta. By two o'clock all my part of Málaga was in the possession of the Italian army. There was not a Spaniard among them.[3]

The easy victory at Málaga of the Italian expeditionary force (Corpo Truppe Voluntarie or C.T.V.) over the Republican militia —consisting largely of ill-armed, half-starved Andalusian peasants —led the commander of the C.T.V., General Roatta, to believe that Republican resistance on the central front could as easily be overcome, Madrid taken, and the war won.

At about the time the Italians were entering Málaga, Franco's troops were being successfully held along the Jarama river to the south of Madrid by Republican forces, composed, in the main, of units of the International Brigades. Thus, just as the first rebel offensive against Madrid from the northwest out of the Guadarramas in November, 1936, had ended in failure, so the second attack on the capital from the southeast across the Jarama in February, 1937, had proved unsuccessful. Now the time was come for a third attempt to capture Madrid. The offensive was to be mounted by the Italians and was to be launched from the northeast, down the Zaragoza road toward Guadalajara, a town less than fifty miles from the capital.

The Italian forces consisted of the First, Second, and Third Blackshirt Divisions and the Littorio Division, supported by tanks, artillery, and aircraft, including some German air units.[4] These were bolstered by two special brigades which included some German ground units.[5] With seventy trucks assigned to each battalion and a reserve truck park to each division, this was a motorized army.[6]

The Italian offensive began on March 6, 1937. In the beginning it appeared that the easy victory of Málaga would be repeated. The Italians advanced rapidly—nearly twenty miles in two days—meeting little organized resistance. But as they pushed on toward Guadalajara the Republican defense stiffened. Then the weather turned foul, with torrential rains and high winds.[7] Italian action in the air was reduced to a minimum. It appears that the Italian command had neglected to prepare forward air fields on well-drained ground.[8] The attack began to falter. Yet, the Italian forces, deployed in open country and unable to advance, were not regrouped and withdrawn to defensive positions. They were left like sitting ducks in weather for ducks.

The Duce was nevertheless in high spirits and sent the following telegram, dated March 13, to General Mancini who was in command on the Guadalajara front:

I am receiving on board the *Pola* sailing toward Libya the communiqués of the great battle in progress in the direction of Guadalajara. I am following the vicissitudes of the battle with confidence, for I am certain that the impetuosity and tenacity of our legionaries will sweep away the enemy's resistance. To rout the international forces will be a success of great value, also politically. Let the legionaries know that I am following hour by hour their action which will be crowned with victory.[9]

Meanwhile, the Republicans had rushed every available man, gun, and airplane to the Guadalajara front, including units of the International Brigades from the Jarama sector. Franco, whether because his forces were exhausted, or because of poor liaison with the Italians, or, perhaps, as some suggest,[10] because he was piqued by the arrogance displayed by the conquerors of Málaga, did not undertake a diversionary action, either along the Jarama or elsewhere. The Republicans, commanded by General José Miaja and Colonels Vicente Rojo and Enrique Lister, the last a Galician quarryman turned soldier who had proved himself an excellent field com-

mander, fought superbly and, on March 14, hurled their first coun-
terattack against the fascists. The Italian offensive was turned first
into a defeat and then into a rout. By March 23 the battle was over,
the Italians having lost thousands in killed, wounded, and prisoners
as well as a vast amount of matériel.

Despite the severe defeat suffered by the Italian forces at Guadalajara, a fourth attempt by the rebel army to take Madrid, if adequately prepared and properly executed, coordinating the actions
of Franco's troops along the Jarama, Mola's army in the Guadarramas, and the C.T.V. along the Zaragoza road, might have prevailed over the brave but sorely beset defenders of the capital. According to J. Álvarez del Vayo, General Emilio Mola, the rebel
commander in the north, urged that a fourth offensive be hurled
against Madrid.[11] But the Madrid front did not erupt. It was in the
north, in the Basque and Asturian regions, that the heaviest fighting
of the spring and summer of 1937 took place. Madrid was spared
another blow, according to J. Álvarez del Vayo, because the Germans, concerned with the needs of their own rearmament program,
insisted that the rebels turn their efforts to the conquest of the iron-
rich Basque country.[12] Señor del Vayo's views on General Mola
and the Germans gain credence from a report which General Wilhelm Faupel, the German ambassador to the Franco government,
sent to the German Foreign Ministry on July 9, 1937, some three
weeks after the fall of Bilbao. As head of the Ibero-American Institute in Berlin, Faupel had long been interested in the Spanish-
speaking world. He had not found it difficult to win the confidence
of the Generalissimo. In his report Faupel noted that Franco had
felt relief at the death of General Mola [13] whom Franco had recently described to Faupel as a "stubborn fellow" ready to take
umbrage at directives which differed from his own proposals.[14]
The report discloses that Faupel believed that a resumption of the
attack on Madrid "should absolutely be avoided." [15] Earlier in his
report Faupel had declared that "the capture of Bilbao signifies
not only a military and a great moral victory but also possession

of one of the most important harbors of Spain, and, above all, of the iron ore mines." [16]

It is also of interest that a memorandum, dated July 10, 1937, by an official (Kreutzwald) of the Economic Policy Department of the German Foreign Ministry noted with respect to the conquest of Bilbao that the mines, blast furnaces, and rolling mills were undamaged and that work in them could be resumed at once.[17] It went on to declare: "In the future, of course, the Spanish smelting works should continue to receive the iron ore necessary for their operation. It was hoped, however, that all other ore would be sent to Germany for the forseeable future, although it was not the intention to disregard the British in the long run." [18]

Navarrese and Italian infantry, strongly supported by German air power, constituted the main forces of the rebels in the campaign against the Basques and Asturians. Bilbao was taken by the Navarrese on June 19, 1937, Santander by the Italians on August 25, 1937. Gijón, the last Republican stronghold in the north, fell on October 22, 1937. It was at the beginning of this campaign, on April 26, 1937, that Guernica, the ancient capital of the Basques, was ruthlessly destroyed from the air by the Germans.

The loss of Andalusia and most of Extremadura in the summer of 1936, followed by the collapse of Republican resistance in the Basque and Asturian regions in the summer of 1937, rendered the plight of the Republic desperate. As was previously noted, the rebel victories in Andalusia and Extremadura deprived the Republic of important wheat-growing and cattle-raising regions. Equally significant, they deprived the Republic of the support of a vast peasant population whose sentiments were, in the main, republican. The rebel conquest of the Basque and Asturian regions constituted not only a heavy economic blow to the Republic but, as in the south, a serious reduction of its popular base. Perhaps even more than the loss of the support of millions of illiterate, half-starved peasants who, the mercurial Andalusians particularly, were prone to pursue anarchist will-o'-the-wisps, the loss of the support of the stalwart, ef-

ficient Basques, who while devout Catholics were nonetheless sincere republicans, and of the hard-fighting Asturians, who in 1934
had given ample evidence of their worth, would be grievously felt
in Republican Spain.

Without the assurance of a steady flow of war materials and supplies from abroad, thanks to the Non-Intervention Agreement and
to the increasingly effective rebel, *i.e.*, Italo-German, blockade,
Madrid had great need of the foodstuffs of the south and of the industrial products of the north, as it had of the enthusiasm, the skill,
and the fighting capacity of the millions of republicans who now
found themselves behind the Franco lines. Yet, if victory could be
forged by one's own fire and on one's own anvil, Madrid was not
completely bereft of means and resources. At the end of 1937 the
Republic continued to possess most of New Castile, including La
Mancha, Murcia, Valencia, part of Aragon, and all of Catalonia.
There was a limited number of factories and shops in and around
Madrid and in Valencia and, perhaps, through improvisation, a
small war industry could be established. Moreover, and of salient
importance, Catalonia, along with the fallen Basque country, was
the most industrialized region in Spain. If its resources, skills, and
energies could be mobilized, organized, and properly directed
Catalonia could be made into the arsenal of the embattled Republic.
Certainly it was not to be expected that Catalan industry could rival
that of the Ruhr or even that of Piedmont, but perhaps it could supply the margin which might enable the Republican Army to remain
in the field until, in the course of events, a different outlook came
to prevail at No. 10 Downing Street. However, the political situation in Catalonia militated against the realization of this hope. The
economic and military potentialities of Catalonia were never to be
adequately utilized. This, coupled with the greater matter of foreign intervention, was to prove the tragedy of Republican Spain.[19]

While an extended analysis of the internal politics of Spain during the Civil War lies beyond the scope of this study, to shed some
light on the profoundly bitter antagonisms which divided and
weakened the Republic would be both germane and useful. Fol-

lowing the defeat of General Goded's soldiers in the streets of Barcelona in July, 1936, important changes occurred in the pattern of political power within Catalonia and in the relations between Catalonia and the rest of Republican Spain. The victory of the Frente Popular in the general elections of February 16, 1936, placed the *Generalitat* [20] in the hands of the Esquerra led by Luis Companys. The Esquerra, or Catalan Left party, derived its principal support from the urban middle classes, professional groups, and moderately prosperous landowners. Apart from its strongly autonomist features, its political program was comparable to that of Manuel Azaña's Left Republican party. Between the Esquerra, and the anarchists there existed, ideologically, a chasm that the strikes and disorders of the past years had widened and deepened.[21] Yet, when Goded ordered his troops into the streets on July 19, 1936, it was to the anarchists and the anarchist-controlled C.N.T. unions that the *Generalitat* turned for support.[22] It was a cruel dilemma that Luis Companys and the Esquerra confronted: surrender to Goded and see the end of the Republic and Catalan autonomy or arm the anarchists and run the risk of proletarian revolution.

The suppression of Goded's revolt and the subsequent defense of the Republic (and of the *Generalitat*) furnished the occasion for an anarchist attempt to establish "libertarian communism" in Catalonia. Amid considerable disorder, church burnings, political assassinations, and other wanton and terroristic acts,[23] the control and operation of transport facilities and other public utilities was assumed by workers' committees, a number of factories seized and collectivized, and landed property (usually of Franco sympathizers who, if they remained alive, had fled abroad or to rebel-held territory) confiscated. Yet, the tumult and the shouting notwithstanding, the "revolution" remained pretty much a spontaneous, sporadic, local, direct-action, single-dimension affair. It lacked a general plan, coordination of effort, and seizure of and mastery over the apparatus of governmental power. Felix Morrow observed that "despite the scope of the power of the proletariat in the militias and their control of economic life, the workers' state remained embry-

onic, atomized, scattered in the various militias and factory committees and local anti-fascist defense committees jointly constituted by the various organizations." [24] The *Generalitat*, although
cowed by the armed strength of the anarchists and forced to ap-
prove the revolutionary measures taken by the workers' committees,
remained in the hands of President Luis Companys and the Esquerra.
Its power, now nominal, could and would be reasserted in more
propitious circumstances. The moderate program of the Esquerra
continued to attract widespread, if temporarily silent, support
throughout Catalonia.

Meanwhile, because of anarchist preoccupation with the domestic situation in Catalonia, the autonomist tendencies of the Esquerra-
dominated *Generalitat*, and the exigencies of civil war, the Catalans
began to assume a position of virtual independence vis-à-vis Madrid.[25] The extent to which this was true can be ascertained from
the fact that before the year had ended the Catalan government had
begun to issue new small-value notes, to circulate within Catalonia.[26] While the efficiency of certain worker-controlled war industries in Catalonia and the fighting capacity of certain anarchist
militia units in action along the Huesca-Zaragoza line and on the
Madrid front cannot be gainsaid, the Catalan contribution to the
common struggle against Franco, nevertheless, was not commen-
surate with Catalan resources and manpower.[27]

The anarchist-led "revolution" in Catalonia and the quasi-inde-
pendence of the *Generalitat*, matters of salient importance in their
effect on the Republican war effort, together constituted the "Catalan issue," upon which turned the political struggle within the
Madrid government.

It has already been noted that at the outbreak of the Civil War
there was not a single Socialist, Communist, or anarchist of Cabinet
rank in the Spanish government. With the resignation of Casares
Quiroga as premier and the formation of a new Cabinet headed by
José Giral on July 19, 1936, the government remained exclusively
Republican. It was not until September 4, 1936, when the military
position of the Republic had seriously deteriorated, that the gov-

ernment was broadened to include other elements of the Frente Popular coalition. Francisco Largo Caballero, the Left Socialist leader, became premier and minister of war. Other Socialists, both Center and Left, occupied the ministries of foreign affairs, home affairs, finance, industry and commerce, marine and air; Communists those of agriculture and public instruction; a Left Republican that of justice; a Union Republican that of communications; a Basque Nationalist that of public works; a member of the Catalan Esquerra that of labor; while the former premier and Left Republican, José Giral, remained in the government as minister without portfolio. Measured by the Azaña-Giral yardstick this was a revolutionary government. Beyond a doubt, the liberal, middle-class Republicans, conceding that the situation demanded a Socialist-led government, would have preferred Indalecio Prieto to Largo Caballero as premier. Prieto, shrewder and abler than his popular rival in the Socialist movement, was a moderate with strong ties to the Basque Nationalists. Largo Caballero, dubbed the "Spanish Lenin," had become premier by virtue of his popularity with the rank and file of the U.G.T. and the support of the Communist party, both organizations being among the most militant defenders of the Republic. Prieto had had to be content with the ministry of marine and air.

The elevation of Largo Caballero to the premiership was a singular misfortune for the Republic. Not only was he revealed to be an unimaginative and inept war leader,[28] he was to remain what he had been—the single greatest obstacle to the emergence of a "government of national union" based on a Republican-Socialist entente. What might have been possible with Prieto as premier proved impossible under Largo Caballero. For he continued to be, in war as in peace, the flamboyant "revolutionary" unable to accommodate himself to the necessities of the times yet forever incapable of revolutionary leadership.

It was during the incumbency of Largo Caballero, particularly following the arrival of large-scale Soviet aid in the autumn of 1936, that the political fortunes of the Spanish Communist party rose to impressive heights. From a minuscular political group without mass support and devoid of influence as recently as the last general elections, Spanish communism was to become before the year had ended a powerful mass organization whose authority and influence were felt throughout Republican Spain. Undoubtedly, much of the credit for this remarkable achievement belongs to the Communists themselves. For they were indefatigable workers and valiant fighters.[29] Moreover, they had a sure grasp of modern political technique and an appreciation of the demands of modern warfare.[30] Their discipline, their moderation with respect to revolutionary change, and their supreme concern with winning the war against Franco made a strong appeal among all sections of the population but, particularly, to those *milicianos* who saw the need for and were prepared to accept discipline, to the urban middle classes and small landowners who, as in Catalonia, felt themselves menaced by anarchist excesses and revolutionary schemes, and to those industrial and agricultural workers who, belonging to neither the U.G.T. nor the C.N.T., were drawn to the Communist party by war-born enthusiasm.

However, in the final analysis, it was the fact that Soviet Russia was the one important source of war materials and supplies to which the Spanish Republicans had access that gave the Communists a unique political advantage and accounted for their soaring prestige and power. What the fortunes of the Second Spanish Republic might have been had English and French war materials been available to Madrid and had Madrid been governed by a Republican-Socialist coalition led by Indalecio Prieto (the second a logical concomitant of the first) is, of course, impossible to say. However, a safe conjecture would be that Spanish communism would not have experienced the phenomenal growth that it in fact did.

The part played by the Communists, both Spanish and foreign, in the Spanish Civil War, has given rise to a plethora of opinions and interpretations, ranging from the most bitter denunciations to the most fulsome accolades. Colonel Segismundo Casado, who commanded the Republican central army from May, 1938, to the end of the war and who in March, 1939, rose against the Negrín government, precipitating the ultimate debacle of the Republic, has written:

I consider that one of the major causes of our defeat was the behaviour of the Communists, and the Russian Technicians, and those Members of the Government, Military Commanders and many others who, through cowardice or ambition, forgot Spain and its magnificent people. Members of the Communist Party put their political ambitions before the necessities of war, and did not mind behaving in a way which was deadly to our cause in order to satisfy them.[31]

Yet an American, Harry Gannes, wrote a pamphlet entitled *How the Soviet Union Helps Spain* in which he declared:

Geographically Spain is the farthest country away from the Soviet Union in Europe. Yet in the battle against fascism, for democracy, freedom and world peace, Soviet Russia and democratic, revolutionary Spain stand inseparably side by side.[32]

And some pages later:

The Soviet Union is the undenied leader of the hosts fighting everywhere for Spanish democracy and freedom. The Soviet Union inspires united action of all world labor and anti-fascists against the Spanish rebel butchers and their fascist instigators. The Soviet Union leads the way.[33]

With Largo Caballero installed as premier and minister of war on September 4, 1936, it might have been assumed that the Left Socialists and the Communists would pursue a common policy with respect to both the extremely fluid internal situation and the conduct of the war. In such an event the Left Socialist-Communist entente might have become the left equivalent of a Prieto-led Republican-Socialist coalition which, lacking Anglo-French support, failed to materialize. A number of developments argued the plausibility of this assumption. To begin with, as early as March, 1936, the Socialist Youth and the Communist Youth had combined in a single organization, Juventudes Socialistas Unificados (United Socialist Youth, called simply the J.S.U.). Then, in Catalonia in

August, 1936, the Socialists and Communists, whose adherents were
few as compared with the anarchists, had united to become the
Partido Socialista Unificado de Cataluña (United Socialist Party
of Catalonia, known as the P.S.U.C.). And, finally, hailing him as
the "Spanish Lenin" and supporting him for the premiership, the
Communists apparently saw in the sixty-seven-year-old trade-unionist a fit war leader. It would seem that J. Álvarez del Vayo, a
Socialist and, for a time, a close friend of Largo Caballero, played
an important role in bringing about amity and collaboration between the Socialists and Communists in Spain.[34]

However, the Socialist-Communist rapprochement did not
amount to more than an ardent flirtation. It was not to flame into
love and to end in marriage but, rather, was to end in mutual re-
criminations and complete estrangement. This came to pass because the program of the Communists in Spain, geared to the purposes of Soviet diplomacy, and that of the Socialists led by Largo
Caballero—if a hodge-podge of old-fashioned trade-unionism, revolutionary quixotism, noble sentiments, and personal vainglory can
be said to have constituted a program—were fundamentally antithetical.

The course that the Communists wished Largo Caballero to
follow was made explicit in a letter from Joseph Stalin to the
Spanish leader dated December 21, 1936. After noting that the
Soviet Union had sought, and would continue to seek, within the
measure of its possibilities, to aid the Spanish Republic in its struggle against a "military and fascist clique" which was nothing but
an instrument of international fascist forces, Stalin gave Largo
Caballero a four-fold piece of "friendly advice." First, it would be
necessary to attract the peasants to the side of the government by
settling the agrarian question and reducing taxes. In an agricultural
country such as Spain, Stalin observed, the peasants are of great
importance. The settlement of the agrarian question and the reduction of taxes would encourage the peasants to enlist in the army
and to form partisan groups behind the fascist lines. Second, it
would be necessary to attract the middle classes to the side of the

government by avoiding confiscation of property and furthering trade. Third, the chiefs of the Republican parties should not be alienated but, on the contrary, should be permitted to participate in the government. The continuance of Azaña and his group in power was of particular importance. In thus giving the lie to her enemies' charge that Spain was a Communist republic, open intervention by her enemies—the greatest menace that confronted Republican Spain—would be forestalled. Fourth, the occasion should be found to declare in the press that the Spanish government proposed to respect the property and legitimate interests of foreigners in Spain who were not citizens of countries assisting the rebels.[35]

The Communist program in Spain was not revolutionary. On the contrary, it sought to achieve the unity of the various sections of the population in the struggle against Franco and to subordinate all other considerations to that struggle. That it realistically embodied the imperatives of the Spanish situation has been both stoutly affirmed and vigorously denied.[36] However, that it reflected the larger purposes of Soviet diplomacy is generally conceded. From Stalin's letter to Largo Caballero it can be seen that the Communist position with respect to the Spanish crisis had greater affinities with the ideas of the Left Republicans and the Prieto Socialists than with those of the Left Socialists, the anarchists, and the POUM. In urging Largo Caballero to quiet the fears of the Republican leaders and to prevent the abdication of "Azaña and his group" from their positions of power, Stalin, in effect, was asking that the "revolution" be placed in abeyance and that the legitimacy of the Republic be insured by the maintenance of its constitutionally established bourgeois leadership. The words and deeds of Communist leaders within Spain were to make it abundantly clear that in the course of a few months the Communist party had moved from the extreme left to the extreme right of the Frente Popular coalition. In pointing up the necessity to refute the allegation that Spain had become a Communist republic and thus to forestall "open intervention" by the fascist powers, Stalin might have had the experience of the Russian Revolution and Civil War in mind. However, be that as it may, his reference to "open intervention" as the "greatest menace that confronted Republican Spain" served notice on Largo Caballero that Soviet Russia was not prepared to engage in an all-out effort in Spain to meet the challenge of an open fascist invasion. And, by the same token, it sought to persuade the Spanish leader that the fate of the Second Spanish Republic would be decided not only in the Guadarramas and along the Jarama but, more significantly, in London and Paris. In a word, the Communist position in Spain and the concept of the Popular Front itself were predicated on identical premises. Thus, Georgi Dimitrov, secretary-general of the Third International, could write that the tasks which confronted the "world proletariat" in the winter of 1936–37 were, in effect, to transform the war in Spain into a broad struggle against fascism and war.[37] In Moscow's view, the war in Spain was the principal link in a chain of developments which must lead to a world coalition against the fascist powers. It was not, then, a matter of proletarian revolution in Spain, nor of a Russian-Italo-German war fought on Spanish soil, but—avoiding the one as quixotic and politically divisive and the other as militarily absurd and disruptive of new-found ties with the West—of bringing out of the Spanish crisis the general unity of anti-fascist forces and a closer, firmer understanding between the Western democracies and the Soviet Union against the growing menace of fascist aggression.

Of the many factors which militated against the fulfillment of Soviet policy with respect to Spain two were of preeminent importance. The first, which has been discussed at length, was the reluctance of the Western democracies to meet the challenge of the fascist adventure in Spain. Indeed, as was noted, Soviet aid to the Madrid government was a source of annoyance and apprehension in London and Paris. The second was the attitude of Largo Caballero and the Left Socialists. The trade-unionist turned revolutionary, despite his readiness to cooperate with the Communists and, after the advent of Soviet assistance, his need to do so, was not prepared to see his leadership and revolutionary expectations sacrificed to the larger purposes of Soviet diplomacy. It must be re-

membered that there was considerable ill-will between Largo
Caballero and Azaña and, again, between Largo Caballero and
Prieto. Much of this ill-will was the result of merely personal antip-
athies and, as such, regrettable in the circumstances. But, in significant measure, it was the result of profoundly discrepant political
philosophies. To negate the revolutionary changes which had followed in the wake of the July uprising and to bolster the sagging
edifice of the bourgeois state constituted a policy vastly repugnant
to Largo Caballero, both personally and ideologically. Thus, while
he might be prone to take steps to limit somewhat the power and
influence of the anarchists—whose C.N.T. was the rival of his
U.G.T.—he was not ready to go as far in this direction as the Communists urged and he was quite unwilling to destroy the POUM—
which, as a Trotskyist organization, had called down upon itself
the Kremlin's most bitter anathemas.[38]

Thus, notwithstanding the auspicious beginnings made in Left
Socialist-Communist cooperation in the spring and summer of 1936,
Largo Caballero and the Communists were not to travel far together.
Indeed, in the first month of the new year a controversy involving
questions of military strategy and command in which Largo Caba-
llero took the side of General José Miaja, the Republican com-
mander on the Madrid front, and the Communists that of General
Emil Kleber,[39] a foreign Communist and the commander of the
International Brigades, revealed the mounting discord between
Largo Caballero and the Communists that soon was to result in an
open break between them.[40] The logic of the situation called for a
Spain ruled either by Indalecio Prieto, supported at home by a
Republican-Socialist coalition and abroad by Anglo-French diplomacy, or by Largo Caballero, supported at home by a Left Socialist-
Communist-Anarchist-POUM coalition and abroad by a Soviet Russia both willing and able to "export" revolution. However, the
historical process is not governed by the niceties of logic. The
course of Anglo-French diplomacy, the weakness of the Republican
parties following the July uprising, and the divergent tendencies
within Spanish socialism prevented the realization of the first pos-

sibility; the foreign policy of the Soviet Union and the fierce antagonisms which existed among the proletarian parties, the second.
What, in fact, emerged was a patchwork of incongruities. Largo
Caballero, thanks to his popularity with the working classes who,
pushing aside the perplexed and hesitant Republican leaders, had
taken the defense of the Republic into their own hands, became
premier. But developments abroad forced Largo Caballero to lean
heavily on the Communists for support. The Communists, however, pursued a policy predicated on the maintenance of the bourgeois Republic and, ultimately, on Anglo-French support of the
Spanish government. Yet, Largo Caballero proved unwilling to tack
to the Communist wind and Anglo-French support of the embattled
Republic was never to materialize. The events in Barcelona in
May, 1937, when the Madrid government sought to reestablish its
authority in Catalonia, led to a final split between Largo Caballero
and the Communists. For, with the forces of the Madrid government triumphant over anarchist and POUM extremists[41] in a week
of street fighting that left hundreds killed and wounded, and Catalan autonomy extinguished in all but name, Largo Caballero was
unwilling to sanction further repressive measures demanded by the
Communists. The Communist argument was that these measures
were necessary to complete the coordination of Catalonia with
the rest of Republican Spain, thus insuring that Catalan resources
would be fully utilized in the Republican war effort.[42] The Premier's position was that a workers' government could not properly
preside over the liquidation of workers' parties and organizations.
On May 11, 1937, an editorial in *Adelante*, a newspaper published
in Valencia and the organ of the Left Socialists, declared:

If the Caballero government were to apply the measures of suppression
to which the Spanish section of the Communist International is trying
to incite it, then it would come close to a government of Gil Robles
or Lerroux; it would destroy the unity of the working class and expose
us to the danger of losing the war and shipwrecking the revolution.
. . . A government composed in its majority of people from the labor
movement cannot make use of methods that are reserved for reactionary and fascist-like governments.[43]

With his military and domestic policies under attack not only by the Communists but by the Republicans and Prieto Socialists too, Largo Caballero felt obliged to resign as premier on May 16, 1937.

The power of the anarchists in Catalonia had been broken but not destroyed. In time, the anarchists and Largo Caballero were to stand together in opposition. Catalonia, in the months to come, as in those past, was not to play her full part in the defense of the Republic.

Meanwhile, the Communists, who had done so much to elevate Largo Caballero to the premiership and then to force his resignation, sought to draw close to the middle-class parties. Here, indeed, was an anomalous situation. The mass working-class parties were, in effect, in opposition. The Communist party owed its power and prestige to the importance of Soviet aid in the defense of the Republic. The middle-class parties lacked mass support and distrusted and feared the Communists. If men such as Azaña, Giral, Besteiro, and Prieto joined hands with the Communists it was only because the defense of the Republic demanded it. However, it was, at best, a tenuous alliance. In these circumstances, the Communist power in Spain, essentially an alien plant in Spanish soil watered and sustained by the flow of Soviet assistance, evolved into what can fairly be described as an *imperium in imperio*, an autonomous entity which while not sufficiently powerful of itself to dominate the situation possessed nevertheless enough strength to prevent other groups from doing so.

Largo Caballero was succeeded in the premiership not by Indalecio Prieto but by Dr. Juan Negrín, formerly a professor of physiology in the University of Madrid and a Socialist who had served as minister of finance in the previous government. The personal animosity of Largo Caballero who, thanks to his popularity with the working classes, remained a powerful figure, and the distrust of the Communists had prevented Prieto from attaining the premiership.[44] However, he was given the important post of minister of defense in the new government. Negrín was to remain as premier until the end of the war. He had the confidence of the Communists and he, in turn, worked closely with them. It was while Dr. Negrín was minister of finance in the Largo Caballero government that "something more than half" of Spain's gold reserves had been shipped from Cartagena and deposited in the Gosbank in Moscow, a move which was to occasion considerable comment in later years but which at the time had seemed justified by the fluid situation in Spain, the pro-Franco sentiments of many English and French bankers, and the fact that Soviet Russia was the Republic's principal source of war materials and supplies.[45] Responsibility in this matter did not rest with Dr. Negrín alone but with the principal members of the government, including, besides the Premier and the Minister of Finance, Foreign Minister del Vayo and Minister of Marine and Air Prieto, all of whom were privy to the plan to send the gold to Moscow.[46] Yet, after the fall of the Republic, it was Negrín's name that was sinisterly linked with the scheme by fellow Republicans in exile who sought far and wide for explanations of their defeat.[47] But Juan Negrín was not a crypto-Communist, a fellow-traveler, a dupe, nor a fool. He had been, and was to remain to the end of the war, merely honestly convinced that cooperation with the Communists was imperatively demanded by the situation in which the Republic found itself.[48]

The Negrín government had been hailed as "the government of victory" but, limited Republican offensives against Brunete in July, 1937, against Teruel in the winter of 1937–38, and along the Ebro in the summer of 1938 notwithstanding, the prospect of victory became increasingly remote. For Franco's war machine, constantly growing in strength, went from success to success, recapturing Teruel, mounting a great offensive in the Levante (March–July, 1938) that carried to the Mediterranean and split Republican Spain into two segments, Catalonia and Madrid-Valencia, and driving the Republican forces back across the Ebro. As the first snow of winter fell in 1938 Franco's final triumph appeared inevitable.

Meanwhile, on April 5, 1938, Indalecio Prieto had resigned as minister of defense. He had sought to reduce the influence of the Communists in the Republican army [49] and the Communists, following the military defeats of the late winter and spring of 1938, had accused him of ineffective leadership and defeatism.[50] Negrín had tried to prevent an open break between Prieto and the Communists.[51] But his efforts had proved in vain. With Prieto's resignation the patchwork of incongruities that was the political fabric of Republican Spain had come apart at the seams. From April, 1938, to the end of the war a three-cornered political struggle raged intermittently behind the Republican lines, a struggle that was to assume violent and tragic proportions with the Casado-Miaja uprising against the Negrín government in Madrid in March, 1939.

In one corner of the triangle stood Largo Caballero and the Left Socialists, along with the anarchists and the POUM, a beaten but disgruntled and potentially revolutionary opposition. In the second were the moderate Socialists, followers of Prieto and Besteiro, along with many Republicans, including President Azaña. These Socialists and Republicans, largely of middle-class background and orientation, had been swept by the course of events to the periphery of the struggle against Franco. Certain individuals among them, not the least important being Prieto himself, had managed to remain at the center of things and had rendered distinguished service to the Loyalist cause. But they had acted as individuals, isolated from the masses and forsaken by their natural allies in the Western democracies.[52] Now, perceiving that the Republic must inevitably go down to defeat, they had come to believe that to continue the war was senseless. They were ready to accept the best terms that they could get from Franco. The war-weariness of the bombed, shelled, and hungry populace gave meaning and strength to their position. In the third corner of the triangle were gathered those Republicans and Socialists, along with the Communists and countless thousands of Spaniards of no particular political allegiance save to the Republic itself, who gave their support to the Negrín government. Negrín was determined to continue fighting in the hope that Franco would be forced, either by pressure from abroad or by the strength of Republican resistance, to agree to terms which guaranteed the lives of the defeated Republicans.[53] On February 1, 1939, in the Catalan town of Figueras, Premier Negrín announced before the

Cortes (this was a rump Cortes and this would be its final meeting) the three conditions on which the Republicans would lay down their arms. These were: evacuation of Spanish territory by all foreign elements; the Spanish people to be allowed to determine their own political regime freely and without foreign pressure of any kind; no reprisals to be taken.[54] However, J. Álvarez del Vayo states that the Negrín government was aware that its first and second conditions could not realistically be insisted upon but that the third could not be relinquished without utterly divesting the Loyalist struggle of moral dignity.[55]

In the past there had been attempts on the part of various states to mediate the conflict in Spain. As early as the third week in August, 1936, certain Latin American states, prominent among them Uruguay and Argentina, had sought to arrange an armistice in Spain.[56] Nothing had come of this effort largely because of the indifference of the great powers which had looked upon it as premature.[57] However, in December, 1936, Great Britain and France, believing that the rapid advances made by General Franco coupled with his defeat before Madrid had disposed both the Loyalists and the rebels to take a less sanguine view of their respective prospects of ultimate victory, had jointly proposed to the interested great powers mediation to bring about a cessation of hostilities in the Peninsula.[58] But the Anglo-French proposal had floundered on the reluctance of Germany and Italy to give it serious support.[59] By this time both Berlin and Rome had recognized the Franco regime and were deeply committed in Spain. Their descent on Spain having gone virtually unchallenged by the Western democracies, the fascist powers had been disinclined to enter into arrangements which, in the circumstances, would have resulted in the restoration of the *status quo ante* with respect to Spain's position in the European balance of power. London and Paris had not pressed the matter and it had come to nothing.

Perhaps the Anglo-French *démarche* of December 5, 1936, had been little more than a gesture which served to put on record the

desire of the British and French governments that peace be re-
established in Spain while it served to demonstrate the unfeasibility
of mediation at this time and thus to preclude the possibility that the
Council of the League of Nations would give serious attention to
the situation in Spain at its forthcoming meeting. For there had
been considerable concern in London and Paris that Spanish Foreign Minister J. Álvarez del Vayo would seek to arraign Germany
and Italy before the tribunal of world opinion at Geneva. That the
wish to circumvent the Spanish delegation at Geneva rather than
the belief that the time was propitious for an armistice in Spain was
the underlying motive of the Anglo-French *démarche* is strongly
suggested by two reports of the American ambassador (Bingham)
in London to the United States Department of State. In a telegram
dated December 3, 1936, Bingham informed his government that
it was the opinion of the British Foreign Office that the Spanish war
could continue "for an extended period" and that Germany was
determined "to secure success for the Franco forces" but that Soviet Russia would seek to gain its ends in Spain "through less obvious means than tests of military strength in the present conflict." [60]
The following day, on the eve of the Anglo-French *démarche*,
Bingham sent another telegram to Washington in which he said:

I do not understand that either the French or British Governments
are hopeful that this *démarche* in Rome, Berlin and Moscow will be
successful, but the British and French Governments are anxious for
their own records that such an action should be taken especially before the meeting of the Council on December 10.

I learned from the French Embassy that the French Government
is particularly apprehensive over the desire of the Spanish Government for the Council meeting in that the Spanish Government may
attempt, supported by smaller governments and nations not directly
concerned, to set up a League Committee in Geneva in connection
with the Spanish situation. The Spanish Government anticipated that
there would be no representative on such a League Committee either
of Italy or Germany. Both France and England are anxious to avoid
such a situation and do not wish the League Council to go farther

than taking note of the Spanish Government's statement and at the same time reinforcing the position and authority of the London Committee upon which the great nations most concerned in the Spanish situation (except for Spain itself) are represented.[61]

That the British government sought to keep the Spanish situation within the purview of the Non-Intervention Committee in London, thus preventing it from becoming the occasion for serious discussion and possibly action at Geneva, is further substantiated by the instructions given Lord Cranborne (Viscount Robert), the British representative on the Council of the League at its December, 1936, meeting, to hold the Spanish issue "within a small compass." [62] It must not be forgotten that Spain was not represented on the London Committee while the Covenant of the League provided the Spanish Republic with the means to present its case to the world. But, perhaps, the British were unduly anxious and sealed a locked door. For the machinery of the League was not to be set in motion, either in December, 1936, or at any other time during the course of the Spanish war. The Spaniards were to find that the hand at the throttle in Geneva was the same that held the gavel in London.[63] However, the concern of the Western democracies that the Spanish situation remain the province of the interested powers in London and not become that of the world organization at Geneva did not lessen their interest in restoring peace to Spain.

On May 15, 1937, the British foreign secretary, Anthony Eden, informed the German ambassador in London, Joachim von Ribbentrop, that it was the intention of the British government, operating through normal diplomatic channels, "to work for a cessation of hostilities in Spain." [64] Two days later, on May 17, 1937, the British ambassador in Berlin, Sir Neville Henderson, delivered a note to the German foreign minister, Baron Constantin von Neurath, in which the British government proposed to the German government that they, together with the other interested powers, seek to arrange a truce in Spain which would permit foreign volunteers on both sides to be withdrawn from that country.[65] At the same time, the British made a similar proposal to the Italians.[66] However, Rome

showed no interest in the suggestion, seeing in it a British maneuver
to circumvent a fascist victory in Spain.[67] The Germans evinced
no greater interest in the matter than the Italians. Four days after
Ambassador Henderson had delivered his government's note to
the German Foreign Minister, Baron von Neurath informed him
that in the view of the German government a truce in Spain at this
time was not feasible and that discussions concerning the withdrawal of foreign volunteers from Spain could best be continued
in the Non-Intervention Committee.[68]

Burgos, no less than Rome and Berlin, viewed the suggestion of
a truce with misgivings. The day following Neurath's reply to
Henderson, General Franco conversed at length with General Wilhelm Faupel, the German ambassador to rebel Spain. Franco appeared to have been excellently informed. He told Faupel that he
strongly opposed an armistice, the upshot of which would be to
place the destinies of Spain once again in "Red" hands. The British
proposal, Franco continued, had stemmed from the activities of
Indalecio Prieto who, after the May Days in Barcelona, had become convinced that the internal difficulties of Republican Spain
rendered imperative an immediate armistice. A few weeks back
Prieto had had a conference with Premier Blum in Paris, at which
time he had sought for means to end the war in Spain. The British
had acceded to Prieto's importunities, Franco explained, out of a
desire to safeguard their interests in the Basque region, which was
under heavy attack by the rebel forces.[69]

On May 24, 1937, the day following the conversation between
Franco and Faupel, Baron von Neurath informed the rebel chargé
d'affaires in Berlin of the German government's rejection of the
British proposal, suggesting to the Spaniard that the attack on Bilbao
should be continued "energetically." [70]

Thus, in the Spanish crisis, the League of Nations had been by-
passed, the Non-Intervention Committee reduced to a debating society, and "normal diplomatic chanels" allowed to become stagnant.

While the mounting adversities of the Republic found the Loyalists increasingly amenable to the idea of peace through compro-

mise,[71] the passing months saw General Franco become more and more adamant in his demand for unconditional surrender. Franco's intransigence reflected three important factors in the Spanish situation. Two of these have been discussed at length; the third remains to be considered. The first was the lassitude and indecision of the Western democracies in the face of the Italo-German descent on Spain. No significant pressure was ever exerted on Franco by London and Paris, either directly or indirectly, to treat with the Republicans. The second was the scale and scope of the assistance that Franco received from the fascist powers which gave him a decisive military superiority over the Republicans and enabled him to go from victory to victory. The third factor, significantly impinged upon by the first and second, was Franco's absolute control over his rear which prohibited the formation and expression of opinion favorable to the conclusion of a peace based on compromise. Now, despite what was said of the anarchy and terror in the Republican rear (which, it should be noted, was true only in a measure and then largely during the early period of the war), the Loyalist government remained structurally democratic, its policies reflecting the precarious equilibrium that existed among competing political parties which, in the main, remained free to actively influence and direct public opinion. And, if the Communists sought to use their political power and influence, and extralegal coercion as well,[72] to convert the Republic into a single-willed, single-purposed, monolithic state, it must be owned that they failed dismally in the end.

The rebel rear was, of course, in no wise democratic. From the beginning Franco strove to root out any resistance, actual or potential, to the rule of the army. Those in the rebel rear who were identified as Republican or were suspected of harboring Republican sympathies found themselves the victims of a reign of terror beside which the harsh and often indiscriminate repressive measures taken against pro-Franco elements in the Republican rear seem almost benign.[73] The eye-witness accounts of such able and honorable men as Georges Bernanos,[74] Sir Peter Chalmers Mitchell,[75] Antonio Ruiz Vilaplana,[76] and others are eloquent on this score. The massacre of hundreds of Republicans, combatants and noncombatants alike, by the rebels after the capture of Badajoz was, in the words of Gerald Brenan, "merely the culminating act of a ritual that had already been performed in every town and village in the South-West of Spain." [77]

The rebel terror was not limited to hostile Andalusia and Extremadura but extended to regions in the north which were traditionally conservative. Antonio Ruiz Vilaplana has written:

Throughout the Nationalist area the military movement assumed an indescribably ferocious character. . . . In Burgos [in the heart of rebel territory], on the day following the proclamation of martial law, all the leaders of working-class organizations and *Casas del Pueblo* [headquarters of Socialist trade-unions], both in the capital and the smaller towns—down to the humblest officials—were arrested and shot.[78]

The rebel terror, Señor Ruiz Vilaplana continued, was directed against all who, in any way, past or present, were associated with organized labor and progressive political groups.[79] Commenting on the bloody farce that the rebel authorities made of the established judicial system, Ruiz Vilaplana said:

a judge was not required to be a Phalangist or a *requeté* or a member of any party: his elimination or his confirmation in office entirely depended upon the degree of his Right and Catholic sympathies, and, above all, on the extent to which he was likely to be adaptable and pliant to the will of the military.[80]

With the phrase "adaptable and pliant to the will of the military" Ruiz Vilaplana described the quintessence and inexpugnable reality of both the Franco judiciary and the Franco political system. For the army not only had forthwith unleashed terror against its political opponents on the Left, it soon made puppets of its political allies on the Right. With the complete suppression of the Republican and Marxist parties, and the virtual disappearance of the discredited CEDA, the two most active political organizations in Franco territory were the Comunión Tradicionalista, led by Fal Conde, and the Falange Española, whose founder, José Antonio Primo de Rivera, had been executed by the Republicans on November 20, 1936, and whose nominal leader now was Manuel Hedilla, an almost illiterate dockworker from Santander. The Tradicionalistas, who as Carlists were devoted monarchists, furnished Franco with some excellent troops, the *requetés*. However, narrow, bigoted, atavistic, the Tradicionalistas enjoyed little political influence beyond Navarra. The Falange Española, like the Communist party, had remained small and insignificant until the July uprising, following which, again like the Communist party, it had experienced a great expansion. Not only did many erstwhile monarchists and other upper and middle class elements enter the Falange but also thousands of former Socialists, Communists, and anarchists, who, finding themselves behind the rebel lines, saw in that swelling, pseudo-revolutionary organization a place of refuge.[81]

Between the tradition-bound, self-contained Tradicionalistas and the amorphous, flamboyantly "revolutionary" Falangistas there was nothing in common save their hatred of the "Red Republic." That the insurgent "movement" was the sheerist eclecticism and political improvisation was made abundantly clear when the Generalissimo moved to merge the completely antipathetic Comunión Tradicionalista and Falange Española into a single organization with himself as its leader. In a conversation with General Faupel on April 11, 1937, General Franco revealed that he had contemplated ordering the execution of Fal Conde for the latter's "treasonable" activities on behalf of a monarchical restoration but, out of consideration for the combat value of the *requetés*, had been content to banish him from the country. (Fal Conde had found refuge in Portugal.) The issue of the monarchy, Franco explained, would have to await the reconstruction of Spain. In Franco's opinion, Hedilla, too, lacked the qualities of leadership. The Falange was a body without a head.[82] Thus, on April 19, 1937, a not too surprising political grotesquerie was consummated. On that day Franco issued a decree ordering the fusion of the Tradicionalistas and the Falangistas into a new organization whose official name was to be Falange Española y Tradicionalista y de las Juntas de Ofensiva

Nacional-Sindicalista and whose leader, with the title of *caudillo*, was to be Franco himself. All other political parties were banned. Not long thereafter the hapless Hedilla and twenty of his supporters were arrested.[83]

However, the political vicissitudes of the rebel rear, unlike those of the Republican rear, were of limited significance because the Franco regime was a military dictatorship (wearing the transparent disguise of fascism),[84] while the Republic remained a democracy (albeit strife-torn), and—this was of the essence—the rebel army was victorious while the Republican army was not. What conflicts and schisms might have developed within rebel Spain had Franco suffered heavy reverses at the front and been thrown back on the defensive is, of course, impossible to say. However, it can be doubted that a regime which lacked popular support and political cohesion and rested, ultimately, on the bayonets of the army could have survived for long misfortunes and disasters such as plagued the embattled Republic for nearly three years.

However, the Spanish war was won and lost not in Burgos and Madrid, not at Teruel and along the Ebro, but in the chancelleries of Europe. Two important conferences of the European powers, held only a year apart, the first, at Nyon, Switzerland, arising out of the Spanish situation and bearing directly upon it, the second, at Munich, Germany, arising out of the Sudeten question but having an important if indirect effect on the struggle in Spain, marked the apogee and the nadir respectively of the great, fixed hope of the Spanish Republicans that events abroad would rescue them from the plight in which events abroad had placed them.

The summer of 1937 had seen the collapse of the Republican front in the Basque country. With Bilbao and Santander in rebel hands and with the French Pyrenean frontier closed, Soviet war materials could reach Republican Spain only by way of the Mediterranean. As early as August 3, 1937, General Franco had urgently requested the Italian government to use its fleet to prevent the passage of Soviet transports through the straits between Sicily and Tunisia.[85] Two days later, Nicolás Franco (the Generalissimo's brother), accompanied by the deputy chief of the rebel admiralty staff, had arrived in Rome for the purpose of expediting joint Italian-rebel arrangements to curb the movement of Soviet vessels through the Mediterranean. For, according to Italian Foreign Minister Ciano, "the Duce was in principle still inclined to do everything he could to put a stop to them [the Soviet transports]—not with surface vessels, to be sure, but only with submarines, in Sicilian waters; in case the submarines had to surface, they would display the Spanish flag." [86] Within a week following the arrival of the Spaniards in Rome, Mussolini had informed Burgos that he "was prepared to carry out the measures requested by Franco for preventing the transit of Russian war matériel through the straits south of Italy." [87] Thereupon the Italian naval campaign in the Mediterranean had been intensified.

In the second half of August, 1937, reports began to appear in the world press which told of "mysterious sinkings" not only of Spanish ships in Spanish waters but also of other vessels far from the Spanish coasts. What could it mean? Was it possible in the day of the steamship and wireless telegraphy that pirates had infested the Mediterranean? Under the date, August 31, 1937, Count Ciano made this entry in his diary:

The naval blockade is producing very remarkable results: four Russian or Red ["russi o rossi"] steamships sent to the bottom, one Greek ship seized, one Spanish ship shelled and forced to seek refuge in a French port.[88]

However, in their enthusiasm, the Italians carried things to the point where on the night of August 31–September 1, 1937, they unsuccessfully attempted to torpedo the British destroyer *Havock* north of the Spanish port of Alicante.[89] This was the eighteenth attack on a neutral vessel by an "unknown" craft in a month.[90] Moreover, it was a direct act of effrontery against the position and prestige of the British navy in the Mediterranean. London and Paris became alarmed. If they remained supine in the face of this cavalier disregard of their rights in the Mediterranean, where would it end?

On September 6, 1937, London and Paris invited all the powers concerned to confer together at Nyon on September 10 on measures to put an end to acts of aggression in the Mediterranean. That same day, September 6, the Soviet government dispatched a note to the Italian government in which Moscow formally charged Italy with responsibility for the torpedoing of a Soviet ship off the Greek coast and demanded compensation for the loss and punishment of the guilty.[91] Rome promptly rejected the Soviet note. On September 8 the Soviet government dispatched a second note, which Rome ignored. However, the Italians, seizing on the Soviet action as a pretext, indignantly refused to attend the conference at Nyon. According to Louis Fischer, the nonparticipation in the conference at Nyon of Italy (and of Germany) was precisely what Soviet Foreign Minister Maxim Litvinov sought to achieve by sending Rome these blunt notes containing charges which—if proof had been demanded by Italy—could not have been substantiated.[92] Apparently, the Italians had been trapped by their own knowledge of their guilt. Moreover, the suggestion of the German government (supported by the Italian government) that the problem of security in the Mediterranean be considered not by a special conference but by the Non-Intervention Committee in London "since its sphere of action is very closely related to the issues in question, and since its organization affords the possibility, if all sides show good will, of reaching a prompt settlement" proved unavailing in this instance.[93] The magic of the hackneyed formula seemed spent.

Thus, despite the abstentions of Italy and Germany, the conference was held at Nyon as scheduled. Within a few days agreement was reached by the participating powers—Great Britain, France, the Soviet Union, Bulgaria, Egypt, Greece, Roumania, Turkey, and Yugoslavia—as to the measures to be taken to put an end to "piracy" in the Mediterranean. This agreement, formally entitled the Nyon Arrangement, was communicated to the secretary-general of the League of Nations on September 21, 1937, by French Foreign Minister Yvon Delbos, who had served as president of the Mediterranean Conference of Nyon.

The Nyon Arrangement, after defining wanton attacks on neutral ships as piracy, declared that the participating powers "will instruct their naval forces to take . . . action . . . with a view to the protection of all merchant ships not belonging to either of the conflicting Spanish parties." [94] The Arrangement then specified the duties and zones of action of the various participating powers. In effect, it declared that the British and French navies would patrol the Mediterranean (save for the Tyrrhenian Sea) and would seek to destroy any submarine (and, as later amended, any surface vessel or aircraft) engaged in piratical acts.[95]

Like Pompey, some two thousand years before, the British and French navies swept the pirates from the Mediterranean. Perhaps it would be more accurate to say that at their approach the pirates simply vanished. No more was heard of "mysterious sinkings." Into *Mare Nostrum* had come the outsider and established his fiat, without Rome, against Rome, and Rome did nothing. The Italian ambassador to Franco Spain, Count Guido Viola di Campalto, complained bitterly to Dr. Erich Heberlein, the German chargé d'affaires in Salamanca, that the Nyon Arrangement was "entirely one-sided discrimination in favor of Red Spain," adding that "the measures for putting a stop to Russian deliveries of war matériel, which so far had proved exceptionally effective, would in the future be made extremely difficult if not impossible by the carrying out of the surveillance decided upon at Nyon." [96] He concluded that to offset the expected increase in Soviet deliveries to "Red" Spain, Italy and Germany would have to give Franco additional support.[97]

The Germans were no more fertile of ideas than the Italians. When Franco's ambassador in Berlin, the Marquis Antonio de Magaz y Pers, inquired at the German Foreign Ministry concerning Germany's position vis-à-vis the Nyon Arrangement, he was told that the German government was "still occupied in studying" the document and that Germany, in a question concerning the Mediterranean, "naturally" expected Italy to take the lead "in regard to the further treatment generally to be accorded the Nyon decisions." [98]

The Nyon Conference and the subsequent Arrangement proved that, if Great Britain and France acted with unity of purpose and with resolution, their rights and interests would not be lightly set aside by others. Nyon could have marked the beginning of the end of appeasement. But it did not. For Nyon was viewed with misgivings not only in Italy and Germany but also in England and France.[99] For one thing, it had engendered fresh demands for the opening of the French Pyrenean frontier;[100] for another, it had placed a heavy strain on Anglo-Italian relations. The Anglo-Italian "Gentlemen's Agreement" was less than a year old. The events of the past few weeks had all but killed it. However, perhaps it could yet be resuscitated and restored to full vigor. A firm Italian commitment not to seek territorial advantages in Spain, particularly in the Balearic Islands, was deemed highly important in London.

On October 2, 1937, the British ambassador in Rome, Sir Eric Drummond, and the French chargé d'affaires, Jules Blondel, delivered a joint Anglo-French note to Italian Foreign Minister Ciano in which the British and French governments invited the Italian government to join them in a fresh examination of the situation arising from the prolongation of the Spanish strife.[101] After Blondel had departed, leaving Drummond alone with Ciano, the British Ambassador expressed his "deep regret" that Anglo-Italian relations, which had been improving, had been permitted to deteriorate of late. He attributed the deterioration, in part, to Italy's refusal to participate in the Nyon conference. Drummond concluded by saying that "the British Government earnestly desired to reestablish Anglo-Italian relations on a cordial plane." [102]

Here, again, the British sought a solution to the Spanish problem through "normal diplomatic channels." In doing so, they destroyed the moral and practical advantages which had accrued to the Western democracies from their forthright stand in the Mediterranean and permitted the diplomatic initiative to pass once more to the fascist powers.

On October 7, 1937, Drummond and Blondel again called on Ciano, soliciting a reply to the Anglo-French note of October 2. Ciano explained that certain matters had delayed the Italian answer.[103] Meanwhile, Rome was keeping Berlin fully informed of developments.[104] On October 9, 1937, Ciano summoned Drummond and Blondel to the Italian Foreign Ministry and gave them his government's reply.[105] The Italian government rejected the Anglo-French proposal to confer concerning the situation in Spain because first, Italy was convinced that the Spanish situation could best be dealt with in the Non-Intervention Committee, and second, Italy would not enter a conference concerning Spain at which the German government was not represented.[106]

With this, the British and French had either to fish or to cut bait. They fished. Long negotiations ensued which eventually resulted in the Italians being admitted to the Nyon Arrangement as "equals" (thus they were put to chasing themselves) and the Non-Intervention Committee restored to its pure and pristine state. Meanwhile, on October 19, 1937, General Franco urged Rome to dispatch another Italian division to Spain "to liquidate the northern front." Rome agreed to send it.[107] By the end of the year Italian naval craft had resumed their blockade activities, but somewhat more circumspectly than in the past.

The issues and negotiations which led to the Munich Settlement of September, 1938, do not fall within the compass of this study. The importance of Munich to the Spanish story lies in its effect on Republican morale. For after Munich only the most sanguine Loyalist could permit himself to believe that a new light would come to shine at No. 10 Downing Street. If the bastion that was Czechoslovakia could be surrendered without a shot being fired, then there was little hope indeed that the Spanish Republic, driven into a corner of Spain, would be succored, at long last, by the Western democracies.

On December 6, 1938, as an aftermath of the Munich Settlement, the French and German governments signed a joint declaration that served to solemnize their new-found friendship.[108] Georges Bonnet, the French foreign minister, took the occasion to observe that "no difference that could imperil the peaceful basis of their relations now exists between the two countries." [109] Six days later

Prime Minister Chamberlain declared before the House of Commons that the British government warmly approved of the rapprochement between Paris and Berlin.[110]

In the midst of such political conviviality the cause of Republican Spain must have seemed a ghost out of a wretched and forgotten past and, like a ghost, been feared and shunned. Well might the Loyalist General Vicente Rojo conclude: "We lost the war definitely in the international field during the last ten days of September when the diplomats concocted the pact of Munich." [111]

IX

Franco Spain—Axis Satellite, 1939-1941

FROM Burgos, on April 1, 1939, Generalissimo Franco issued the following communiqué: "To-day, after capturing and disarming the Red Army, the National troops have attained their last military objectives. The War is over." [1]

Actually, Madrid had been occupied on March 28 and all serious resistance had ended by the following day. The Casado-Miaja coup d'état against the Negrín government had produced chaos in the Republican rear, while the efforts of the Casadists to induce Franco to mitigate his demand for unconditional surrender had proved unavailing.[2] Colonel Casado has sought to explain Franco's obduracy in the following terms:

Why, without reason to justify it or precedent to make it advisable, did the Nationalist Command angrily suspend peace negotiations?

In my judgment they behaved in this way because the Nationalists, like their allies and protectors the totalitarian states, wanted to achieve a political and military victory of a spectacular kind. Their excessive insolence actually only snatched the victory from their hands, since the Republican Army did not surrender.[3]

What Casado meant, of course, was that the Republican army did not surrender on terms, but simply dissolved, that is, in effect, surrendered unconditionally.[4] But in noting the relationship between Franco and the fascist powers Casado pointed to the source and substance of Franco's insistence on unconditional surrender.

Not only had Franco been joined with the Italians and Germans in a comradeship of arms, not only had he ostentatiously patterned the structure, the institutions, and the program of his Spain on Italian fascism (and, to a lesser extent, on German nazism), the Generalissimo had signed formal treaties with the Italian and German governments which, in effect, established Franco Spain as a junior member of the Axis.

As early as November 28, 1936 (ten days after formal recognition had been extended to the Franco regime by Italy and Germany), Rome and Burgos had entered into a secret agreement of a far-reaching character. This agreement consisted of a preamble and six sections. The preambulatory statement declared that Italy and Spain, "united in solidarity in the common struggle against Communism," were "animated by the desire to develop and reinforce their own relations" and to do all within their power to further the social and political stabilization of Europe. In the first section Italy pledged her "support and aid for the conservation of the independence and integrity of Spain" and for the reestablishment of social and political order within Spain. In the second section the Italian and Spanish governments promised to maintain close contacts with each other and to act in concert on all matters of common interest, particularly in the western Mediterranean. The third section prohibited each of the contracting parties from entering a combination of or agreement among powers hostile to the other and from giving any kind of assistance to such a combination. All previous agreements entered into by either government which were incompatible with the foregoing injunction were to be considered null and void. The fourth section called for joint Italo-Spanish action aimed at abolishing or radically modifying Article 16 of the Covenant of the League of Nations (which related to the use of sanctions against an aggressor state) and stipulated that should one of the contracting parties find itself at war or the victim of collective punitive action the other would adopt an attitude of "benevolent neutrality," making available supplies and facilities to the first-mentioned party. The fifth section declared that, with the above contingency in view, the two governments would determine "the method to be adopted for the exploitation of their own economic resources, particularly raw materials, and of the means of communication." It added that "the technical agencies of both Governments will shortly conclude the agreements necessary to this end." The last section called for the development of "all forms of economic relations and sea and air communications" between the two nations, conceding "each other all possible facilities for exchange of goods, for the mercantile marine and for civil aviation."[5]

It is apparent from this Italo-Spanish agreement that the experience of even moderate economic sanctions during the Italo-Ethiopian War had proved traumatic in Rome. At that time the Spanish government had faithfully supported the League in its action against Italy. Now Rome sought to assure itself of Spain's "benevolent neutrality" in a similar contingency. More than this, Rome sought to gain access to Spanish sources of raw materials and to bind Spain to Italy in a particularly close relationship.

Although the agreement was to remain secret, Rome, in deference to Italo-German friendship, forthwith informed Berlin of its contents.[6] This was done with Franco's knowledge.[7]

The German government, when it had learned the terms of the Italo-Spanish agreement, had feared that Italian influence in Spain might become preemptive. On December 5, 1936, the German foreign minister, Baron von Neurath, had sent a telegram to the German ambassador in Rome, Ulrich von Hassell, that was marked "urgent" and "secret" and by not a little chagrin at the conduct of the Italians. It read:

The agreement which the Italian government concluded with the government of General Franco is evidently a political and economic agreement of considerable scope. By accepting it Franco, whose hands are tied at the present time, becomes dependent on Italy in the future to an extent which precludes similar agreements with third powers, including Germany. Remarks like those Ciano made to you, that the agreement was not of an exclusive nature, must therefore be considered meaningless. In view of the close interrelationship between German and Italian policy in the Spanish crisis and after the Berlin conversations with Ciano, it would have been the duty of the Italian government to consult us before concluding an agreement of such proportions. Naturally we are reserving all rights with regard to the demands we shall make of Franco, which are preponderantly of a commercial character.[8]

Baron von Neurath had concluded by observing that while the German government recognized that Italy, "if only for geographic reasons," had a greater interest in Spain than Germany, it expected that in the future this greater Italian interest be reflected in the amount of aid that Italy would give to Franco.[9] However, the Germans had not long remained content to play second fiddle to the Italians in Spain. During the course of the war they, as well as the Italians, had continually sought through formal agreements with the Franco government to strengthen their position in Spain.

On March 20, 1937, the German government and the Franco government entered into a political and economic agreement which, like the Italo-Spanish agreement of November 28, 1936, consisted of a preamble and six sections and provided, but in a less explicit manner, for the assumption of similar mutual obligations.[10] Then, after considerable negotiation, the Germans and the Spanish insurgents signed protocols (July 16, 1937) which obligated Spain to pay interest of 4 per cent annually, exclusively in reichsmarks, on the debt incurred as a result of "special deliveries" made by Germany to the Spanish Nationalist government. It was further agreed that Germany would be permitted to obtain raw materials from Spain and Spanish Morocco, to be charged against the German claims, thus facilitating the liquidation of the Spanish obligation. It was also agreed that Germany would assist in the reconstruction of the Spanish economy, "particularly in opening up and utilizing the mineral resources and other raw materials" in Spain and Spanish Morocco.[11]

The German investment of men and arms in Spain brought immediate and handsome dividends. In January, 1938, Herr Johannes Bernhardt, director of Hisma, submitted a report to the German government, noting that during the past year his firm had shipped from rebel-held Spanish territory, including Spanish Morocco, to Germany a total of 2,584,000 tons of ores, including 1,620,000 tons of iron ores and 956,000 tons of pyrites.[12]

As the war began to draw to a close, pressure was exerted on General Franco by Germany and Italy and even by Japan to adhere to the Anti-Comintern Pact (signed originally by Germany and Japan on November 25, 1936, and adhered to by Italy on November 6, 1937).[13] However, Franco demurred at openly joining the pact, not, of course, from any ideological disagreement but out of expediency. He explained that, while in view of Spain's bitter struggle against Bolshevism for the past two years, Spain's accession to the pact "was a matter of course," it would be best to keep the matter secret for the nonce, lest the hostility of England and France be aroused. These countries, Franco insisted, could do Spain great injury, even at this late date.[14] Franco carried his point and it was without public fanfare of any kind that Spain adhered to the Anti-Comintern Pact on March 27, 1939.[15]

Four days later the German government and Franco Spain signed a treaty of friendship, a political, military, economic, and cultural instrument that was to remain in force for five years and unless terminated six months before the date of expiration was to be renewed for another period of five years, and so forth.[16] Article 6 of the treaty read:

In case one of the High Contracting Parties should become involved in warlike complications with a third power, the other High Contracting Party will avoid anything in the political, military, and economic fields that might be disadvantageous to its treaty partner or of advantage to its opponent.[17]

It is of interest that the treaty stipulated that, in view of the close friendship that existed between Germany and Italy on the one hand and between Spain and Italy on the other, Germany and Spain in matters pertaining to international affairs "will be mindful . . . of assuring also the collaboration of the Royal Italian government." [18]

Thus, when on the following day, April 1, Franco proclaimed

the triumphant end of the war, Spain was already held fast in a web of political and economic agreements which had been spun by Rome and Berlin. In the weeks and months to come the fascist powers continued to spin assiduously. In Rome, on April 16, 1939, Mussolini, Ciano, and Field Marshal Hermann Göring discussed the possibility of securing naval and air bases in the Balearic Islands and elsewhere in Spain in the event of a general war.[19] On May 6 and 7, 1939, in Milan, Ciano and Joachim von Ribbentrop (who had been appointed foreign minister by Hitler on February 4, 1938) conferred at length. Concerning Spain Ribbentrop said:

The German Government is satisfied with the attitude of Franco. It agrees that it is necessary to continue to work in common with Italy to strengthen still further the bonds between the Axis and Spain; it might even be necessary to reach a proper alliance since, while not making any unreasonable claims on the Spanish armed forces, it would be very useful for us to be able to pin down some French Army Corps for the defence of the Pyrenean frontier.[20]

The following day, May 8, Madrid announced Spain's withdrawal from the League of Nations. Given the new dispensation in Spain and the impotence and moribundity of the League itself, Madrid's action came as no surprise. Yet, in the light of the Spanish Republic's fervent support of the world organization in the past, Franco's gesture of solidarity with the fascist powers was the sign and the measure of an important shift in the European balance of power.

Political solidarity and economic cooperation went hand in hand. On May 29, 1939, the Italian ambassador in Spain, Count Guido Viola di Campalto, reported to his government that in the course of a recent conversation with General Franco Italo-Spanish economic relations had been discussed. The Generalissimo had observed that in the past the Italian and Spanish economies, owing to their basic similarity, had been not complementary, but competitive. Franco had gone on to suggest that cartel arrangements be devised with respect to citrus fruits and other products, such as already existed for mercury.[21]

In June, 1939, Herr Helmut Wohlthat, an official of the German Economics Ministry, led a delegation of experts to Spain to negotiate with the Spanish government on economic and financial questions and to inspect German economic enterprises in Spain.[22] The Italian ambassador in Berlin, Bernardo Attolico, had informed his government of Herr Wohlthat's departure for Spain, adding that Wohlthat, "already known for the treaty he concluded with Rumania," would seek to negotiate with Spain "an economic-commercial agreement of vast scope." [23] As it proved, however, Wohlthat's mission to Spain did not result in a new agreement.[24]

Early in June, 1939, Ramón Serrano Suñer, the Generalissimo's brother-in-law and Spain's minister of the interior, accompanied returning Italian troops to Italy. In July Count Ciano visited Spain in turn. On July 6, 1939, in anticipation of Ciano's state visit to Spain, Mussolini wrote to Franco. The Duce informed the Caudillo that Ciano would discuss with Franco what Mussolini thought concerning, first, the international situation, second, Spain's position vis-à-vis the international situation, and, third, various problems which concerned Spain and Italo-Spanish relations. Mussolini, assuring Franco of his "unalterably profound friendship," took the opportunity to declare that the restoration of the Monarchy in Spain would constitute a grave menace to the regime that Franco had established with such great sacrifice of blood, that Franco must expect nothing from France and England which were "by definition the irreconcilable enemies of YOUR Spain," and that Franco must move decisively close to the people who are the one great strength of nations.[25] On the occasion of the third anniversary of the *alzamiento*,[26] July 18, 1939, Mussolini and Franco exchanged greetings and felicitations, full of mutual praise and assurance of "indestructible" friendship.[27]

On the eve of the German invasion of Poland, the bonds between Franco Spain and the Axis powers were many and strong. The comradeship-in-arms of Spaniards, Italians, and Germans, the gratitude felt by the Caudillo toward the Duce and the Führer, the pacts of friendship and the economic agreements which bound

Spain to Italy and Germany, the fact that the Falange was openly fascist and the only political party permitted in the new Spain, all attested to the unity that existed among the triumvirate of fascist states. Indeed such was their intimacy that on August 9, 1939, the Generalissimo discussed at length with General Gastone Gambara, the head of the Italian Military Mission in Spain, the possibility, in the event of war, of closing the Straits of Gibraltar to warships by the use of new mortars (with which the Spaniards were experimenting) and of reducing Gibraltar itself by the use of artillery of heavy caliber.[28]

Yet, for all that, there were unmistakable signs that the new Spain was disposed to pursue an independent policy if her interests demanded it. The Axis powers had bought and paid for Franco but were unable to stuff him in their pocket. As early as October 9, 1937, even under the duress of great military need, Franco had taken steps to safeguard Spain from despoilment by his allies. On that day he issued the following decree:

Article I. Until provision is made to the contrary, all acts disposing of mining property, or the purchase, sale, or transfer of shares in mining companies or leases, shall be suspended.

Article II. All titles to mining property, leases, exchanges, sales, or purchase of material, or of properties used in the exploitation of mines or the immediate processing of their products, obtained since July 18, 1936, are declared to be null and void.

Article III. Any arrangements contrary to this decree are dissolved.[29]

This decree was clearly aimed at the so-called Montaña Project, the name given by Johannes Bernhardt's Hisma organization to efforts to establish German control over Spanish mining properties and thus to assure the Reich of a valuable source of raw materials. The Germans were furious. In a long report to his government, dated Burgos, November 4, 1937, Johannes Bernhardt said:

The objective of our economic interest in Spain must be the deep penetration into the main sources of Spanish wealth, namely, agriculture and mining. Whereas the products of agriculture fall to the share of the German Reich more or less without effort, since the Spaniards are forced to find a market, the mining problem is of tremendous importance in every respect.

Reduced to a clear formula, it may be said that the success or failure of our efforts in Spanish mining will determine whether our assistance to Spain was successful or misplaced. Clearly recognizing that the Montana problem is the real objective of our economic effort, we must resolve this problem with all the means available. It must be stated here that these means must be found and applied in all fields and that we must, therefore, exert diplomatic, military, and cultural influence in order to attain this single objective of establishing ourselves economically. . . .

After having saved the Spanish people from destruction and prepared the way for their recovery, we must insist on written pledges of the acquired rights on a long-term basis.[30]

Under heavy German pressure the Spaniards were forced to give way. On November 16, 1937, Franco assured the German ambassador, Dr. Eberhard von Stohrer, that the decree "had been issued because of the danger that the Red government might sell out everything." [31] Thus, while the decree was not officially rescinded, the Germans were allowed to circumvent it.

It is of considerable interest that during the Czechoslovakian crisis (September, 1938) General Franco had assured Great Britain and France that in the event of a general war Nationalist Spain would remain strictly neutral.[32] Franco's haste in assuring London and Paris of his neutrality "had left somewhat of a nasty taste" in Berlin and Rome.[33]

At Burgos, on January 24, 1939, an agreement was signed between Germany and Spain that, providing, among other things, for the exchange of teachers, students, and cultural missions, established the basis for the development of extremely close intellectual and cultural ties between the Reich and the new Spain.[34] Given the marked superiority of German resources and facilities, this agreement, the principle of reciprocity notwithstanding, prepared the way for an extensive German cultural penetration of Spain. However, on February 16, 1939, before the agreement could be ratified and implemented, the Vatican protested to the Franco government that the German-Spanish cultural agreement violated the Spanish-Papal Concordat of 1851.[35] The Spanish clergy and the Traditionalists were averse to the establishment of close cultural ties with Nazi Germany.[36] Their attitude, coupled with the Vatican's protest, caused the Franco government to postpone action on the agreement, procrastinating until the matter was left abeyant. Of course, the lack of a formal agreement did not prevent the Germans from seeking to extend their influence in every direction, but it did serve to insulate Spain against a constant current of Nazi ideas emanating from Berlin.

Not only with respect to mining concessions and cultural missions had the Franco government sought, with varying success, to preserve the Spanish patrimony; it should be emphasized that by the summer of 1939 both the Italian C.T.V. and the German Condor Legion had been repatriated. At the same time Italian bases and installations in the Balearics and German bases and installations in the Canaries and Spanish Morocco had been evacuated and were now manned by Spaniards. (However, as was previously noted, the Italians and Germans continued to negotiate with Franco for permission to reoccupy these positions in the event of a general war.) Thus, despite prognostications to the contrary, there were no foreign troops stationed on Spanish soil, apart from military missions and other technical experts, at the outbreak of the Second World War.

Spanish national pride, verging on xenophobia, is a reality nurtured by the comparative isolation of Spain from the main currents of European life. There is evidence to suggest that during the Civil War the Spaniards admired the military efficiency of the Germans but disliked them as a people, while, despite certain affinities, they neither admired nor liked the Italians.[37] Spanish national pride was an important, albeit intangible, factor that militated against open, outright domination of Spain by the Axis powers.[38] Then, too, it was not to be expected that General Franco, although profuse in adulation of his fascist allies, would permit his gratitude to them to seriously influence his decisions concerning the course that Spain would follow in the future. It was incumbent on Franco, as it must be on any Spanish leader, to seek a *modus vivendi* with Great Britain and France, nations which geography and history have decreed of paramount importance to the Spanish economy and state.

The Germans themselves had been aware that English policy during the Civil War reflected London's conviction that Spain "in any case" would be dependent on British financial and economic assistance after the conflict had ended.[39] On October 16, 1937, the German Foreign Ministry, in informing the German Embassy in Nationalist Spain of current economic negotiations between London and Burgos, observed:

Even if we may assume that General Franco does not intend to satisfy England's wishes to the detriment of Germany's interests, nevertheless any negotiations by Spain with a third country are potentially dangerous to the position of preeminence which we have won in Spain in the economic field. This is especially true with relation to England; for German and British interests, as is well known, confront one another on Spanish soil, particularly in the case of iron ores, which are especially important for Germany, and also in the case of copper and pyrites, *so that it requires a special effort to maintain as long and as fully as possible the preeminence we have won with regard to these raw materials.*

That England cannot permanently be kept from the Spanish market as in the past is a fact with which we have to reckon. England's old relations with the Spanish mines and the Generalissimo's desire, based on political and economic considerations, to come to an understanding with England place certain limits on our chances of reserving Spanish raw materials to ourselves permanently.[40]

There was a note of resigned struggle in these observations that was eloquent of England's powerful economic position in Spain. Toward the close of 1937, moreover, French business circles urged Paris to establish commercial relations with Burgos.[41] At this same time, the highly influential Duke of Alba, the Spanish Nationalist representative in Great Britain, was actively seeking to strengthen relations between London and Burgos and, through his connections in rebel Spain, including Señor Merry del Val, the former Spanish ambassador in London, to weaken the ties between Franco and the Axis.[42]

Perhaps as powerful a motivation as any other for Franco's eschewal of an adventuristic policy was the great need of Spain for peaceful reconstruction after the appalling loss of life,[43] the vast destruction, the enduring bitterness occasioned by nearly three years of war. Moreover, although Franco's triumph had been complete, the consolidation of his regime would require time and attention to internal matters. For the people of Spain, although filled with the horror of war and decisively defeated, remained overwhelmingly Republican. Perhaps at some time in the future a foreign adventure might serve to deflect the thoughts and emotions of the people from the poverty and struggle of their daily existence, but for Franco to engage in war before his regime had been consolidated would be to risk all that had been gained by the *alzamiento*.[44] On October 25, 1937, and, again, on May 19, 1938, Dr. Eberhard von Stohrer, the German ambassador to Franco Spain, estimated that about 40 per cent of the population behind the rebel lines was "politically unreliable." [45] With the conquest of regions such as New Castile, Catalonia, and Valencia which had been under Republican rule throughout the Civil War the percentage of dissidents probably rose appreciably. Count Ciano, in his account of his visit to Spain in July, 1939, related that Spanish prisons were filled with some 200,000 "Reds" whose trials were being conducted at a speed that he described as "almost summary." An air of tragedy hung over Spain, he said. The firing squads were being kept terribly busy: in Madrid alone there were between 200 and 250 executions a day; in Barcelona 150; and in Sevilla, "a city that was never in the hands of the Reds," 80. He commented on the "impressive spirit of calm coolness" of the Spanish people in the face of these events. During his stay in Spain, he continued, while some 10,000 men already sentenced to death were in prison awaiting execution, only two ("soltanto due, dico due") appeals

for clemency were addressed to him by the families of the condemned men. He added that Franco granted them forthwith.[46]

The situation in Spain and the position of Spain in the summer
of 1939 can be epitomized in a few sentences. Franco's victory
had secured the political, economic, and social supremacy of the
traditional ruling elements in Spanish life—the landed aristocracy,
the financial and industrial oligarchy, the army, and the episcopacy.
Franco's regime was a military dictatorship which, by appropriat-
ing the symbols and the *mystique* of the Falange, had assumed the
aspect of a fascist state. Moreover, thanks to the indispensable assistance given Franco by Hitler and Mussolini during the Civil
War, strong ties now existed between Spain and the Axis powers
which had been given formal expression in treaties of friendship
and economic agreements. However, such was the geographic,
strategic, and economic relationship of Spain to Great Britain and
France that Spain's security and economic solvency necessitated a
rapprochement with the Western democracies, particularly Great
Britain. This imperative need, with roots in geography and history,
was accentuated by the loss and destruction suffered by Spain in
nearly three years of civil war and by the Republican sentiments
of a majority of Spaniards as well. Thus, while the Franco regime
was oriented toward the Axis powers and might be prone, in
optimum circumstances, to pursue an aggressive foreign policy in
concert with the fascist bloc, the vital interests of the Spanish nation imposed on the Spanish leadership the practical obligation not
to alienate completely the Western democracies and therefore, for
the time being at least, to remain at peace.

What with Germany and Italy in alliance and the independence
of Poland guaranteed by Great Britain and France, the crisis in
German-Polish relations in the summer of 1939 posed the threat of
a general war. On August 17, Mussolini informed Franco that war
between Germany and Poland appeared imminent and promised
to keep him advised of developments.[47] The Italian chargé d'affaires
in Spain, Count Guido Roncalli di Montorio, after conveying
Mussolini's message, reported that Franco had been visibly moved

by the information.[48] On August 21, the Caudillo apprised the
Duce of his readiness to take the initiative "in calling the attention of Europe to the absurdity of a terrible conflict, the consequences of which would be disproportionate to the causes which
had given rise to it." [49] Two days later, on August 23, Berlin and
Moscow signed a pact of nonaggression and friendship. It was
the occasion of much soul-searching in Madrid, as well as elsewhere.[50] The Spaniards—as Mussolini later explained to Hitler—
with their hatred of Bolshevism, "with their passionate and fanatical
logic," did not understand "the tactical necessities of politics." [51]
Be that as it may, the German-Russian agreement served to buttress Spain's determination to avoid involvement in the impending conflict.

At 5:25 A.M. on September 1, 1939, forward units of the
Wehrmacht crossed the Polish frontier. Unlike Berlin, Rome did
not want war now. [52] Having depleted its reserve stocks of military equipment and raw materials during the Ethiopian and Spanish
campaigns, Italy, in the opinion of its experts, would not be able
to engage in a major war before 1943.[53] Thus, Mussolini, even
with the Germans and Poles locked in battle, persisted in his efforts to arrange an international conference, on the Munich pattern, to settle the questions of Danzig and the Polish Corridor.[54]
The Italian formula called for an immediate armistice—the troops
remaining in the positions they presently occupied—and the summoning of a conference within two or three days.[55] However,
London, supported by Paris, insisted, as a fundamental condition
for the summoning of a conference, that the German forces be
withdrawn behind the German frontier.[56] To this the German
government would not agree.[57] On September 3, 1939, Great
Britain (at 11:00 A.M.) and France (at 5:00 P.M.) declared war
against Germany. Mussolini continued to entertain the notion that
the actual fighting could be limited to Poland and that his would
be the role of mediator.[58] In a telegram dated Burgos, September 3,
1939, Franco informed Mussolini of his desire to cooperate with
the Duce in seeking to restrict hostilities.[59] That same day the

Generalissimo, "with the authority given . . . [him] through having suffered for three years the weight of a war for the liberation
of . . . [his] country," addressed an appeal to the governments
concerned to do all in their power "to localize the actual conflict." [60] The efforts of both Duce and Caudillo proved unavailing.
The war was to continue and to spread, ultimately engulfing most
of the world. It is of interest that, while Italy assumed the status
of a "nonbelligerent" (September 1, 1939), a heretofore unde-
scribed twilight zone of neutrality that proclaimed Italy a non-
fighting ally of the Reich, Spain, adhering to traditional formulae,
announced that it was strictly neutral (September 4, 1939).

Spanish neutrality was attenuated, however, by the influence
of the Falange on the government, the pro-Axis orientation of the
press, the important economic agreements which existed between
Spain and Germany, and the extremely cordial relations of Madrid
with Rome and Berlin. The Generalissimo, as Caudillo, was the
titular leader of the Falange and, in the final analysis, the arbiter of
its role in Spanish life. But it was his brother-in-law, "*El Cuña-
disimo,*" Ramón Serrano Suñer, who, as head of the Junta Política
of the Falange, enjoyed practical management of Spain's only legal
political party. Moreover, as minister of the interior, he controlled
the police and the press. Thus he occupied a position of considerable power and influence in the new Spain. Unlike many Spaniards
who had been prominent in the *alzamiento*, he was a convinced
fascist and a vociferous advocate of the Axis cause in Spain. Count
Ciano observed that with Serrano Suñer "it is always feeling that
dominates him: he hates and loves impetuously." [61] Serrano Suñer,
according to Ciano, hated France and, to a lesser extent, England.[62]
While he was convinced that Spain needed peace for the immediate
future, Spain, ultimately, would have to settle accounts with
France and England.[63] "Spain will be at the side of the Axis because she will be guided by feeling and by reason. A neutral Spain
would, in any event, be destined to a future of poverty and
humiliation." [64]

Thomas J. Hamilton in his book on the Franco regime, *Ap-*

peasement's Child, described Serrano Suñer as the Spanish Laval, and their respective roles vis-à-vis Nazi Germany would seem to justify the analogy.[65] It was undoubtedly Serrano Suñer's influence in the government and vast power over the press which caused Sir Samuel Hoare, the British ambassador in Madrid, to write to Winston Churchill on June 27, 1940: "I try to keep an appearance of calm but it is not always easy in face of a completely Germanised press and many Germanised departments of State." [66]

In the early months of the war, however, the Minister of the Interior's pro-Axis activities were somewhat counterbalanced by the pro-British sentiments of Colonel Juan Beigbeder who, until he was succeeded by Serrano Suñer on October 17, 1940, served as Spain's minister of foreign affairs. It was Colonel Beigbeder who remarked to British Ambassador Hoare in June, 1940, when Allied fortunes were at their nadir: "The British bull has not yet come into the arena. Will it fight? And if so, how will it fight? No one can say that it is dead until the *corrida* is over." [67]

Sir Samuel Hoare was to write: "That I was lucky to begin my official work with this sympathetic and attractive friend was soon very evident. How fortunate, I did not fully understand until he was ousted from his post by Serrano Suñer." [68]

It behooved London and Paris, of course, to encourage the Spaniards to remain out of the war. This they could do by making various conciliatory gestures toward Madrid, by taking into account the commercial needs of Spain in the enforcement of the Anglo-French naval blockade of Germany, and, above all, by the swift reestablishment of traditional economic and financial relations with Spain.

As early as the week of February 18–26, 1939, Paris and Burgos had negotiated an agreement (the Bérard-Jordana agreement) by the terms of which France accorded the Franco regime *de jure* recognition and promised to return to Spain gold, works of art, ships, and military equipment which the Spanish Republicans had deposited in France or had taken there after the fall of Catalonia.[69] Paris and Burgos also agreed to cooperate in Morocco to prevent activities in their respective zones detrimental to the security of either government.[70]

With the outbreak of war in September, 1939, the British and Spanish governments exchanged notes which amounted to an informal war trade agreement.[71] In effect, Spain accepted British control measures while Great Britain permitted Spanish imports to pass through the blockade.[72] London was confronted with the delicate task of determining the point beyond which Spanish imports no longer served only to insure the viability of the Spanish economy and continued neutrality, but made possible the accumulation of reserve stocks or the transshipment of surpluses to the Axis powers. That in such circumstances there would be quibbling, bickering, and worse between London and Madrid was inevitable.[73] Yet, by and large, Great Britain and France (and, after the fall of France, Great Britain and the United States) played this game of "just so much" with skill and success.

Meanwhile, on January 18, 1940, France and Spain concluded a rather extensive trade agreement that, normalizing economic relations between the two neighbors, complemented the earlier Bérard-Jordana agreement.[74] However, it was to Great Britain, even more than to France, that Spain had to look for the economic and financial asssistance that would permit a rapid recovery from the ravages of three years of civil war. On March 18, 1940, London and Madrid entered into an agreement by the terms of which an adjustment was made with respect to old debts, England loaned Spain a sum of £2,000,000 for reconstruction purposes, and Spain promised not to reexport goods obtained in the sterling area.[75]

The refashioning and strengthening of the economic bonds between Spain and the Western democracies notwithstanding, the Franco government remained the steadfast friend of the Axis powers. On several occasions Madrid assured Berlin "of its great desire, despite the war, to carry into effect as much as it is possible the economic collaboration envisaged prior to the outbreak of war" and repeatedly urged, despite the difficulties of efficient transit imposed by the war, negotiations to that end.[76] In Madrid, on December 22, 1939, Spanish and German representatives signed a protocol that reaffirmed the basic principles which underlay Spanish-German economic relations, these having been embodied in previous economic agreements and in the treaty of friendship of March 31, 1939.[77]

In the spring of 1940 the volume of Spanish imports of gasoline, fuel oil, and lubricants increased considerably. There is evidence to suggest that the Franco government, beyond accumulating reserve stocks of its own against any eventuality, was clandestinely supplying "nonbelligerent" Italy with oil.[78]

In the months preceding the fall of France (June, 1940) the effort of "neutral" Spain, in collaboration with "nonbelligerent" Italy, to undermine the influence of the United States in Latin America and to foster an attitude of benevolent neutrality among the Hispanic American nations, particularly in Argentina, was not entirely unsuccessful. At any rate, the Spanish effort in this regard elicited the gratitude of the German government.[79] A more flagrant act of unneutrality was Spain's concern to keep the Germans regularly supplied with information gathered by Spanish diplomatic representatives abroad. In a cipher letter dated Madrid, October 19, 1939, German Ambassador Stohrer wrote to his government:

1. As has been indicated in my reports, the Foreign Minister [Colonel Beigbeder, perhaps the most Anglophile of Franco's Ministers!] and the Under State Secretary [J. Peche y Cabeza de Vaca] provide me regularly with information found in the telegraphic and written reports from the Spanish diplomatic missions abroad.

It might be possible to make even better use of this cooperation if I were kept informed of any specific questions on which we want to get information, in so far as they concern matters which presumably would come to the attention of the Spanish diplomatic representatives abroad and particularly in the enemy countries.

2. To strengthen security, I shall henceforth refer to information supplied to me by the Minister or the Under State Secretary, by: "Wilhelm reports" or "August reports."

Please acknowledge receipt of this message by telegraph. [80]

The Führer, as he observed in a letter to the Duce dated Berlin, March 8, 1940, had no reason to be displeased with the Caudillo.[81]

Thus, the position of Spain in the period of the "sitzkrieg" was one of neutrality, but a technical neutrality at best, made necessary by Spain's need for peace and the economic and financial assistance of the Western democracies. The sympathies of Spanish official-dom, particularly among Falange stalwarts, were openly pro-German. The Spaniards, moreover, violated both the spirit and letter of neutrality by giving what assistance they could, material and moral, to Germany. When, in the spring of 1940, the "sitz-krieg" was transformed into the blitzkrieg the problems which confronted the Caudillo and the Duce were basically similar. These were: to determine whether the Germans or the Anglo-French would prevail; to determine, in the light of the above, whether the war would be of brief duration or long and costly; and to deter-mine, in the expectation of a quick German victory, if and when to enter the fray.

The swiftness and magnitude of the German victories in Nor-way, Holland, Belgium, and France presaged an early end to the war. What doubts the Latin dictators might have harbored con-cerning the ultimate triumph of their Teutonic colleague were re-solved. For Mussolini the question was no longer whether but when to enter the lists. Even this matter was quickly settled in his mind. On May 13, 1940, with the German breakthrough in the Ardennes, Mussolini said to Ciano: "Some months ago I said that the Allies had lost the victory. Today I tell you that they have lost the war. We Italians are already sufficiently dishonored. Any delay is in-conceivable. We have no time to lose. Within a month I shall de-clare war." [82]

Franco saw matters in the same light. On August 15, 1940, the Caudillo wrote to the Duce:

Since the beginning of the present conflict, it has been our inten-tion to make the greatest efforts in our preparations, in order to enter the foreign war at a favorable opportunity in proportion to the means at our disposal, since the lack of the most vital provisions and the interruption of communications with Italy and Germany hindered every operation at the moment.

The rapid and devastating victories in Flanders altered the situation; the defeat of France liberated our frontiers, lessening the grave tension which we along with our Moroccans have been bearing since the Civil War.

From this moment, our horizon became brighter, our operation became possible and could become very effective, once the difficulties of provisioning have been removed.[83]

However, while the positions of the Duce and the Caudillo with respect to the war were essentially analogous, their respective situations were not. Italy was a "great power." Spain was not. Italy was bound to Germany in a formal military alliance. Spain was not. Italy had not been a battleground since 1918. Spain lay in ruins. The fascist regime had long been consolidated in Italy and Mussolini was its undisputed chief. Under a black mantle of utter exhaustion, bitterness, hatred, and political divisions ran deep in Spain. An adventure at this time could give fresh meaning to the old Spanish saying: *el vencido vencido y el vencedor perdido*. Thus when Italy entered the war on June 10, 1940, Franco saw fit, two days later, only to occupy the position of "nonbelligerency" abandoned by Mussolini.

But events marched quickly in the summer of 1940. It was a time of decision. Franco thought to grow teeth in the jaw of "nonbelligerency"; small, soft teeth, to be sure. On June 14, his troops occupied Tangier, ostensibly in the name of the Sultan of Morocco and for the purpose of preserving order now that Italy's entry into the war had created an awkward situation concerning international control of the city that, by the terms of the Tangier Statute (1928), was shared by Great Britain, France, Italy, and Spain. The Spanish press, however, seized the occasion to chant a *Te Deum* to the new Spain, the occupation of Tangier being made to appear a heavy defeat for the Western allies.[84] Less than a fortnight later, on June 27, German troops arrived at the Pyrenees. German soldiers, in uniform, crossed the frontier and fraternized with the Spaniards in San Sebastián and Bilbao and in the towns and villages of Navarra.[85] With France vanquished and England driven from the continent the triumph of German arms appeared complete. Before the month was out the Spanish government informed the German government that it was ready, under certain conditions, to enter the war at the side of Germany and Italy.[86] Hitler began to give serious thought to "Operation Isabella-Felix," the cover name for the proposed assault on Gibraltar by German and Spanish forces.[87]

Spanish ambitions went beyond the irredentism evoked by Gibraltar. They encompassed a good share of French North Africa. In his letter to Mussolini of August 15, 1940, Franco declared his readiness, "under certain conditions," to enter "the struggle against the common enemies." [88] He also sought to win Italian support for his claims to territories "whose present administration is a consequence of that Franco-English policy of domination and exploitation, of which Italy also bears so many scars." [89]

Mussolini replied on August 25, expressing his conviction that "the Spain of the Falange Revolution" would inevitably join the Axis powers in the common struggle. The Duce, avoiding any definite commitment regarding Spanish aspirations, went on to observe that moral justification of Spain's claims must arise from Spain's participation in the war. "There is no doubt," he declared, "that after France, Great Britain will be defeated; the British regime exists only on one single element: the lie." Then, as the senior triumvir, Mussolini advised Franco that "a victorious revolution must set itself extreme goals of an international type, such goals, therefore, as can, at a given moment, require the complete attention and the total effort of a people." [90]

Concerning North Africa, there was more of an identity of purpose than a community of interest between the Latin dictators. After all, with France and Great Britain eliminated from the region, Italy and Spain would confront each other as rival claimants to the spoils of empire. However, before jackals eat the lion dines. Ultimately, the matter rested with Berlin.

The Germans fully appreciated that the Axis position in south-eastern Europe, the Near East, and North Africa depended on Axis control of the Mediterranean.[91] Axis supremacy in the Mediterranean would guarantee access to vast sources of raw materials. Moreover, it would provide "new and strategically favorable bases" for attacks against the British Empire.[92] At a conference in Berlin on September 6, 1940, attended by the Führer, Grand Admiral Erich Raeder, commander in chief of the German navy, and General Alfred Jodl, it was decided that preparations for "Operation Isabella-Felix" should begin immediately. The possibility of American intervention in the war rendered time of the essence. Hitler emphasized that the conquest of Gibraltar "should not be considered of secondary importance, but *as one of the main blows against Britain.*" [93]

With Franco ready, "under certain conditions," to enter the "common struggle" and Hitler convinced that the Mediterranean was an extremely important theater of war, it would appear that Spain's entry into the war and joint Hispano-German action against Gibraltar were imminent, awaiting only clarification of and agreement on the "certain conditions" alluded to by the Caudillo. In German Ambassador Stohrer's report of August 8, 1940, these conditions were categorized as follows: first, satisfaction of Spain's territorial demands, including all of French Morocco and "that part of Algeria colonized and predominantly inhabited by Spaniards (Oran)"; second, German military support; and, third, German economic assistance, including large amounts of gasoline and grain.[94]

In mid-September Serrano Suñer traveled to Berlin as the special envoy of the Caudillo. On September 17 the Falangist leader conferred for an hour with Hitler and Ribbentrop.[95] Serrano Suñer said that he had come to Berlin to clarify the conditions under which Spain was ready to join Germany in war. "Whenever Spain's supply of foodstuffs and war material was secure she could immediately enter the war." [96] Hitler replied by observing that Germany appreciated Spain's sympathetic stand during the First

World War and that "this feeling of appreciation had been the most profound cause for the German conduct during the Civil War." Hitler went on to say that in the present conflict England had been definitely driven from the Continent and that Spain need have no fears of English landings. He added that "the attack on Gibraltar should be by *Stukas* and special troops, in the manner of the attack on Fort Eben Emaël, and not by reliance on artillery." Germany would supply the necessary specialists and special weapons. Turning to Spanish territorial ambitions, the Führer noted that the African problem was twofold, involving, first, the winning of the war and, second, "the future configuration of the relationships in Europe and Africa." The Führer went on to elucidate this rather cryptic phrase by pointing up Germany's economic and strategic interests in Africa.[97]

It was evident that sentimentalized aspirations which harked back to the days of Spanish greatness counted for little in the hard game of *Machtpolitik*. Serrano Suñer left Berlin (for Rome) without fixing a date for Spain's entry into the war.

It must have been a trying time for Franco. The *Luftwaffe* was subjecting London and the entire southeastern corner of England to heavy attacks. It was still September. From day to day the news could be expected that German forces had effected a crossing of the Channel and were pushing inland, that London was encircled, that the swastika flew over Buckingham Palace. If events marched with the swiftness of earlier campaigns, then the Generalissimo would have waited until it was too late to satisfy Spanish aspirations. But what if Spain, inviting the Germans to cross the Pyrenees, launched an attack on Gibraltar and the expected invasion of the British Isles did not materialize? The British remained capable of inflicting terrible blows on Spain. In a long, exhaustive struggle what could Spain become but the abject vassal of the Nazi Reich? The next few weeks would tell the story. For by the middle of October the invasion of England would have been either consummated or postponed to a more seasonable occasion. Meanwhile, it behooved Franco to maintain a warlike pose but without committing himself to action.

On September 22, 1940, Franco wrote to Hitler, thanking him for the cordial reception given his envoy.[98] The Caudillo went on to aver that his views concerning the problems confronting Spain and the part Spain was to play in the war "matched" those of the Führer, except for "small details." Among these "small details" was Ribbentrop's suggestion to Serrano Suñer that Spain permit Germany to establish permanent bases in Morocco. These would be, Franco declared, "unnecessary in peacetime, and superfluous in wartime" inasmuch as Spain would be firmly bound to Germany in the future. Other "small details" constituted a veritable catalogue of Spanish woes. Franco observed that even with the English fleet driven from the Mediterranean "not all questions of the provisioning of Spain will be solved thereby since there are many products and raw materials which Spain lacks, and which are not to be found in the Mediterranean basin." He also expressed fear that, without German assistance, it would be difficult for Spain to prevent the English from seizing the Canary Islands. Spanish action in the western Mediterranean, Franco continued, could be successful only to the extent that English naval strength in the Mediterranean had been seriously impaired, a contingency that rested on Italian success in Egypt. Having depicted Spain's lamentable limitations, Franco concluded by reaffirming his loyalty to Hitler and the Axis cause, saying, "I hope, in defense of this cause, to be able to renew the old bonds of comradeship between our armies." [99]

On September 28, 1940, the Italian foreign minister, Count Ciano, was in Berlin where he conferred with Hitler and Ribbentrop.[100] The Führer expressed a desire to meet with the Duce to discuss the situation in general and the Spanish question in particular. He considered such a meeting to be important because "far-reaching decisions" had to be made. The Führer revealed to Ciano that the Spaniards had recently proposed to him that: one, Germany deliver to Spain between 400,000 and 700,000 tons of grain

for the coming year; two, Germany supply Spain with all necessary fuel; three, Germany supply the Spanish army with the equipment it lacked; four, Germany furnish aircraft and artillery as
well as specialists and special weapons for the conquest of Gibraltar; and, five, Germany agree to Spanish acquisition of all of
Morocco, Oran, and territory beyond Río de Oro. "Spain is to
promise to Germany, in return, her friendship." Such a sacrifice
on the part of Germany, Hitler declared, could not be made only
to secure the "good graces" of the Spaniards. Between allies there
should be reciprocity, Hitler observed, but in this there was no
reciprocity. If the French learned that they were to lose Morocco,
Hitler continued, they would probably be driven into the arms
of the English. At any rate, he preferred to have the French remain in Morocco and defend it against the English rather than give
it to the Spaniards and entrust them with the task. The Führer
then mentioned that Franco had suggested a personal meeting with
him. Before agreeing, he would like to discuss matters with the
Duce. Hitler went on to say that Germany and Italy had done
much for Spain in 1936, despite the fact that Germany was in the
midst of rearming and Italy had just emerged from the Ethiopian
War. "Without the help of both the countries there would today be
no Franco." Germany had risked much in Spain and had expended
considerable blood and treasure. Ciano, in turn, declared that at
the beginning of the Spanish conflict Franco had asked Italy for
12 airplanes with which to win the war "in a few days." Ciano
continued: "These 12 airplanes became more than one thousand
airplanes, 6 thousand dead, and 14 billion lire." The German and
the Italian agreed that with the Spaniard it was necessary to come
to a definite understanding.[101]

Meanwhile, Serrano Suñer had gone from Berlin to Rome where,
on October 1, 1940, he conferred with Mussolini and Ciano.[102]
He repeated to the Duce what he had said to the Führer. Mussolini
informed him that Italy, "in view of the scanty grain harvest,"
could not help provision Spain for the present. However, "a con-
centration of air strength can be assured here and now." Mus-

solini expressed his confidence that Spain would make its contribution to the victory of the Axis. He promised to give further thought to the practical problems attendant on the matter.[103]

On October 4, Hitler and Mussolini, accompanied by Ribbentrop and Ciano, met at the Brenner.[104] Hitler declared that to acquiesce in Spanish territorial demands would be to sacrifice legitimate German aspirations in Morocco. Furthermore, it could well result in driving French Africa into the Free French camp, a serious matter in that it would confront the Axis with an extension of the zone of military operations. The Spanish claim to Gibraltar was one thing, Spanish acquisition of Morocco quite another. Mussolini expressed agreement with Hitler's views and suggested that Spain be informed that they (Hitler and Mussolini) supported her claim to Gibraltar but, while they agreed in principle to a "territorial alteration" in Morocco, they believed that this could not be precisely defined until the war had ended. Hitler approved of Mussolini's proposals.[105]

The following day, October 5, Ciano informed Serrano Suñer of the conclusions reached at the Brenner meeting in so far as they concerned Spain.[106] Ciano noted in his diary that the Spaniard was "only half satisfied." And he added: "Why hadn't he [Serrano Suñer] yet seen that for a long time the Germans have had an eye on Morocco?" [107]

In the Führer's parlor car at the railroad station in Hendaye, a French town on the Spanish border, Hitler and Franco met for the first time. The date was October 23, 1940. Thus it was late in the season for warlike operations in the English Channel. This was a salient fact. Franco opened the conversation by expressing his satisfaction at meeting Hitler and by giving him thanks for all that Germany had done for Spain. "Spain would gladly fight at Germany's side" in this war but, for the present, the weight of Spain's great needs prevented it. Her food situation, for example, was truly desperate. Yet, Spain was spiritually allied with the Axis powers and had recently assumed a position of nonbelligerency, as Italy had done the previous autumn. The Führer re-

plied that he was glad to see Franco in person after having been
with him so often in spirit during the Spanish Civil War. Turning
to the present situation, the Führer declared that England, "with
the first break in the weather," was doomed. He went on to speak
of the menace of the Free French movement in Africa. In view
of this, he observed, it was necessary to strengthen the fascist
tendency in France, represented by Marshal Henri Pétain and
Pierre Laval, and to bring France to take a definite stand against
England. The French were divided and hesitant because they did
not know what the peace would bring. Yesterday he had told
Laval that either France or England would have to pay for the
war—England if France joined in the effort to bring down the
British Empire, France if a negotiated peace were made with England. Tomorrow he would speak with Pétain in these same terms.
It was necessary, the Führer continued, to establish a broad front
against the British. "In setting up this front, the Spanish desires
and the French hopes were obstacles in the path." England's determination to fight on and General Charles de Gaulle's existence
rendered impossible a final territorial settlement at this time.[108]

The conference produced no tangible result. Germany's promises to Spain remained vague, Spain's entry into the war uncertain.[109]

On October 28, 1940, five days after Hitler met Franco at
Hendaye, the Duce hurled his legions into Greece. Mussolini had
not informed Hitler of his decision to make war on the Greeks.
He wanted to confront Hitler with a *fait accompli* as Hitler had
done him on a number of occasions. However, within a fortnight
the Greeks had not only checked the Italian advance, they had
themselves, in some sectors, assumed the offensive.[110] Thus, with
the threat of an invasion rapidly receding,[111] and with the Italians
in retreat in Greece and bogged down in Egypt, fortune began to
smile, however faintly, on a hard-pressed England.

If the cautious Caudillo had been reluctant to submit his regime
to the test of war before, he was even less prone to embark on an
adventure now. But Hitler saw in the discomfiture of his Italian

ally in the eastern Mediterranean a further reason to begin operations in the western Mediterranean.[112] The Germans increased their
pressure on the Spaniards. At the end of October, 1940, they asked
the Spaniards for permission to station German tankers "in out-
of-the-way bays" of the Spanish coast from which German de-
stroyers could be refueled, a practice that Madrid already coun-
tenanced in regard to German submarines.[113] Early in December,
1940, the Spanish government gave its approval but requested
that the Germans exercise the "greatest caution." [114] In the past
such small, clandestine concessions had enabled the Spaniards to
retain German good will without themselves being drawn into
the war. However, Hitler was now determined to force Franco's
hand. There must be an end to equivocation; either Franco would
openly join the Axis in war and accept its risks or he would remain
out of the fray and away from the conference table when peace
came. The Führer sent his chief of intelligence, Admiral Wilhelm
Canaris, to Madrid.

Canaris met with Franco on December 7.[115] He was brief and
direct. The Führer believed that the time had come to begin operations against Gibraltar. In order to be in position to attack by the
end of January, German troops would have to enter Spain on
January 10. The Führer considered this to be the most favorable
time because the troops now available for the operation were
"directly thereafter" to be employed in other tasks. German economic aid to Spain would begin with the movement of German
troops into the country. But the staccato pronouncements of the
German did not sway the Spaniard. It would be impossible for
Spain to enter the war on the suggested date. Many factors prevented it—lack of foodstuffs, particularly grain, lack of fuel, lack
of transport facilities, incomplete military preparations, inadequate
defenses in the Canary Island, the striking power of the English
fleet in the Mediterranean, and so forth. Canaris asked Franco
whether he was prepared, then and there, "to set a different later
date." Franco replied that he was not because solution of Spain's
problems rested only in part on Spain herself. The Caudillo de-

clared that he was doing all in his power to speed Spain's preparations. Much had been done, but much remained to be done. He
concluded by asking Canaris to convey his "most cordial greetings"
to the Führer.[116]

The Teutonic warlord had imperiously summoned his vassal to
war, but nothing had come of it save, perhaps, the sure knowledge
of the little Galician's obstinacy. On February 6, 1941, an angry
Hitler wrote to Franco.[117] He began by stating that he sought to
clarify a situation that was important not only to Germany and
Italy but that *could have been of decisive importance to Spain.*[118]
The German, Italian, and Spanish regimes, Hitler noted, had common interests and would share a common fate. On the other hand,
Spain would be forever apart from and the victim of the Anglo-
Saxon world. "It is my heartfelt conviction that the battle which
Germany and Italy are now fighting out is thus determining the
future destiny of Spain. Only in the case of our victory will the
present regime continue to exist. Should Germany and Italy lose
this war, however, then any future for a really national and independent Spain would be impossible." The fact of the matter, Hitler
said bluntly, was that Franco, conjuring up first one explanation
and then another, had refused to join the Axis in war. Germany
had been ready to help Spain solve the problems which beset her,
contingent, of course, on Spain's entry into the war. *"If it should
later be asserted that Spain could not enter the war because she
received no supplies, that would not be true!"*[119] Hitler regretted
"most profoundly" Franco's refusal to act because the conquest
of Gibraltar and domination of the Straits "would have changed
the Mediterranean situation in one stroke," bringing relief to Italy
and final victory that much nearer. The Führer asserted that Spain
would have received more supplies from Germany than she had
received from abroad since January 10. He declared that Spain's
territorial ambitions would have been satisfied in a measure com-
patible with "an acceptable new arrangement of the African co-
lonial possession for Europe and its countries." Hitler then observed that "the timing of a military operation must be determined

by the power that will have to carry the main burden of the struggle." He concluded by saying that England was doomed and that the German Army, "the mightiest military machine in the world," stood ready for any task that might be given it.[120]

Before writing to Franco on February 6, Hitler had urged Mussolini to meet with the Spanish leader and urge him to take the Gibraltar road. This had been at a meeting of the senior triumvirs at Berghof on January 19.[121] However, it was not until February 12 that Mussolini and Franco met at Bordighera, a town on the Ligurian Riviera. (At Bordighera Franco took the same position with Mussolini that he had taken with Canaris.) [122]

Why had Hitler not waited until after the Bordighera conference to dispatch his bristling letter to the Caudillo? Did he lack faith in Mussolini's ability to persuade the hard-headed Galician? Then why had he suggested it? Perhaps an explanation of Hitler's contradictory actions is to be found in developments which had nothing to do with Spain. As early as July, 1940, Hitler and his chieftains had considered the threat to German security represented by Soviet Russia.[123] Following unsatisfactory discussions with Soviet Foreign Minister Vyacheslav Molotov in November, 1940, the Germans had made tentative plans for "Operation Barbarossa" (the cover name for the projected invasion of Russia).[124] The ensuing weeks had seen a hardening of the view that a forcible solution to the "eastern problem" was necessary. At a conference in Berghof extending through January 8 and 9, 1941, and attended by Hitler, Foreign Minister Ribbentrop, General Franz Halder, Rear Admiral Kurt Fricke, and others, it was concluded that:

Stalin must be regarded as a cold-blooded blackmailer; he would, if expedient, repudiate any written agreement at any time. Britain's aim for some time to come will be to set Russian strength in motion against us. If the U.S.A. and Russia should enter the war against Germany, the situation would become very complicated. Hence any possibility for such a threat to develop must be eliminated at the very beginning. If the Russian threat were nonexistent, we could wage war on Britain indefinitely. If Russia collapsed, Japan would be greatly relieved; this in turn would mean increased danger to the U.S.A.[125]

However, when Hitler met with Mussolini at Berghof on January 19 a final decision to invade the Soviet Union had not yet been reached. Where the next blow against England would be struck remained a fluid matter. Hence Hitler's request that Mussolini prod Franco in the direction of "Operation Isabella-Felix." The evidence suggests that it was in the period between January 19 and February 4 that Hitler definitely decided to launch the attack on Russia and set in motion plans to that end, abandoning for the time being the Spanish project.[126] Hence his letter to Franco of February 6.

In the light of the German decision to make war on Russia, the letter Franco sent Hitler on February 26 must be seen as anticlimactic.[127] Explanations of Spanish inaction interlaced with asseverations of Spanish loyalty to the Axis cause were no longer of great moment. Yet, despite the disappointment and resentment in Berlin,[128] the Germans continued to cultivate the friendship of the Spaniards. There were, of course, many excellent reasons why the Germans should strive to maintain amicable relations with the Spaniards. To begin with, if it were preferable to have Spain as an active ally as over against a "nonbelligerent" friend, it was at least as desirable to have Spain retain the status of "nonbelligerency" rather than revert to that of "strict neutrality." The Germans appreciated that Spanish faith in the invincibility of German arms served as surety in this matter, the economic blandishments of Great Britain notwithstanding. Thus, it behooved Berlin not to lose all by seeking to gain all. Germany had need of Spain as a source of raw materials, particularly tungsten and manganese, and of clandestine services, such as the refueling and provisioning of submarines. Furthermore, with Russia defeated, Germany would be able to turn her full strength against Great Britain. The war in the Mediterranean, North Africa, and the Atlantic would acquire added significance, particularly if the United States entered the conflict. In these circumstances, Spain's strategic importance would be greatly enhanced. From bases in Spain, Spanish Morocco, and the Canary Islands, German forces could safeguard the approaches to "Fortress Europa." In a word, with the defeat of Russia, "Operation Isabella-Felix" could conceivably become again a matter of supreme urgency.

Hitler had long been convinced of the strategic importance of the conquest of Gibraltar and domination of the Mediterranean. It will be recalled that in his letter to Franco of February 6, 1941, he had written that the conquest of Gibraltar and command of the Straits "would have changed the Mediterranean situation in one stroke." In a conversation with Italian Foreign Minister Ciano at Muenchenkirchen on April 20, 1941, Hitler spoke in the same tenor. He was harshly critical of the Generalissimo and said that if Spain had acted with greater loyalty toward the Axis powers the British by this time would have been driven from Gibraltar, and their position in the Mediterranean seriously weakened. He added that this had not come to pass and that it was unlikely that it would come to pass, "at least not in time to be of any use." [129]

It is evident that in the German view time had been of the essence with respect to "Operation Isabella-Felix." With the invasion of England postponed and the invasion of Russia still tentative, action against Gibraltar and in the western Mediterranean would have employed otherwise idle German forces in a strategically important enterprise. In a conversation with Ciano at the Brenner on June 2, 1941, Ribbentrop asserted that the main responsibility for the delay in Axis operations had to be attributed to Spain, declaring that in January–February, 1941, the conquest of Gibraltar "could easily have been carried out by the German forces prepared for the purpose." [130] He added that, nevertheless, the Axis powers should strive to insure the friendship of Spain.[131]

On June 3, 1941, Ciano wrote at length to Serrano Suñer. He said in part:

I am writing to you on my return from the conversation on the Brenner. I think that you will be happy to learn that Spain was discussed with lively interest both by us and by the Germans and that the Axis attributes fundamental importance to friendship with your country.

The events of the last weeks have had an important effect on the course of the war. The Balkans are now liberated from English influence. [Yugoslavia had been conquered and Greece finally crushed in April, 1941.] The British Navy has lost many of its bases and is caught in an ever tightening vice by the forces of the Axis. A day will come—and it is not far distant—when the entire Mediterranean will be liberated from the presence of the English fleet.

Can Nationalist and Falangist Spain remain indifferent and absent in the face of events of such great import for our life and our future as Mediterranean Powers? As a sincere and proved friend of Spain I do not think so.[132]

Ciano concluded by observing that he appreciated the reasons which had prevented Spain from taking an active part in the war up to now but expressed his conviction that the time had come for Spain to pursue a more audacious course.[133]

In a handwritten postscript to Ciano's letter, Mussolini said:

I confirm the above.

Spain must *at least* adhere to the Tripartite Pact [a military alliance between Germany, Italy, and Japan signed September 26, 1940] and that before other adhesions take place. By subscribing to the Tripartite Pact, Spain comes once more into line as far as tomorrow's European settlement is concerned.

I take the occasion to remember myself to you and to add my most cordial expressions of friendship.[134]

Yet, while the Axis leaders continued to cultivate close ties with the Spaniards in the spring of 1941, no real effort was made to induce Franco to engage in joint military operations in the western Mediterranean. It is significant that it was not the Germans but the Italians who, hard-pressed in the Mediterranean and North Africa and without positive information concerning the imminent German invasion of Russia, evinced the greater interest in this matter. The German attitude toward Spanish participation in the war at this time was reflected in the remarks Ribbentrop made to Ciano in Venice on June 15, 1941, apropos the latter's letter to Serrano Suñer and the Spaniard's reply. Rippentrop said that such a gesture was useful in that it served to maintain contact with

Spain. However, the German was skeptical as to Spanish intentions of joining the Axis powers in war, observing that the Spanish position was exactly what it had been six months before. Ribbentrop added that it would be necessary to permit the Spaniards "full liberty of action and not to push them until the general situation in Europe has become clearer." [135] With the German invasion of the Soviet Union but a week off, an eruption in the western Mediterranean would have proved a most untoward development. [136]

Just as the announcement of the Reich-Soviet rapprochement of August 23, 1939, had been the occasion for considerable soul-searching and dismay in Madrid, so the news of the German invasion of the Soviet Union on June 22, 1941, strengthened the ideological bond between Falangist Spain and Nazi Germany. Probably at no time since the end of the Civil War was pro-German sentiment more evident in Spain than in the summer of 1941. [137]

Within a few days of the German attack on the Soviet Union, the Spanish government organized a division of "volunteers" for service on the Russian front. This "Blue Division," as it came to be called because of the dark blue shirts worn by the "volunteers," originally comprised some 20,000 men. However, it received replacements from Spain from time to time so that some 47,000 men in all passed through its muster rolls. Its first commander was General Muñoz Grande. The "Blue Division," upon its arrival in Germany in July, 1941, was reorganized along the lines of a German infantry division and designated the 250th Spanish Infantry Division. The Spaniards first saw action in the Novgorod-Teremets sector in October, 1941. In addition to the "Blue Division," Madrid dispatched the "Salvador" air squadron (consisting of nine aircraft) to the Russian front. The Spaniards suffered heavy losses against the Russians, but small detachments of Spanish troops remained on the Russian front until February, 1945. [138]

Not only did Madrid dispatch "volunteers" to fight with the Nazis on the Russian front, it agreed, in August, 1941, to send 100,000 workers to the Reich. [139] Yet, while the German invasion

of the Soviet Union furnished Franco with the opportunity to slip
into the war through the rear door, as it were, the maneuver earned
him but slight gratitude in Berlin. The contribution of the "Blue
Division" to the Axis cause could not be equated with the successful realization of "Operation Isabella-Felix." In a conversation with
Mussolini in the evening of August 25, 1941, at the Führer's Headquarters, Hitler spoke in bitter terms of Spain and declared that
that nation had proved a real disappointment to him. To which
Mussolini added that it would be useless to press Spain to intervene for the time being. The "Spanish card" could best be played
at a later time.[140]

In November, 1941, in Berlin, the Spanish foreign minister,
Serrano Suñer, conferred first with Ribbentrop and then with
Hitler. Count Ciano was present at both conferences. Ciano noted
that:

No pressure was applied for Spanish intervention. Hitler complained
at not having been able to attack Gibraltar last winter, and that gave
Serrano the cue to tell of all the difficulties with which his Government
is struggling, beset as it is by monarchists, seditious militarists and by
dormant Reds. He ended by saying that Spain will intervene because
she cannot do otherwise, but that the work of moral and material
preparation is very far from being complete.[141]

Thus, Spain's intervention in the war remained as doubtful and
remote five months after as it had been six months before the outbreak of German-Russian hostilities.[142] The Axis powers were no
longer anxious to draw Spain into the conflict. Indeed, until the
campaign in Russia was concluded, a "nonbelligerent" Spain could
better serve the Axis cause than an impoverished, divided, weak
Spain at war. Meanwhile, against the time when the "Spanish card"
could be played, the Axis leaders would continue to maintain close
relations with Franco. However, the course of the war in Russia
rendered that eventuality increasingly improbable and finally impossible.

In the perspective of subsequent developments it can be seen
that after January, 1941, the position of Spain vis-à-vis the war

had changed significantly. In the summer and autumn of 1940 Spanish intentions had been of crucial importance to both Berlin and London. After January and, particularly, after June, 1941, Germany was preoccupied with the "eastern problem." While Germany and Italy continued to cultivate the friendship of Spain both for reasons of immediate advantage and against the time when Spain might serve as a *point d'appui* for military operations in the western Mediterranean, the center of gravity of the war had shifted from the Atlantic and the Mediterranean to the eastern front. Thus, the strategic importance of Spain had been considerably diminished. With the Allied landings in North Africa in November, 1942, and, particularly, with the collapse of Fascist Italy in 1943, Spain lapsed back into the obscurity from which the events of the Civil War and the first years of the Second World War had lifted her. Spain ceased to be a menace of any kind. Indeed, she increasingly accommodated herself to the demands and purposes of the Anglo-Saxon powers.

Madrid's refusal to permit the German forces to enter Spain on January 10, 1941, was a decision of far-reaching significance. The factors which had militated against the realization of "Operation Isabella-Felix" were many. The physical exhaustion of the country, potential political dissidence, the retaliatory power of the English fleet, Spanish dependence on British economic and financial assistance, the failure of the Germans to invade England, the Italian military debacle, the conflict of interests in Morocco, Spanish *dignidad*, and the sense of caution of the Caudillo all were important. However, at least as important as any of these was the very nature of Franco Spain. The revolt of the generals in July, 1936, had brought the Germans and Italians into Spain. In the furnace of war a bond had been forged between the fascist powers and Burgos. With Franco's victory in March, 1939, Spain emerged in the trappings of a fascist state. But the "New Spain" was in fact the old Spain—a backward, agricultural country, with masses of illiterate peasants, little industry, and a small, insignificant middle class, a semi-feudal land ruled by grandees, bishops, and generals. The

complex economic and psychological situation out of which had
come Italian fascism and, even more so, German nazism, did not
pertain to Spain and to Spanish falangism. Unlike German and
Italian imperialism which sprang from compelling economic, psychological, and demographic circumstances, Spanish imperialism
was atavistic and romantic. Franco's main concern was not to expand in Africa—in itself an excellent thing, to be sure—but to remain in power. His fascist associations proved momentarily be-
guiling. Yet, in a fundamental sense, he did not look outward on a
vast, complex, modern world which he might hope to dominate
and influence but inward on a small, stagnant land that he would
not have change.

It is this, as much as anything, that explains the course followed
by Franco Spain in the Second World War and after—from refueling German submarines to interning Italian ships, from sending
a "Blue Division" to fight in Russia to abandoning "nonbelligerency" and returning to neutrality (October 3, 1943), from crusader
against American "materialism" to American ally in the Cold War.
Franco Spain is not a new political expression in however perverse
a sense. Like that of Miguel Primo de Rivera before it, the more
ruthless regime of Francisco Franco is but the rule of the cacique
writ large.

X
Conclusions

THE Second Spanish Republic endured for eight years, years marked by high idealism and progressive change as well as by disorders, strikes, and abortive uprisings culminating in thirty-two months of bitter internecine war. The strategic position and mineral wealth of Spain impinged importantly on the European power-struggle and rendered significant beyond the Pyrenees the thrust and direction of Spanish politics. Yet, while evidence exists of the intrigues and machinations of foreign powers in Spain prior to July, 1936, the military insurrection resulted from social tensions within Spain itself, specifically from the conflict between an ancient ruling class and a group of reformers who drew their principal support from middle-class liberalism, Basque and Catalan separatism, organized labor, and the distress of an impoverished, landless peasantry. On this essentially Spanish struggle there was imposed the imperialistic rivalry of the great powers, fought out on Spanish soil and, in the main, with Spanish blood.

Of the six major and two minor powers principally concerned with the war in Spain, namely, Great Britain, France, the United States, Germany, Italy, the Soviet Union, Portugal, and Mexico, four played primary and four secondary roles in the Spanish drama. Mexico extended to the Spanish Republic its full moral support. However, physical distance, scant industrial resources, and Mexico's reluctance to offend its northern neighbor by circumvention of the American arms embargo severely limited the material assistance which Mexico could give Spain. The democratic government of Lázaro Cárdenas was a staunch but weak friend of democratic Spain.

The Portugal of Dr. Antonio Salazar, on the other hand, was a fervent champion of the rebel cause in Spain. Geographical propinquity and a wanton disregard of international law permitted Lisbon to give valuable aid to the rebel generals, particularly during the critical first weeks of the Civil War. However, given the paucity of Portuguese resources, Lisbon's assistance to Franco was, in the main, adjunctive to that of the great fascist powers.

Physical distance, isolationist sentiment, and the lack of vitally important interests in the Peninsula kept the United States on the periphery of the Spanish struggle. However, the vast resources, the great power and prestige of the American Republic gave importance to its role, whether active or passive. It is beyond cavil that if Washington had displayed a nice regard for established practice with respect to a situation of civil war, the Madrid government would have found its position greatly improved. Many factors— from widespread isolationist sentiment through the powerful pressure of conservative and Catholic opinion to concern with the effect of a Republican victory on United States holdings in Latin America —motivated Washington to depart from tradition and to impose first a "moral" and then a legal embargo on the shipment of arms to Spain. Not the least important of these was the desire in a world threatened by armed aggressors to draw close to the great European democracies and to this end to support British diplomacy in Spain.

Given France's contiguity with Spain, French military resources, the centuries-old concern of French diplomacy to insure the friendship and good will of the nation south of the Pyrenees and thus to forestall "encirclement" by hostile powers, and the fact that in July, 1936, the political regime in Paris and that in Madrid were inspired by similar ideals and purposes, it was entirely plausible that France would extend immediate assistance to the embattled Spanish Republic. This expectation was strengthened by the traditions and practices of European diplomacy as they pertained to a situation of civil war. Moreover, the ability of the Spanish government to purchase with gold war materials and supplies in French markets would have served to keep the matter within commercial channels,

enabling Paris to avoid overt political action. The initial impulse
of the French government was to accede to the request of Madrid
that it be permitted to purchase what it needed in French markets.
However, in less than a fortnight this impulse had been turned into
an initiative for the conclusion of a nonintervention agreement
among the powers principally concerned with the war in Spain.
The decision of the French government (July 25, 1936) not to
permit war materials to go to Spain was, perhaps, the most important single act in the history of the diplomacy of the Spanish Civil
War. For France, more than any other power, possessed the means
to influence decisively the course of events south of the Pyrenees.
Given the failure of the rebel generals' coup d'état, it was not improbable that the Madrid government, if it had been permitted to
purchase the necessary matériel in France, would have been able
to crush the rebellion within a few weeks or months. The factors
which had induced Paris to abandon the notion of succoring the
Spanish Republic and to initiate the policy of nonintervention were
many. Pacifist sentiment, fear of a general conflagration arising out
of the Spanish strife, the desire to win the friendship of Italy against
the possibility of German aggression, the hostility of French conservative and Catholic circles to the Frente Popular as well as to
the Front Populaire all were important. Perhaps of paramount importance in the fateful decision of the French government, however, was Paris' fervent desire to maintain the friendship and good
will of London which it saw as the *sine qua non* of French security.
There is sufficient evidence to indicate that it was British diplomatic pressure that coalesced into a final negative the various elements which impinged on the French decision of July 25, 1936.
In seeking not to alienate British opinion the French government
abandoned the thought of an independent policy toward Spain.
It was never seriously to reconsider it. In the months and years to
come the Quai d'Orsay, in matters relating to Spain, was, in effect,
an adjunct of No. 10 Downing Street.

If French interests demanded that a friendly regime exist beyond
the Pyrenees, German interests would better be served if the gov-

ernment in Madrid looked not to Paris but to Berlin. In Hitler's dream of a "Thousand Year Reich" the strategic position of Spain —bastion (through the Balearic Islands) on the sea routes of the western Mediterranean, bridge to Africa, and promontory (through the Canary Islands) into the Atlantic—was a matter of compelling importance. German intervention in the Spanish Civil War was prompted, primarily, by strategic considerations. Another important factor was the desire of Germany to win a position of economic preeminence in the Peninsula. This would serve a twofold purpose; firstly and immediately, to gain access to Spanish mineral resources to meet the needs of German rearmament, and secondly and ultimately, to make of Spain a fertile field for German business enterprise. German intervention was also motivated by ideological and political factors but these were, relatively, of minor importance. The German military effort in Spain was characterized by its swift development, its high quality (concerned in the main with air power and other technical aspects of modern warfare), and its decisive influence on the conduct and course of the war.

It can be doubted that Mussolini would have embarked on his Spanish adventure, or would have persisted in it, without, or bereft of, German support. As with Germany, so with Italy strategic considerations constituted the principal motivation for intervention in the Spanish struggle. However, while economic factors were less significant in Italian than in German intervention, ideological and political motives were probably stronger with the Italians than with the Germans. The Italian military effort in Spain was qualitatively inferior to but quantitatively greater than that of the Reich. As the war continued and the *Tercio* and the Moorish levies were decimated, Italian ground forces came to constitute the hard core of the rebel army. There is evidence to suggest that the fascist powers had been convinced that, with their assistance, General Franco would be able to achieve a swift victory. The stubborn resistance of the Republican forces (buttressed by Soviet assistance) and the consequent prolongation of the war led to a greater expenditure of blood and treasure by the fascist powers than they had contemplated. In the case of Italy, particularly, the war placed a heavy burden on her intrinsically weak economy. Yet, by boisterous advertisment of its role in Spain, Rome had involved the prestige of the Fascist regime in the outcome of the struggle. After Guadalajara, moreover, Rome found it necessary to redeem Italian military honor. The Spanish Civil War marked the real beginning of Italo-German amity and collaboration which resulted first in an entente styled the "Rome-Berlin Axis" and ultimately in a formal military alliance between the two powers.

The advent to power of Adolf Hitler on January 30, 1933, was an important factor in the reorientation of Soviet foreign policy as well as in the redefinition of immediate Communist political objectives. By the end of 1935 the Soviet Union had concluded military pacts with France and Czechoslovakia and the Popular Front movement had come into being. With the outbreak of the Spanish Civil War, Moscow, however reluctantly, supported the French initiative for a nonintervention agreement. However, as the fascist powers proceeded to make a farce of the agreement while the democracies remained bound by it, Moscow, without a formal denunciation of the plan, began actively to support the Spanish Republicans. Given the passivity of the democracies, the inevitable result was that the Spanish Republic became increasingly beholden to the Soviet Union and that Communist power and influence grew apace in the Republic. However, the Soviet Union had not intervened in the Spanish conflict for ideological and political reasons, although these had not been entirely unimportant. Nor was the Soviet Union in search of strategic or economic gain in Spain. Fundamentally, Soviet intervention in Spain was prompted by the desire to bring an end to the policy of appeasement and to refurbish the system of collective security. Moscow was not concerned with the maintenance of the Spanish Republic per se, nor did it seek a trial of strength with the fascist powers in Spain: it sought to bolster the Spanish Republic against the fascist onslaught until Great Britain and France, alert to the threat to their security, would jettison the policy of appeasement and would themselves move to succor the Madrid government. The war in Spain, then, provided the supreme test of the new Soviet diplomacy aimed at rapprochement with the Western democracies and collective security against fascist aggression, and, concomitantly, of the political viability of the Popular Front movement. However, Soviet policy in Spain not only failed of its ultimate objective; it served to arouse the anxiety and consternation of London and Paris as well as the open hostility of Berlin and Rome. Following the Munich Agreement Soviet aid to Spain virtually ceased.

The available evidence makes it abundantly clear that while Great Britain did not commit soldiers, technicians, and weapons to Spain, as did Germany, Italy, and, to a lesser extent, the Soviet Union, its role in the Spanish drama was fully as important. The conclusion is inescapable that the defeat and destruction of the Spanish Republic must be attributed as much to British diplomacy in the years from 1936 to 1939 as to German aircraft and Italian infantry. British influence in the determination of French policy toward Spain was decisive, in that of the United States, important. There can be no doubt that the chief architect of appeasement in Spain was Great Britain. The motivations which underlay British policy toward Spain were many. To begin with, in England, as in France, pacifist sentiment was widespread. In giving its support to the non-intervention plan the British government announced that it thus hoped to localize the Spanish conflict and to prevent it from developing into a general war, an aim that received the approbation of a large number of people on both sides of the Channel. The British government, moreover, desired to establish a *modus vivendi* with Italy in the Mediterranean and, ultimately, to restore the cordiality which from the time of the *Risorgimento* had characterized Anglo-Italian relations but which had been dissipated by events attendant on the Italo-Ethiopian War. The British government, furthermore, was prepared to reach an understanding with Germany that would serve to insure the tranquillity of Western Europe. London saw a firm regional understanding as a realistic and viable undertaking but was inclined to view an ambitious system of collective security as transcending both the means and the legitimate interests of the Western democracies and therefore as essentially unworkable. The deflection of German energies and aspirations eastward would not occasion dismay in London. Then, too, Englishmen owned a vast amount of property in Spain. A government in Madrid in which Socialists, Communists, and anarchists sat might well prove a source of considerable difficulty. London was confident that, despite General Franco's present fascist associations, such were the long established economic and financial ties between Great Britain and Spain that the British position in the Peninsula, in the event of Franco's victory, would remain secure.

When, in little more than a year after the war in Spain had come to an end, German panzer units smashed through the Ardennes and sealed the fate of France and Falangist Spain appeared on the verge of following Fascist Italy into the victor's camp, there were those who said that Great Britain had gambled and lost in Spain and now would have to pay. Yet, such were the fixed relationships between Great Britain and Spain, such the physical exhaustion, the economic weakness, and the silent but deep-going political hatreds and divisions within Spain itself, such the conflicts and contradictions within the Nazi New Order (which, for example, saw Germans, Italians, Spaniards, and Vichy French staking rival claims to choice pieces of the North African littoral), and such the defensive strength of Great Britain and the military might of the Soviet Union that Great Britain was never seriously menaced by Franco's victory. Indeed, in some respects, it would appear that it was the fascist powers which had gambled and lost in Spain. However, be that as it may, the real losers were Europe and the Spanish people.

Notes

I: THE SPANISH BACKGROUND

1. Jellinek, p. 33. 2. *Ibid.*, p. 34. 3. Brenan, p. 120.
4. *Ibid.*, pp. 120–21.
5. The native vines required less care and lived almost twice as long. The terms of the *rabassa morte* had been originally established with the native vines in mind. Obviously, the introduction of the American vines aggravated the plight of the *rabassaire*.
6. Jellinek, pp. 39–40. 7. Brenan, p. 333. 8. *Ibid.*, p. 100.
9. Gannes and Repard, p. 182. 10. Ortega y Gasset, p. 167.
11. Borkenau, pp. 4–6. 12. Brenan, p. 126. 13. *Ibid.*, p. 156.
14. de la Mora, p. 41. 15. Borkenau, pp. 19–21. 16. *Ibid.*, p. 9.
17. Brenan, p. 53. 18. *Ibid.* 19. *Ibid.* 20. *Ibid.*
21. *Ibid.* 22. Borkenau, pp. 10–11. 23. *Ibid.*, pp. 19–21.
24. See Mosca. 25. Álvarez del Vayo, *The Last Optimist*, p. 10.
26. Brenan, p. 60. 27. Jellinek, p. 55.
28. Álvarez del Vayo, *The Last Optimist*, pp. 15–16.
29. Brenan, p. 59. 30. *Ibid.*
31. Earl J. Hamilton, "The Decline of Spain," *The Economic History Review*, VIII (1938), 168–79.
32. Jellinek, pp. 71–73. 33. *Ibid.*, p. 99. 34. *Ibid.*, p. 107.
35. *Ibid.*, p. 73. 36. *Ibid.*, p. 75. 37. Bowers, p. 12.
38. Earl J. Hamilton, "The Decline of Spain," *The Economic History Review*, VIII (1938), 168–79.
39. See Skinner, p. 517. 40. Jellinek, p. 73.
41. See U.S. Bureau of Foreign and Domestic Commerce, Economic Series—Number 20, Sammons and Abelson, *American Direct Investments in Foreign Countries—1940*, p. 4.
42. Jellinek, p. 72.
43. In a speech at Barcelona on July 18, 1938, Manuel Azaña, the President of the Spanish Republic, declared that the Communist party in 1936 was the most recently formed and the least numerous of all the Spanish proletarian parties, receiving less than 4 per cent of the

total vote cast in the general elections of February 16, 1936. Quoted in Bowers, pp. 317–18.

44. Brenan, p. 311.   45. Bowers, p. 177.

II: THE SPANISH REPUBLIC AND THE REVOLT OF THE GENERALS

1. Peers, *The Spanish Tragedy*, p. 11.   2. Jellinek, pp. 121–22. 3. Smith, pp. 320–21.

4. *Constitución de la República Española*, Article 1.

5. *Ibid.*   6. *Ibid.*, Article 2.   7. *Ibid.*, Article 3.

8. *Ibid.*, Article 6.   9. *Ibid.*, Article 26.   10. *Ibid.*   11. *Ibid.*

12. *Ibid.*   13. *Ibid.*, Article 27.   14. *Ibid.*, Article 46.

15. *Ibid.*   16. *Ibid.*, Article 48.   17. *Ibid.*   18. *Ibid*

19. Jellinek, p. 147.

20. Buckley, pp. 152–53. See also Arrarás, p. 129, and de Madariaga, *España*, p. 533.

21. Jellinek, pp. 179–81. See also de la Mora, pp. 196–97.

22. Jellinek, p. 189.   23. *Ibid.*, p. 285.   24. Buckley, p. 150.

25. Álvarez del Vayo, *Freedom's Battle*, p. 4.

26. Godden, *Conflict in Spain*, and Loveday, *Spain, 1923–1948*, are representative of this school of thought.

27. Schuman, *Europe on the Eve*, pp. 92–94.

28. *Report of the Seventh World Congress of the Communist International.* See particularly the Report delivered by G. Dimitrov on August 2, 1935, and the Resolution on the Report of Dimitrov adopted on August 20, 1935. There is no question but that the Communists became vociferous champions of the Popular Front movement, so much so that W. G. Krivitsky mistook zeal for invention. See Krivitsky, *In Stalin's Secret Service*, p. 78. Dr. Franz Borkenau observed with respect to Communist claims concerning the origins of the Spanish Popular Front that "they [the Communists] were as yet too insignificant for their moves to be important; the Popular Front would have won even without them; and their claim to have 'founded' the Popular Front in Spain is unfounded." See Borkenau, *op. cit.*, p. 58.

29. Godden, pp. 33 ff.

30. de la Mora, pp. 202–03. See also Bowers, pp. 159–61. Mr. Bowers wrote: "*One historic thing Azaña did that day—he laid the foundation for a coalition of the parties of the Left for the elections that could not much longer be denied.*" p. 161. Bowers' italics.

31. Charles A. Thomson, "Spain: Issues Behind the Conflict," *Foreign Policy Reports*, v. 12, no. 20, January 1, 1937.

32. Álvarez del Vayo, *Freedom's Battle*, pp. 4–5.

33. de la Mora, p. 207.

34. Quoted in Álvarez del Vayo, *Freedom's Battle*, p. 5.

35. *Ibid.*, p. 5.

36. Charles A. Thomson, "Spain: Issues Behind the Conflict," *Foreign Policy Reports*, v. 12, no. 20, January 1, 1937.

37. *Ibid.*   38. Schuman, *Europe on the Eve*, p. 265.

39. Charles A. Thomson, "Spain: Issues Behind the Conflict," *Foreign Policy Reports*, v. 12, no. 20, January 1, 1937.

40. de la Mora, p. 207.   41. *Ibid.*, p. 209.

42. The Duchess of Atholl, pp. 48–49.

43. de la Mora, p. 209.

44. To meet the danger from the Right Largo Caballero suggested to Azaña in June, 1936, that arms be distributed to the working class. Given the fact that the Left Socialists had refused to enter and share the responsibilities of the Azaña government, this was a fatuously unrealistic proposal. For, obviously, Azaña could not agree to it unless he were prepared to see the power of the State pass into the hands of the Socialists. See Brenan, pp. 313–14.

45. *Ibid.*, pp. 302–04.   46. *Ibid.*, p. 304.   47. Sencourt, pp. 77 ff.

48. Brenan, p. 307. See also Bowers, p. 214.

49. Schuman, *Europe on the Eve*, pp. 254–58.

50. Krivitsky, pp. 77–79. My italics.   51. Brenan, p. 304.

52. Brenan doubted if it would ever come, save as a consequence of an attempted military uprising. Brenan labeled Largo Caballero "a social democrat playing at revolution." See *ibid.*, pp. 304–05.

53. Bowers, pp. 197 ff.   54. *Ibid.*, pp. 211 ff.

55. This and the foregoing information, as well as the material directly quoted, was drawn from the English translation of the complete *procès-verbal* of the interview between Mussolini and the Spanish monarchist leaders. Reproduced in the Duchess of Atholl, Appendix, pp. 273–74. The Duchess has a photostat of this document in her possession. This document is also reproduced in Klotz, pp. 118–20. Dr. Klotz informed the Duchess of Atholl that the document was found in a file relating to Antonio Goicoechea in the Madrid office of the *Acción Popular*. According to Dr. Klotz, an expert had vouched for its being in Goicoechea's handwriting.

56. Salvemini, *Mussolini Diplomatico*, p. 87.

57. Garratt, p. 217.   58. *Ibid*.

59. Quoted in Schuman, *Europe on the Eve*, p. 266.

60. *Ibid*., pp. 265–67.

61. de Madariaga, *España*, pp. 357–60. See also Brenan, p. 57.

62. Brenan, p. 58.

63. Jellinek, pp. 76–77. See also Garratt, pp. 189–90.

64. Jellinek, p. 282.   65. Buckley, pp. 207–08.

66. Dzelepy, *The Spanish Plot*, pp. 5–7.   67. Garratt, p. 193.

68. Manuel, p. 176. See also Jellinek, p. 283.

69. Jellinek, p. 282. See also Álvarez del Vayo, *Freedom's Battle*, p. 50.

70. Álvarez del Vayo, *Freedom's Battle*, p. 50.

71. Charles A. Thomson, "Spain: Civil War," *Foreign Policy Reports*, v. 12, no. 21, January 15, 1937.

72. *Ibid*. See also Álvarez del Vayo, *Freedom's Battle*, p. 10.

73. Álvarez del Vayo, *Freedom's Battle*, p. 10.

74. Jellinek, p. 282.

75. Álvarez del Vayo, *Freedom's Battle*, p. 50.

76. *Ibid*., p. 22.   77. Foltz, pp. 39–40.

78. Quoted in Álvarez del Vayo, *Freedom's Battle*, p. 6.

79. Arrarás, pp. 154–57.   80. *Ibid*.   81. *Ibid*., p. 159.

82. This is the opinion of most observers. See Álvarez del Vayo, *Freedom's Battle*, pp. 13–14.

83. Álvarez del Vayo, *Freedom's Battle*, pp. 13–14.

84. *Ibid*., p. 19.   85. *Ibid*.   86. Arrarás, p. 163.

87. *Ibid*., p. 164.   88. Jellinek, pp. 296–97.   89. *Ibid*.

90. Major Pollard explained his role in this drama in these words: "My family is Catholic, and I could not allow my Spanish friends to be murdered by the Reds. I knew Franco was the man who could save Spain." Quoted in Jellinek, p. 297.

91. Arrarás, p. 178.   92. Quoted in *ibid*., p. 183.

III: THE GENERALS RECEIVE FOREIGN ASSISTANCE

1. The original Spanish text of this document is reproduced in Peers, ed., "Documents of the Civil War," *Bulletin of Spanish Studies*, Institute of Hispanic Studies at the University of Liverpool, v. 13, no. 52, October, 1936, p. 192.

2. Peers, *The Spanish Tragedy*, p. 211.   3. de la Mora, pp. 216–17.

4. Jellinek, pp. 254–55.   5. de Madariaga, *España*, pp. 599–600.

6. *Ibid.*, p. 600.

7. The foregoing account of the life and activities of Johannes Bernhardt was drawn, in the main, from Foltz, pp. 46–47.

8. *Documents on German Foreign Policy, 1918–1945* (Washington: United States Government Printing Office, 1950), Series D, v. III, "Germany and the Spanish Civil War, 1936–1939," no. 1, p. 3. Hereafter referred to as *German Documents.*

9. Foltz, p. 47.

10. *German Documents*, v. III, no. 4, pp. 5–7.

11. *Ibid.*, no. 2, pp. 3–4.

12. From a document of the Präsidialkanzlei of the Führer and Chancellor dated July 5, 1939, and entitled "Recommendations for Decorations in Connection with the Conclusion of the Spanish Civil War." Reproduced in part in the Editors' Note, *ibid.*, p. 2.

13. *Ibid.*, no. 10, pp. 10–11.   14. *Ibid.*   15. *Ibid.*, no. 16, p. 16.

16. del Vayo, *Freedom's Battle*, p. 73.

17. Buckley, pp. 233–34.

18. *German Documents*, v. III, no. 41, p. 40.

19. *Ibid.*, no. 39, p. 38.   20. *Ibid.*, no. 29, pp. 29–30.

21. *Ibid.*, no. 27, pp. 26–28.   22. *Ibid.*

23. *New York Times*, August 4, 1936.

24. *Foreign Relations of the United States, 1936* (Washington: United States Government Printing Office, 1954), v. II, "Europe," pp. 481–82. Hereafter referred to as *Foreign Relations of the United States, 1936.*

25. del Vayo, *Freedom's Battle*, p. 54. See also Buckley, pp. 410–11.

26. del Vayo, *Freedom's Battle*, p. 54.

27. *Ibid.*, pp. 54–55.   28. *Ibid.*

29. E. N. Dzelepy, *Spanish Plot*, pp. 28–29.

30. *New York Times*, July 31, 1936. See also *German Documents*, v. III, no. 18, p. 17 and *Foreign Relations of the United States, 1936*, II, 450–52.

31. *New York Times*, August 1, 1936.

32. *Ibid.*, August 4, 1936.

33. *Foreign Relations of the United States, 1936*, II, 481–82.

34. Even a moderate liberal such as Salvador de Madariaga avers that the union of Spain and Portugal must be "an obvious, natural, biological development in the history of the Peninsula." See de Madariaga, *España*, p. 768.

35. On August 3, 1936, the American minister in Portugal, R. G. Caldwell, reported to the American secretary of state, Cordell Hull,

that "from the beginning of the Spanish revolution [*i.e.*, the military insurrection] there have been clear indications that the Portuguese government has regarded the success of the revolutionary movement as a matter almost of life and death." See *Foreign Relations of the United States, 1936*, II, 456–57.

36. *German Documents*, v. III, no. 25, pp. 24–25.

37. A contraction of *Compañía Hispano-Marroquí de Transportes*, of which Johannes Bernhardt was the organizer and director.

38. *German Documents*, v. III, no. 52, p. 53. Du Moulin-Eckart's italics.

39. *Ibid.*, no. 53, pp. 54–56.　　40. *Ibid.*　　41. *Ibid.*

42. *New York Times*, August 1, 1936.

43. Sir Robert Hodgson, a writer not unfriendly to the rebel cause, states that "in all some 20,000 Portuguese took part in the war and fought with great bravery, their losses in the course of the campaign totalling some 8,000." See Hodgson, p. 70.

IV: THE FRIENDLESS NEIGHBOR: THE ORIGINS OF "NONINTERVENTION"

1. *Constitución de la República Española*, Article 6.

2. *Ibid.*, Article 77.　　3. de Madariaga, *España*, p. 567.

4. Perhaps this point of view is best exemplified by Point Three of the Twenty-Six Points of the Falange which as the official creed of Spanish fascism embodied the aims and aspirations of Spanish imperialism: "We have a will to empire. We demand for Spain a pre-eminent place in Europe. We will not put up with international isolation or with foreign interference. With regard to the Hispano-American countries, we will aim at unification of culture, of economic interests and of power. Spain claims a pre-eminent place in all common tasks because of her position as the spiritual cradle of the Spanish world." Quoted in Hamilton, pp. 76–77.

5. de Madariaga, *España*, pp. 564–65.

6. Álvarez del Vayo, *Freedom's Battle*, p. 233.

7. Padelford, p. 1.　　8. *Ibid.*, p. 4.

9. de Madariaga, *España*, pp. 601–03. See also Álvarez del Vayo, *Freedom's Battle*, p. 122.

10. Buckley, p. 234.

11. *Foreign Relations of the United States, 1936*, II, 458.

12. Muggeridge, pp. 21–22.

13. *New York Times*, July 28, 1936.　　14. *Ibid.*, August 5, 1936.

15. *Foreign Relations of the United States, 1936*, II, 461.

16. *Ibid.* 17. *Ibid.* 18. *Ibid.*

19. *Le Temps*, August 17 and 18, 1936.

20. See the letter dated Paris, July 25, 1936, from Fernando de los Ríos, special envoy to the French capital, to José Giral, the Spanish premier, the French text of which is reproduced in Brasillach and Bardèche, pp. 216–18.

21. *Foreign Relations of the United States, 1936*, II, 447–49. See also *German Documents*, v. III, no. 3, p. 4.

22. *Foreign Relations of the United States, 1936*, II, 447–49.

23. *Ibid.* 24. *Ibid.* 25. See Chapter 1, footnote 43.

26. See Bowers, pp. 288 ff.

27. *New York Times*, July 27, 1936.

28. See David Thomson, "Third Republic *versus* Third Reich," *The Contemporary Review*, CLIX (1941), 668–75.

29. *Ibid.*

30. *Foreign Relations of the United States, 1936*, II, 447–49 and 450–52. See also *German Documents*, v. III, no. 3, p. 4.

31. See Vera Micheles Dean, "European Diplomacy in the Spanish Crisis," *Foreign Policy Reports*, v. 12, no. 18, December 1, 1936, pp. 222–32.

32. *Foreign Relations of the United States, 1936*, II, 447–49.

33. It is of considerable interest that, when, on July 23, 1936, the German ambassador in Paris, Count von Welczeck, informed his government of the French government's intention to supply arms to Spain, the director of the Political Department of the German Foreign Ministry, Dr. Hans Dieckhoff, instructed Prince Otto Christian von Bismarck, the counselor of the German Embassy in London, to discuss this matter with the British Foreign Office "as soon as possible." See *German Documents*, v. III, no. 3, p. 4.

34. *Foreign Relations of the United States, 1936*, II, 447–49.

35. *Ibid.*

36. Elizabeth R. Cameron, "Alexis Saint-Léger Léger," in Craig and Gilbert, p. 391.

37. At his trial before the court of Riom, Blum strongly affirmed that as premier he had always put the interests of the "national community" before those of party or faction. See *Léon Blum devant la Cour de Riom*, pp. 90–92 and p. 193 ff.

38. Quoted in Dzelepy, *Spanish Plot*, p. 72.

39. *Foreign Relations of the United States, 1936*, II, 454–55.

40. *Ibid.*, pp. 464–66. See also *German Documents*, v. III, no. 34, pp.

34–35; Dzelepy, *Spanish Plot*, p. 94; Álvarez del Vayo, *Freedom's Battle*, pp. 66–69; Simone, p. 186; Paul-Boncour, v. 3, p. 73.

41. John C. deWilde, "The Struggle Over Spain," *Foreign Policy Reports*, v. 14, no. 2, April 1, 1938, pp. 14–24.

42. See Chapter IV, footnote 33.

43. Quoted in Martín Blázquez, p. 147.

44. Salvemini, *Prelude to World War II*, pp. 486–87.

45. *Ibid.*, p. 510. Unlike Salvemini, Langer and Gleason see appeasement as a two-way street, with both London and Moscow seeking to divert "the dynamism of the Nazi Revolution" away from itself and toward the other. See Langer and Gleason, *The Challenge to Isolation* (New York: Harper and Brothers, 1952), pp. 55–56.

46. Great Britain, 5 *Parliamentary Debates* (Commons) (London: His Majesty's Stationery Office, 1935), v. 295 (1934–35), 919–20.

47. Eden, *Foreign Affairs*, pp. 149–53.

48. *German Documents*, v. III, no. 11, pp. 11–13.

49. Martín Blázquez, p. 146.

50. *Ibid.*, p. 186.

51. Salvemini, *Prelude to World War II*, p. 485.

52. *Ibid.*, pp. 414–17.

53. Two years later the German West Wall had not yet been completed. At the height of the Czechoslovakian crisis Hitler ordered nearly 500,000 men from all parts of Germany to be organized into labor battalions and sent to the Rhineland to speed the work. See Fischer, pp. 556–57.

54. Concerning the relations between France and England with respect to Spain, the American ambassador to Spain, Claude G. Bowers, wrote: "The almost pathetic anxiety of the French to hold on to their understanding with England has been taken advantage of in London to force France into policies clearly dangerous to France." See *Foreign Relations of the United States, 1937*, I, 422–25.

55. J. Fred Rippy, "The Most Profitable British Mining Investments in the Hispanic World," *Inter-American Economic Affairs*, v. 8, no. 2, Autumn, 1954, pp. 43–53.

56. See Chapter IX.

57. *Foreign Relations of the United States, 1938* (Washington: United States Government Printing Office, 1955), I, 201–02.

58. *Ibid.*, 1937, I, 317–18.

59. *Ibid.*, 1938, I, 177. Paul-Boncour believed that the policy of nonintervention could be justified only if Germany and Italy, as well as

Great Britain and France, adhered to it faithfully. See Paul-Boncour, p. 70 ff.

60. *Foreign Relations of the United States, 1938*, I, 177.

61. Salvemini, *Prelude to World War II*, p. 508.

62. Eden, *Foreign Affairs*, pp. 168–73.

V: THE NONINTERVENTION AGREEMENT: INTERVENTION AND COUNTER-INTERVENTION

1. Switzerland, in view of her position as a "permanent neutral," did not formally adhere to the nonintervention agreement, but the Swiss government did place a ban on the exportation of war materials to Spain.

2. Muggeridge, pp. 26–28.   3. *Ibid.*, pp. 30–31.

4. *German Documents*, v. III, no. 29, pp. 29–30.

5. *Ibid.*   6. *Ibid.*, no. 32, pp. 32–33.   7. *Ibid.*, no. 34, pp. 34–35.

8. *Ibid.*, no. 37, pp. 36–37.   9. *Ibid.*, no. 38, pp. 37–38.

10. *Ibid.*, no. 42, pp. 41–42.

11. *Foreign Relations of the United States, 1936*, II, 485–87.

12. *Ibid.*   13. *Ibid.*   14. *Ibid.*, pp. 491–92.

15. *Ibid.*, pp. 515–16.   16. Harper, p. 220.

17. Beloff, I, 93 and II, 3. See also Fischer, pp. 441–42.

18. Harper, p. 219. See also Beloff, I, 89 ff.

19. *Foreign Relations of the United States, 1936*, II, 515–16.

20. Quoted in a telegram dated Moscow, August 29, 1936, from the American chargé d'affaires in Moscow, Loy Henderson, to the American secretary of state, Cordell Hull. See *Foreign Relations of the United States, 1936*, II, 515–16.

21. Reproduced in translation in Padelford, Appendix I, pp. 205–06.

22. *Ibid.*, p. 214.   23. *Ibid.*, pp. 217–18.   24. *Ibid.*, pp. 224–26.

25. *Ibid.*   26. *Ibid.*   27. Malcolm pp. 29–30.

28. *German Documents*, v. III, no. 65, pp. 65–66.

29. *Ibid.*, no. 55, pp. 56–57.   30. *Ibid.*, no. 71, pp. 72–73.

31. *Ibid.*, no. 64, pp. 63–65.   32. *Ibid.*   33. *Ibid.*, no. 60, p. 60.

34. *Ibid.*   35. See Padelford, p. 58.

36. *Foreign Relations of the United States, 1936*, II, 510–11.

37. *Ibid.*   38. *Ibid.*

39. *German Documents*, v. III, no. 73, p. 75.

40. *Ibid.*   41. Padelford, p. 60. Professor Padelford's italics.

42. In this regard the establishment of the London committee was a

masterstroke, for it appeared to create a controlling agency which would implement the nonintervention agreement. The Germans, until reassured, balked at the phrase "control committee" current in newspaper accounts. See *German Documents*, v. III, no. 72, p. 74. However, Prince Otto Christian von Bismarck, in his report to the German Foreign Ministry on the first meeting of the Non-Intervention Committee in London, observed that the establishment of the committee was pretty much a matter of appeasing public opinion in France and England. He said in part: "Today's meeting left the impression that with France and England, the two powers principally interested in the committee, it is not so much a question of taking actual steps immediately as of pacifying the aroused feelings of the Leftist parties in both countries by the very establishment of such a committee. In particular during my conversation today with Vansittart [Sir Robert, later Lord Vansittart, permanent under secretary of the British Foreign Office] in regard to another matter, I had the feeling that the British government hoped to ease the domestic political situation for the French premier by the establishment of the committee." See *German Documents*, v. III, no. 79, pp. 82–84.

VI: THE NONINTERVENTION AGREEMENT: INTERVENTION AND COUNTER-INTERVENTION (*continued*)

1. See *German Documents*, v. III, no. 52, p. 53; no. 57, pp. 58–59; no. 58, p. 59; no. 61, p. 61; and no. 62, pp. 61–62.

2. *Foreign Relations of the United States, 1936*, II, 484.

3. *Ibid.*, p. 517.   4. *German Documents*, v. III, no. 77, p. 78.

5. Vera Micheles Dean, "European Diplomacy in the Spanish Crisis," *Foreign Policy Reports*, v. 12, no. 18, December 1, 1936, pp. 222–32.

6. *German Documents*, v. III, no. 80, pp. 84–89.

7. *Ibid.*   8. *Ibid.*   9. *Ibid.*, no. 101, pp. 113–14.

10. *Ibid.*, no. 83, p. 91.   11. *Ibid.*, no. 93, p. 104.

12. This Junta de Defensa Nacional (Committee of National Defense), that claimed the right to empower the Franco regime, had been established on July 23, 1936, and had been originally composed of seven high-placed rebels—five generals and two colonels—under the presidency of General Miguel Cabanellas. See *Foreign Relations of the United States, 1936*, II, 449.

13. *German Documents*, v. III, no. 92, p. 103.

14. *Ibid.*   15. *Ibid.*   16. *Ibid.*, no. 96, pp. 105–07.

17. *Ibid.*, no. 113, pp. 123–25.   18. *Ibid.*

19. *Ibid.*, no. 691, pp. 784–87.

20. *Foreign Relations of the United States, 1936*, II, 575–76.

21. *Ibid.*

22. *Foreign Relations of the United States, 1936*, II, 558.

23. Charles A. Thomson, "Spain: Civil War," *Foreign Policy Reports*, v. 12, no. 21, January 15, 1937, pp. 258–68. See also *Foreign Relations of the United States, 1936*, II, 586–87.

24. *Foreign Relations of the United States, 1936*, II, 582–83.

25. *Ibid.*, 593–94.

26. Charles A. Thomson, "Spain: Civil War," *Foreign Policy Reports*, v. 12, no. 21, January 15, 1937, pp. 258–68.

27. *German Documents*, v. III, no. 40, pp. 38–40.

28. *Foreign Relations of the United States, 1936*, II, 517.

29. Peers, ed., "A Diary of the Civil War," *Bulletin of Spanish Studies*, v. 13, no. 52, October, 1936, p. 189.

30. Muggeridge, p. 45.

31. *Ibid.*

32. Álvarez del Vayo, *Freedom's Battle*, p. 111.

33. *German Documents*, v. III, no. 95, p. 105.

34. Muggeridge, pp. 53–54.   35. *Ibid.*   36. *Ibid.*

37. *Foreign Relations of the United States, 1936*, II, 582.

38. *German Documents*, v. III, no. 156, p. 169.

39. *Ibid.*

40. *Ibid.*, no. 170, p. 191. See also *Foreign Relations of the United States, 1936*, II, 620–21.

41. *Foreign Relations of the United States, 1936*, II, 620–21.

42. *German Documents*, v. III, no. 170, p. 191.

43. Charles A. Thomson, "Spain: Civil War," *Foreign Policy Reports*, v. 12, no. 21, January 15, 1937, pp. 258–68.

44. *New York Times*, October 30, 1936.

45. *Foreign Relations of the United States, 1936*, II, 574–75.

46. *Ibid.*, 576–77.   47. *Ibid.*, 611.   48. *Ibid.*

49. *German Documents*, v. III, no. 129, p. 139.

50. In late December, 1936, some 1000 Irish volunteers led by General O'Duffy arrived in rebel-held Cáceres. Most of them had come by way of Lisbon. See *Foreign Relations of the United States, 1936*, II, 620–21.

51. See Padelford, p. 17.   52. Eden, pp. 196–205.

53. *Foreign Relations of the United States, 1936*, II, 516–17.

54. *Ibid.*

55. *German Documents*, v. III, no. 156, p. 169 and no. 161, p. 178.

56. *Foreign Relations of the United States, 1936*, II, 584.

57. *Ibid.*, 584, 625. See also *German Documents*, v. III, no. 67, p. 68 and Louis Fischer, pp. 351–52 and pp. 448–49.

58. Muggeridge, p. 164 ff. The Italians sought to make the most of this sophistry, Ciano, on one occasion, instructing the German ambassador in Rome, Ulrich von Hassell, in its usefulness! See *ibid.*, pp. 126–27.

59. Louis Fischer, pp. 448–49.

60. This is, in the main, an argument from silence. Discounting obviously unfounded charges made by the Germans and Italians for propaganda purposes, and uncritically repeated by Franco apologists, there is very little mention in the voluminous literature on the Spanish Civil War of French war materials arriving in appreciable quantities in Republican Spain. What can be said of the Russians cannot be said of the French. The government forces were chronically critically short of arms and supplies; the bulk of their equipment, particularly heavy weapons, came from Soviet Russia; therefore, the amount of French matériel sent by France to Spain must have been quite meager. Concerning the lack of arms among the government forces, there is virtual unanimity of opinion among serious students of the Spanish Civil War. J. Álvarez del Vayo wrote that during the rebel offensive in the Levante (April–July, 1938) the proportion of war material between the rebels and the Republicans was 8–10 to 1 in medium and heavy cannon, 5–6 to 1 in light cannon, 10 to 1 in bombing planes, and 8 to 1 in pursuit planes. See Álvarez del Vayo, *Freedom's Battle*, pp. 189–90. This vast disproportion was to become even greater toward the close of the conflict.

61. Álvarez del Vayo, *Freedom's Battle*, p. 63.

62. However, during the critical battle of Irún in early September, 1936, the French authorities, by refusing to permit six freight cars loaded with munitions from Catalonia to be moved from Hendaye into Spain, facilitated the victory of Mola's rebel forces who captured Irún only after the Loyalists had exhausted their ammunition. See Bowers, p. 282.

63. Nelson, p. 20 ff.   64. Muggeridge, pp. 229–30.

65. Álvarez del Vayo, *Freedom's Battle*, p. 233 ff.

66. *Foreign Relations of the United States, 1936*, II, 505–06.

67. *Ibid.*   68. Martín Blázquez, p. 193.

69. See *Foreign Relations of the United States, 1936*, II, 626.

70. London *Times*, October 8, 1936.

71. Statement made by the Soviet ambassador in London, Ivan

Maisky, on October 23, 1936. See London *Times*, October 24, 1936.

72. Álvarez del Vayo, *Freedom's Battle*, p. 65.

73. *German Documents*, v. III, no. 63, pp. 62–63. See also *ibid.*, no. 97, pp. 108–10.

74. Muggeridge, pp. 39–41.

75. *German Documents*, v. III, no. 88, pp. 97–100.

76. *Ibid.*   77. *Ibid.*   78. Martín Blázquez, p. 243.

79. Krivitsky, p. 79.   80. *Ibid.*, pp. 80–81.   81. *Ibid.*, pp. 81–82.

82. *Ibid.*, pp. 84–85. See also Fischer, p. 405.

83. Krivitsky, p. 84.   84. *Ibid.*, p. 85.   85. *Ibid.*, pp. 86–87.

86. *Ibid.*   87. Martín Blázquez, p. 244.   88. *Ibid.*, p. 245.

89. Krivitsky, p. 87.   90. Martín Blázquez, pp. 245–46.

91. Claude G. Bowers wrote: "There was never at any time more than five hundred Russians in Spain. When the commission of the League of Nations supervised the withdrawal of all foreigners in loyalist Spain, on the request of the loyalist government, they found but one hundred and fifty Russians." See Bowers, p. 316. Louis Fischer put the number of Russians in Spain at 700. See Fischer, p. 498. W. G. Krivitsky said that Soviet military personnel in Spain was never more than 2000. See Krivitsky, p. 95. And David T. Cattell has written: "It is doubtful whether the entire Russian military forces in Spain ever reached more than four to five thousand." See Cattell, *Communism and the Spanish Civil War*, p. 82.

92. Krivitsky, p. 92 ff. See also Fischer, p. 389.

93. Krivitsky, p. 93.   94. Fischer, p. 354.

95. Louis Fischer maintained that the first unit of the International Brigades, numbering 1900 men, mostly Frenchmen, committed to battle on November 8 and a second unit, numbering 1550 men, committed to battle on November 14 "saved the military situation." See Fischer, pp. 393–94. However, Henry Buckley, the English journalist, who was in Madrid at the time, believed that it was not the Internationals but the Spanish *milicianos* who saved the city. Buckley argued that the height of the battle was reached between November 7 and 11, that is, when there were less than 2000 Internationals in a total defense force of some 80,000 Republicans. Buckley noted, too, that the main thrust of the rebel attack was aimed at positions manned by the *milicianos*. See Buckley, pp. 256–57. Robert Garland Colodny, who fought in Spain with the Loyalists, holds views similar to Buckley's. See Colodny, pp. 66–70 and p. 144.

96. See Krivitsky, p. 83. See also Fischer, p. 394 and Bowers, p. 316.

97. Krivitsky, p. 92 ff. See also Fischer, p. 389.

98. The phrase is Krivitsky's. See Krivitsky, p. 95.

99. Fischer, p. 576.

100. *The Volunteer for Liberty* (New York: Veterans of the Abraham Lincoln Brigade, 1949), Introduction.

101. *German Documents*, v. III, no. 542, p. 615.

102. *Ibid.*   103. Fischer, p. 405. See also Strong, p. 66.

104. Fischer, p. 576.   105. *Ibid.*   106. *Ibid.*

107. As Max Beloff succinctly observes: "Russia was not in Spain to endow it with an immediate Communist revolution." See Beloff, II, 28.

108. Martín Blázquez, p. 205.

109. David T. Cattell, *Spanish Civil War*, pp. 162–63.

110. Morrow, pp. 32–33.

111. Fischer, p. 403. See also Martín Blázquez, pp. 250–52.

112. Krivitsky, pp. 78–79.

113. Dimitrov, p. 12. Dimitrov's italics. This pamphlet was expanded from an article that first appeared in *Pravda* on November 7, 1936.

114. *Foreign Relations of the United States, 1936*, II, 539–40.

115. *Ibid.*, p. 539.

116. According to Loy Henderson, it was Maxim Litvinov who urged the Soviet government to keep this announcement somewhat equivocal, in order not to completely alienate France and England. See *ibid.*, pp. 541–42.

117. According to Louis Fischer, the Loyalists, when the war ended in 1939, owed the Soviet government $120,000,000, which, of course, was never paid. See Fischer, p. 365.

118. Section II of the secret Protocol signed at Burgos on July 16, 1936, by representatives of Nazi Germany and the Franco government read: "In order to give the German government a certain assurance with regard to the liquidation of the obligations mentioned under I [obligations incurred by the rebels for 'special deliveries' made them by the Germans], the Spanish Nationalist government will arrange that goods, especially raw materials, which the German government desires to obtain from Spanish sovereign territory, including the Spanish protectorate in Morocco, are delivered to Germany according to periodic agreements between the two governments and charged against the German claims in question, and furthermore, that payments in discharge of these claims, which will be agreed upon periodically between the two governments, will be made available to the German government for application to economic purposes in the above-named areas." See German Documents, v. III, no. 397, pp. 421–22.

119. Reliable figures as to the amount of war materials sent by So-

viet Russia to Republican Spain are not available. The statement in the text is based on the virtual unanimity of opinion among competent observers and on the well-established fact that the Loyalist forces chronically suffered from an acute shortage of armaments while the somewhat smaller rebel forces enjoyed a relative abundance of ma-tériel, particularly with respect to aircraft, tanks, and artillery. See Álvarez del Vayo, *Freedom's Battle*, p. 273 ff.

120. According to David T. Cattell, "it would be quite true to say that without the Communists as the unifying and driving factor, the Loyalist forces would have been defeated long before 1939." See David T. Cattell, *Spanish Civil War*, pp. 87–88.

121. *Foreign Relations of the United States, 1936*, II, 574–75.

122. Great Britain, 5 *Parliamentary Debates* (Commons) (London: His Majesty's Stationery Office, 1936), v. 317 (1936–37), 1923.

123. *German Documents*, v. III, no. 100, pp. 111–13.

124. Álvarez del Vayo, *Freedom's Battle*, p. 77.

125. Fischer, p. 497. See also Beloff, II, 181 ff.

126. Fischer, p. 497.

127. In the opinion of David T. Cattell the Munich agreement was a heavy blow to Loyalist morale. He wrote: "The Czechoslovakian crisis marked the final realization by the Loyalists that the democracies had never intended to help them. They had long suspected this but there had always been a faint hope which kept them going and kept them appealing to the humanitarianism of the democratic peoples. Their cause after September, 1938, had become absolutely hopeless against the might of the Fascist powers." See David T. Cattell, *Spanish Civil War*, p. 203.

128. *Ibid.*, p. 204. See also Krivitsky, p. 115.

VII: THE UNITED STATES AND THE SPANISH CIVIL WAR

1. *Foreign Relations of the United States, 1936*, II, 437–39.
2. *Ibid.*, pp. 440–77.   3. Padelford, pp. 176–77.   4. *Ibid.*
5. *Ibid.*, p. 179.
6. *Foreign Relations of the United States, 1936*, II, 478 and 479.
7. *Ibid.*, 449.   8. Padelford, p. 171.
9. *Foreign Relations of the United States, 1936*, II, 471.
10. *Ibid.*, pp. 474–75.   11. *Ibid.*   12. *Ibid.*
13. *Ibid.*, pp. 475–76. See also Hull, I, 478.
14. *Foreign Relations of the United States, 1936*, II, 471–72.

15. *New York Times,* August 12, 1936.

16. Padelford, pp. 174–75.

17. *Foreign Relations of the United States, 1936,* II, 530–31.

18. *Ibid.,* 531.   19. *Ibid.,* 536–38.   20. *Ibid.*   21. *Ibid.*

22. *Ibid.,* 618–20. See also Hull, I, 490.

23. *Foreign Relations of the United States, 1936,* II, 618–20.

24. Hull, I, 490.

25. *Foreign Relations of the United States, 1936,* II, 618–20.

26. *Ibid.*

27. *New York Times,* December 30, 1936. That President Roosevelt personally felt strongly on the matter can be seen from the statement he made at the press conference of December 29, 1936. Contrasting the attitude of most businessmen with that of Mr. Cuse, he said: "Well, these companies went along with the request of the Government. There is the 90 percent of business that is honest, I mean ethically honest. There is the 90 percent we are always pointing at with pride. And then one man does what amounts to a perfectly legal but thoroughly unpatriotic act. He represents the 10 percent or less of business that does not live up to the best standards. Excuse the homily, but I feel quite deeply about it." See Rosenman, V, 620–26.

28. *New York Times,* December 30, 1936.

29. Hull, I, 490.

30. *Foreign Relations of the United States, 1936,* II, 623–24.

31. *Ibid.*   32. *Ibid.*   33. *Ibid.*   34. Hull, I, 490.

35. U.S., *Congressional Record,* 75th Cong., 1st Sess., 1936, v. 81, Part 1, pp. 84–86.

36. *Ibid.,* pp. 76–77.   37. *Ibid.,* p. 77.   38. *Ibid.,* pp. 78–79.

39. *Ibid.*   40. *Ibid.*   41. *Ibid.,* p. 86.   42. *Ibid.*

43. *Ibid.,* p. 87.   44. *Ibid.,* pp. 91–92.   45. *Ibid.*   46. *Ibid.*

47. *Ibid.,* p. 93.   48. *Ibid.*

49. *Ibid.,* p. 87. This was achieved by the Neutrality Law of May 1, 1937.

50. *Ibid.,* pp. 98–99.   51. *Ibid.*   52. Hull, I, 491.   53. *Ibid.*

54. *Ibid.*   55. *New York Times,* March 9 and 10, 1937.

56. Hull, I, 399. For a brief but trenchant discussion of American isolationist sentiment during this period see Langer and Gleason, *The Challenge to Isolation,* pp. 11–15. For an extended treatment of American public opinion and the war in Spain see Taylor, p. 39 ff.

57. Hull, I, 491–92. See also Taylor, pp. 45–46.

58. *New York Times,* September 1, 1935.

59. Hull, I, 406.   60. *Ibid.,* p. 475.

61. *Foreign Relations of the United States, 1936*, II, 447–49. See also Hull, I, 476.

62. *Foreign Relations of the United States, 1936*, II, 457–58.

63. Hull, I, 477–78.   64. *Ibid.*   65. *Ibid.*, p. 476.

66. *Ibid.* See also *Foreign Relations of the United States, 1936*, II, 447–49.

67. Hull, I, p. 479.   68. *Ibid.*, p. 399.   69. Rosenman, V, 279.

70. *Ibid.*, pp. 276–79.   71. Hull, I, 481.

72. Rosenman, V, 285–92.   73. *Ibid.*, 291.

74. *German Documents*, v. III, no. 127, pp. 136–37.

75. See U.S. Bureau of Foreign and Domestic Commerce, Economic Series—Number 20, Robert L. Sammons and Milton Abelson, *American Direct Investments in Foreign Countries—1940* (Washington: U.S. Government Printing Office, 1942), p. 4.

76. See U.S. Bureau of Foreign and Domestic Commerce, Economic Series—Number 1, Paul D. Dickens, *American Direct Investments in Foreign Countries—1936* (Washington: U.S. Government Printing Office, 1938), p. 11.

77. See the pamphlets *Catholics and the Civil War in Spain* (New York: Three Arrows Press, 1937) and *Catholics Speak For Spain* (New York: North American Committee To Aid Spanish Democracy, 1937).

78. "Joint Letter of the Spanish Bishops to the Bishops of the Whole World Concerning the War in Spain." Quoted in Hughes, p. 309.

79. Quoted in *Spain*, a semi-monthly publication of Spanish War Events edited by Francis X. Connolly, Ph.D., May 1, 1938, p. 13.

80. Quoted in Salvemini and LaPiana, *What To Do With Italy?*, p. 148.

81. Henry L. Stimson, Letter to the *New York Times*, January 24, 1939.

82. Bowers, p. 418.   83. *Ibid.*, p. 419.   84. Welles, p. 61.

VIII: FALSE HOPES AND BITTER TRUTHS: THE CIVIL WAR ENDS

1. Hodgson, pp. 78–79.

2. Álvarez del Vayo, *Freedom's Battle*, p. 51 ff.

3. Mitchell, p. 271.

4. This information is contained in the *Spanish White Book: The Italian Invasion of Spain* which consists of official documents and papers seized from Italian units in action at Guadalajara and which was

presented by the Spanish government to the League of Nations in
March, 1937.

5. *Ibid.*

6. *Ibid.* The French General, Duval, labeled untrue the charge that
these Italian forces constituted a part of the Italian regular army, declaring that "the Italian Legion is in no way comparable to the [Italian]
regular army; the one has almost nothing in common with the other."
See Duval, p. 124. However, it should be noted that the available
evidence does not support General Duval's contention and that his
book, with a preface written by General Weygand, is openly sympathetic with the rebel cause.

7. Buckley, p. 296. Mr. Buckley, an English journalist, was with the
Loyalist forces during the battle of Guadalajara.

8. *Ibid.*, p. 297. Roberto Cantalupo, the Italian ambassador to the
Franco government, in his account of the battle of Guadalajara, makes
much of the foul weather. The Loyalist air force, he avers, operated
from dry fields south of Madrid while the Italian air force was bogged
down in wet, muddy fields. Unlike Buckley, he does not mention the
lack of adequate preparations on the part of the Italian command. See
Cantalupo, p. 182 ff.

9. *Spanish White Book: The Italian Invasion of Spain*, March, 1937.

10. Claude G. Bowers noted that pro-Franco Spaniards were unable
to conceal their satisfaction at the discomfiture of the Italians. See
Claude G. Bowers, p. 330. Henry Buckley wrote that he was informed
by correspondents who had been with Franco at the time that the
Italian defeat at Guadalajara had been the occasion for considerable
merriment among rebel officers. See Buckley, p. 300. It is of interest
that Roberto Cantalupo sought to ascribe the failure of the Italian
offensive to the inactivity of Franco's forces along the Jarama. See
Cantalupo, p. 188.

11. Álvarez del Vayo, *Freedom's Battle*, pp. 58–59.

12. *Ibid.*

13. General Mola had been killed in an air crash on June 3, 1937.

14. *German Documents*, v. III, no. 390, pp. 408–12.

15. *Ibid.*   16. *Ibid.*   17. *Ibid.*, no. 391, pp. 412–13.   18. *Ibid.*

19. Salvador de Madariaga ascribes the defeat of the Republic not to
the foreign assistance received by the rebels but to the bitter divisions
within the Republican camp. Señor de Madariaga describes the Republic as *"una turba de tribus malavenidas"* ("a rabble of querulous
tribes"). See de Madariaga, *España*, pp. 688–91. However, most students of the Spanish Civil War, while acknowledging that the Re-

public's lack of unity had a deleterious effect on its war effort, stress the importance of the foreign aid received by the rebels in seeking to explain the Republic's defeat.

20. *Generalitat* was the term used to designate the government of the Autonomous Region of Catalonia. The word, applied originally to a politico-economic institution of medieval Catalonia, can be traced back to the thirteenth century. See Peers, *Catalonia Infelix*, pp. 32–33.

21. Peers, *Catalonia Infelix*, pp. 205–06 and 217–18.

22. Cattell, *Spanish Civil War*, p. 47.

23. Peers, *Catalonia Infelix*, p. 251 ff.   24. Morrow, p. 25.

25. The seat of the Republican government was moved from Madrid to Valencia on November 6, 1936. The choice of Valencia, rather than Barcelona, as the war-time capital of the Republic is in itself significant.

26. Peers, *Catalonia Infelix*, p. 269.

27. *Ibid.*, p. 274. See also Cattell, *Spanish Civil War*, p. 139.

28. Major José Martín Blázquez had this to say of Largo Caballero as minister of war: "From the first moment . . . his complete and absolute lack of preparation for his task was painfully evident, and it was clear that he had not the slightest idea of military problems. True, those who knew him would have been greatly astonished if he had turned out to be an organizing genius. But the incapacity that he immediately revealed was such to produce the gravest concern." See Martín Blázquez, pp. 201–02.

29. *Ibid.*, p. 125 and p. 128. See also Buckley, p. 421.

30. Cattell, *Spanish Civil War*, p. 84. See also Buckley, pp. 401–02.

31. Casado, pp. 76–77.

32. Gannes, *How the Soviet Union Helps Spain*, p. 3.

33. *Ibid.*, p. 46.

34. Regarding this matter, it is of interest to note that Salvador de Madariaga labeled J. Álvarez del Vayo "the principal agent of Communism in Spain." See de Madariaga, *España*, p. 281. However, J. Álvarez del Vayo, while acknowledging his sympathy for the Russian Revolution and his advocacy of unity of action between the Socialists and Communists in Spain, vigorously denied the charge of "fellow traveller." See Álvarez del Vayo, *The Last Optimist*, pp. 288–89.

35. The English text of this letter, along with a facsimile of the French original and an explanatory article by Luis Araquistain, former Spanish Republican ambassador to France and a friend of Largo Caballero, was published by the *New York Times* on June 4, 1939.

36. Palmiro Togliatti, at the time a Member of the Executive Committee of the Communist International, wrote in a pamphlet entitled

The Spanish Revolution that: "the Communist Party of Spain has fought not only to bring about joint action by the working class, but also to establish a broad anti-fascist People's Front, which reflects the peculiar form of development assumed by the Spanish revolution at its present stage." See Ercoli [Palmiro Togliatti] p. 19. However, Felix Morrow wrote: " 'El gobierno de la victoria,' Pasionaria [Dolores Ibarruri, Spanish Communist leader] had christened it [the Negrín government]. Six months demonstrated the grotesque ludicrousness of that christening. The one conceivable 'justification' for its repressions against the workers and peasants might have been its military victories. But precisely from its reactionary politics flowed its disastrous military policies. Whether Spain remained under this terrible yoke and went down to the depths, or freed herself from these organizers of defeat and went forward to victory—whatever happened, history had already stamped the government of Negrín-Stalin with its true title: 'the government of defeat.' " See Morrow, p. 177.

37. Dimitrov, p. 12.

38. Cattell, *Spanish Civil War*, p. 132 and p. 153 ff. See also Brenan, pp. 327–28.

39. Walter Krivitsky states that he was well acquainted with Kleber and that Kleber, whose real name was Stern, was born in Bukovina when that region formed part of the Austro-Hungarian Empire. He later joined the Russian Bolsheviks, became a staff officer in the Red Army, and was attached to the military section of the Comintern. See Krivitsky, pp. 97–98.

40. Cattell, *Spanish Civil War*, pp. 130–31.

41. The leaders of both the Anarchists and the POUM sought to dissuade their followers from violent resistance and, in the main, were successful. See Morrow, p. 82 ff. See also Cattell, *Spanish Civil War*, pp. 143–44.

42. In the view of many anti-Stalinist revolutionaries the May Days in Barcelona represented a counter-revolutionary blow struck by the Communists and their bourgeois allies in a bid for absolute power. See Morrow, p. 103. However, David T. Cattell is inclined to doubt that in this instance the Communists were as much concerned with the acquisition of power as they were in harnessing Catalan resources and energies to the common task of defeating Franco. See Cattell, *Spanish Civil War*, pp. 160–63.

43. Quoted in Lambda, pp. 15–16.

44. Cattell, *Spanish Civil War*, p. 158. See also Fischer, pp. 416–18.

45. The phrase "something more than half" is used by J. Álvarez del Vayo. See Álvarez del Vayo, *The Last Optimist*, p. 284. Salvador de Madariaga gives the amount as 510,079,592 grams of gold, the equivalent of 1,581,642,100 gold pesetas or £63,265,684. See de Madariaga, *España*, p. 641.

46. Álvarez del Vayo, *The Last Optimist*, pp. 280–87.

47. Salvador de Madariaga, *España*, pp. 640–42.

48. Álvarez del Vayo, *The Last Optimist*, pp. 289–92. See also Henry Buckley, p. 396 ff.

49. Cattell, *Spanish Civil War*, p. 191.

50. *Ibid.*, pp. 195–99.   51. *Ibid.*

52. Henry Buckley observed: "The Republicans [in the political sense of the term] had remained in a comatose state throughout the war. Although individuals had done great work, as political forces they had been little in evidence. . . . The Catalan Left Party showed the same lack of spirit and the same complete lack of constructive leadership." Buckley added that the great European democracies were much to blame for the weakness and apathy of the Spanish Republican parties. See Buckley, pp. 402–03.

53. J. Álvarez del Vayo, whom Negrín made foreign minister again after Prieto had left the government, has said: "We did not want an endless and blind struggle, but we were not willing to die a dishonourable death without so much as attempting to secure a peace guaranteeing the lives of those who had committed no other crime than that of defending their country's independence. . . . No government with a clear conception of duty towards its people could do less than defend the city [Madrid] until the great democracies which were ready to recognize Franco should promise to impose the condition of humane treatment, nor could they do other than go on defending it if this guarantee were not given." See Álvarez del Vayo, *Freedom's Battle*, pp. 293–94.

54. Álvarez del Vayo, *Freedom's Battle*, p. 296.

55. *Ibid.*, pp. 296–97. However, believing that further resistance was impossible and useless, President Azaña appealed to the French and British governments to help bring an end to the war (February 4, 1939), declaring: "The reality is that we have lost the war. We are conquered; nothing remains but for us to accept the consequences." See Bonnet, v. 2, p. 82.

56. *Foreign Relations of the United States, 1936*, II, 488–99.

57. *Ibid.*

58. *Ibid.*, 583–613. See also *German Documents*, v. III, no. 141, pp. 151–52; no. 146, pp. 156–57; no. 147, pp. 158–59; no. 149, p. 163; no. 150, pp. 163–65; and no. 152, pp. 165–66.

59. The position taken by the German government was that it had already shown "by its recognition of the Nationalist Government that it sees no other factor in Spain besides this Government which could still claim to represent the Spanish people." See *German Documents*, v. III, no. 152, pp. 165–66.

60. *Foreign Relations of the United States, 1936*, II, 585.

61. *Ibid.*, 585–86.

62. *German Documents*, v. III, no. 147, pp. 158–59.

63. In discussing the problems faced by the Spaniards at Geneva, J. Álvarez del Vayo writes: "Dr. Negrín had once again [September, 1937] confronted the Assembly with the problem created by an act of aggression against a state member of the League. The Spanish delegation could not hope for any very heroic decision on the part of either Council or Assembly. It knew that they would not dare to name the aggressor, and that in no event would the measures laid down in the Covenant be applied. It merely wished to give the British and French Governments an opportunity of bringing their influence to bear on Berlin and Rome, in order to enforce the withdrawal of non-Spanish combatants from Spain." Then Señor del Vayo relates how pressure was exerted on him, as the chief Spanish delegate, to vote for "another platonic resolution, lacking in all meaning and practical value." He continues: "After a particularly heated, and at times painful, discussion, a formula was reached whereby the British and French Governments promised to revise their policy of Non-Intervention if 'in the near future' Germany and Italy had not withdrawn their troops from Spain. 'What,' I asked before registering our vote, 'do the honourable delegates of Great Britain and France mean by 'the near future'?' 'Probably an earlier date than the Spanish delegate thinks,' replied Mr. Elliot, immediately seconded by M. Delbos. But when eighteen months later, on March 6, 1939, I left Spain with the Negrín Government, the 'near future' had still not been converted into the present." See J. Álvarez del Vayo, *Freedom's Battle*, pp. 42–44.

64. *German Documents*, v. III, no. 257, p. 289.

65. *Ibid.*, no. 260, pp. 290–91.   66. *Ibid.*, no. 261, pp. 291–92.

67. *Ibid.*   68. *Ibid.*, no. 262, pp 292–93.

69. *Ibid.*, no. 264, pp. 293–95.   70. *Ibid.*, no. 265, p. 295.

71. On May 1, 1938, Premier Negrín proclaimed the Republic's "war aims." These were thirteen in number and soon became known as the

"Thirteen Points," in conscious emulation of President Woodrow Wilson's famous "Fourteen Points" of World War I. Negrín's program for the reconstruction of Spain was moderate and conciliatory, and obviously intended to attract the support not only of Spaniards on both sides of the lines but of the Western democracies as well. Louis Fischer writes that the idea for the promulgation of the Republic's war aims was given him by the English photographer, Ivor Montagu, and that Fischer passed it on to Foreign Minister del Vayo who, in turn, suggested it to Premier Negrín. See Louis Fischer, pp. 491–92.

72. See Cattell, *Spanish Civil War*, p. 132 ff.

73. Charles Foltz, Jr. estimates that the Loyalists executed some 75,000 persons during the war; whereas, the rebels executed some 400,000 during the same period and some 500,000 more in the period from 1939 to 1947. See Charles Foltz, Jr., p. 98. Writing of a period when authority was weakest in the Republican rear, Gerald Brenan opines "that for every person executed in Government territory, two or three were executed in the Rebel zone during the first six months of the war. For Andalusia the proportion was probably even higher." See Brenan, p. 322.

74. Georges Bernanos, a French writer, a Catholic, and, in the beginning, a rebel sympathizer, vividly describes what he saw of fascist terror on the Balearic Islands in his book, *Les grands cimetières sous la lune*.

75. Sir Peter Chalmers Mitchell, as was previously noted, was living in Málaga when that city fell to the fascist forces. His account of the event in *My House in Málaga* is a dispassionate indictment of the rebels and their methods.

76. Antonio Ruiz Vilaplana held an important position in the Spanish judiciary and at the time of the military revolt was serving in Burgos, continuing at his post under the rebel authorities for more than a year. He tells of the rebel terror in his book, *Burgos Justice*.

77. Brenan, p. 322. He adds to a footnote on the same page: "I have in my possession a file of cuttings from Portuguese newspapers which abundantly proves this. Every rebel column in Andalusia was accompanied by Portuguese journalists and their accounts made no effort to conceal the terrible savagery with which the war was being conducted. But when the reports of the culminating massacre at Badajoz got into the English and American press, the Portuguese censorship was tightened up and no more stories of this sort were published."

78. Ruiz Vilaplana, p. 29.   79. *Ibid.*, p. 29 ff.

80. *Ibid.*, pp. 142–43.   81. Foltz, p. 76 ff.

82. *German Documents*, v. III, no. 243, pp. 267–70.

83. *Ibid.*, no. 248, pp. 277–79.

84. In describing the "new" Falange, Foltz said that it "was neither revolutionary, nor Nazi, nor Fascist, nor anything save a mask to be worn by the Spanish Family [the "Establishment"]. After April, 1937, everything done by the Falange was directed and supported by the oligarchy of noblemen, churchmen, financiers, and soldiers who ran Spain. After April, 1937, the program of the revolutionary Falange was carried out—in the Spanish Family's way." See Foltz, pp. 86–87.

85. *German Documents*, v. III, no. 407, p. 432.

86. *Ibid.*, no. 408, p. 433.   87. *Ibid.*, no. 409, p. 433.

88. Ciano, pp. 9–10.

89. *German Documents*, v. III, Editors' Note, p. 438.

90. *Ibid.*   91. *Ibid.*, no. 415, pp. 440–41.   92. Fischer, p. 445.

93. *German Documents*, v. III, no. 417, pp. 442–43.

94. *The Nyon Arrangement and the Agreement Supplementary to the Nyon Arrangement*, League of Nations, Geneva, September 23, 1937, League of Nations Publications, C. 409.M273. 1937, VII.

95. *Ibid.*   96. *German Documents*, v. III, no. 419, pp. 433–44.

97. *Ibid.*   98. *Ibid.*, no. 420, p. 444.

99. Brasillach and Bardèche, p. 318.   100. *Ibid.*

101. *German Documents*, v. III, Editors' Note, p. 451.

102. Muggeridge, p. 137.   103. Ciano, p. 31.

104. *Ibid.* See also *German Documents*, v. III, no. 428, p. 452; no. 433, pp. 455–56; and no. 434, p. 456.

105. Ciano, p. 32.   106. *German Documents*, v. III, no. 428, p. 452.

107. Ciano, p. 37.

108. *Le livre jaune française: Documents diplomatiques, 1938–1939* (Paris: Imprimerie nationale, 1939), no. 28, p. 38.

109. *Ibid.*, no. 29, pp. 39–41.   110. *Ibid.*, no. 31, pp. 41–42.

111. Quoted in Cattell, *Spanish Civil War*, Notes, p. 248.

IX: FRANCO SPAIN—AXIS SATELLITE, 1939–1941

1. Quoted in Peers, *Spain in Eclipse*, p. 86.

2. See Casado, pp. 226–37.   3. *Ibid.*, p. 247.

4. Franco's demand for unconditional surrender had been well advertised. The Casadists found their *raison d'être* in believing that they could accomplish what the Negrín government could not or would not. See *ibid.*, pp. 284–86.

5. The full text of this agreement is reproduced, in English, in Muggeridge, pp. 75–77.

6. *German Documents*, v. III, no. 133, pp. 143–44 and no. 137, pp. 147–48.

7. *Ibid.*, no. 133, pp. 143–44.   8. *Ibid.*, no. 142, pp. 152–53.

9. *Ibid.*   10. *Ibid.*, no. 234, pp. 256–57.

11. *Ibid.*, no. 397, pp. 421–22.   12. *Ibid.*, no. 507, pp. 565–66.

13. See *ibid.*, no. 748, pp. 857–58.   14. *Ibid.*

15. *Ibid.*, no. 768, p. 881.   16. *Ibid.*, no. 773, pp. 884–86.

17. *Ibid.*   18. *Ibid.*   19. See *ibid.*, Editors' Note, p. 900.

20. Muggeridge, p. 258.

21. *I documenti diplomatici italiani* (Roma: La Libreria dello Stato, 1952), Ottava Serie, 1935–1939, v. 12, no. 56, p. 48. Hereafter referred to as *I documenti diplomatici italiani*.

22. *German Documents*, v. III, no. 809, pp. 919–31.

23. *I documenti diplomatici italiani*, v. 12, no. 192, p. 170.

24. *German Documents*, v. III, no. 809, pp. 919–23.

25. *I documenti diplomatici italiani*, v. 12, no. 488, p. 368. Mussolini's use of the upper case.

26. The military revolt.

27. *I documenti diplomatici italiani*, v. 12, no. 602, p. 452; and no. 603, pp. 452–53.

28. *Ibid.*, v. 12, no. 813, p. 607.

29. This decree is reproduced in *German Documents*, v. III, no. 435, p. 457.

30. *Ibid.*, no. 464, pp. 499–503.   31. *Ibid.*, no. 469, p. 508.

32. See *ibid.*, no. 666, pp. 749–50.

33 *Ibid.*, no. 673, p. 757. However, with the dismemberment of Czechoslovakia a *fait accompli*, Hitler, in a conversation with the French ambassador, François-Poncet, on October 18, 1938, alluded to Franco's action during the Czechoslovakian crisis, observing reassuringly that "Spain has need to maintain good relations with France." See *Le livre jaune français: Documents diplomatiques, 1938–1939*, no. 18, pp. 24–30.

34. *German Documents*, v. III, no. 716, pp. 821–26.

35. *Ibid.*, no. 739, p. 843. See also *ibid.*, note 1, p. 826.   36. *Ibid.*

37. See *ibid.*, no. 477, p. 521 and no. 715, pp 820–21. See also Ruiz Vilaplana, p. 223 ff.

38. In this regard the German ambassador to Nationalist Spain, Dr. Eberhard von Stohrer, reported to his government (February, 1938) that "it would mean completely misunderstanding the Spanish

mentality if we assumed that Nationalist Spain would ever be prepared to yield to any country at all even so much as a foot of national soil." See *German Documents*, v. III, no. 529, pp. 590–99. In his commentary on Stohrer's report Dr. Karl Schwendemann, Head of the Spanish-Portuguese section of the Political Department of the German Foreign Ministry, wrote: "From the ideology of the Spanish Nationalist movement as well as from the Spanish character it is apparent that any subordination to the will of one or more allies, particularly if it is forced, would meet with the strongest internal resistance." See *ibid.*, no. 544, pp. 615–19.

39. *Ibid.*, no. 382, p. 400. See also *Foreign Relations of the United States, 1937* (Washington: United States Government Printing Office, 1954), v. I, pp. 369–70 and pp. 374–76.

40. *German Documents*, v. III, no. 440, pp. 461–62. My italics.

41. *Ibid.*, no. 473, pp. 512–16.   42. *Ibid.*, no. 488, pp. 532–33.

43. An accurate figure on fatalities during the Civil War is not available. Most estimates put the total number killed at about one million in a population of about twenty-five millions. See Foltz, pp. 97–98.

44. In March, 1939, as the Civil War was drawing to a close, the Generalissimo informed the Italian General Gambara that "if an armed conflict should develop in Europe in the foreseeable future, Spain would have to remain neutral." See *German Documents*, v. III, no. 755, pp. 856–66.

45. *Ibid.*, no. 455, pp. 480–84 and no. 586, pp. 657–63.

46. *I documenti diplomatici italiani*, v. 12, no. 611, pp. 458–62.

47. *I documenti diplomatici italiani* (Roma: La Libreria dello Stato, 1953), Ottava Serie, 1935–1939, v. 13, no. 74, p. 50. Hereafter referred to as *I documenti diplomatici italiani*.

48. *Ibid.*, v. 13, no. 109, p. 74.   49. *Ibid.*, v. 13, no. 128, p. 85.

50. See Peers, *Spain in Eclipse*, pp. 143–44.

51. *Documents on German Foreign Policy, 1918–1945* (Washington: United States Government Printing Office, 1954), Series D, 1937–1945, v. VIII, no. 504, pp. 604–09. Hereafter referred to as the *German Documents*.

52. See Gibson, entry for August 27, 1939, pp. 130–32 and (final) entry for December 23, 1943, pp. 580–84.

53. *I documenti diplomatici italiani*, v. 12, no. 59, pp. 49–51. See also Gibson, entry for April 29, 1939, p. 74 and entry for May 2, 1939, p. 76.

54. *I documenti diplomatici italiani*, v. 13, no. 571, p. 352; no. 572, pp. 352–53; no. 581, p. 356; and no. 586, p. 358.

55. *Ibid.*, no. 571, p. 352.

56. *Ibid.*, no. 589, p. 359. See also *Le livre jaune français: Documents diplomatiques, 1938–1939*, no. 363, pp. 410–11.

57. *I documenti diplomatici italiani*, v. 13, no. 626, pp. 380–381. See also *Le livre jaune français: Documents diplomatiques, 1938–1939*, no. 367, pp. 412–13.

58. Gibson, entry for September 6, 1939, pp. 139–40.

59. *I documenti diplomatici italiani*, v. 13, no. 641, p. 388.

60. *Ibid.*, no. 642, p. 388. See also Doussinague, pp. 12–13.

61. Gibson, entry for June 5, 1939, pp. 93–94. Serrano Suñer himself declared that he was an Italophile "spontaneously" and a Germanophile "reflectively." See Serrano Suñer, pp. 108–09.

62. Gibson, entry for June 6, 1939, p. 94.   63. *Ibid.*

64. *Ibid.* In Serrano Suñer's view there was a positive correlation between Anglo-French hegemony and Spanish weakness and poverty. "The Anglo-French group dominant during our worse political periods had sentenced Spain to be a nation of the third rank, a mere satellite, a market, a source of valuable raw materials." See Serrano Suñer, p. 142.

65. Hamilton, p. 109.   66. Hoare, pp. 20–21.

67. *Ibid.*, p. 33. See also Doussinague, p. 42.   68. Hoare, p. 33.

69. See Bonnet, v. 2, p. 82 ff. See also de Madariaga, *España*, pp. 715–16.

70. Bonnet. See also de Madariaga, *España*.

71. See Gordon and Dangerfield, pp. 101–02.   72. *Ibid.*

73. At one point (November, 1939) the Spaniards made the threat to convoy their vessels through the blockade. However, it proved to be an empty gesture. See *German Documents*, v. VIII, no. 388, p. 449.

74. See *Manchester Guardian Weekly*, January 26, 1940.

75. See *ibid.*, March 29, 1940.

76. *German Documents*, v. VIII, no. 282, p. 322.

77. *Ibid.*, no. 482, pp. 568–69.

78. Feis, pp. 37–38. Spain's main source of oil was the United States oil companies and their subsidiaries, foremost among them being the Texas Company. Under the chairmanship of Captain Thorkild Rieber, the Texas Company had supplied the Franco forces with oil from the beginning of the Civil War and, of course, after Franco's victory, its contract had been renewed. From 1936 to the middle of 1940 Texaco shipped to Spain and its possessions in excess of 2,000,000 metric tons of oil, this figure representing more than half of the total oil shipments made by American companies to Spain and its possessions in that same period. See *ibid.*, p. 269 ff.

79. *German Documents*, v. VIII, no. 265, p. 304.

80. *Ibid.*, no. 284, pp. 324–25.   81. *Ibid.*, no. 663, pp. 871–80.

82. Gibson, entry for May 13, 1940, p. 249.

83. *The Spanish Government and the Axis* (Washington: United States Government Printing Office, 1946), European Series 8, Official German Documents, no. 2, pp. 6–7. Hereafter referred to as *The Spanish Government and the Axis.*

84. Hoare, pp. 34–35.   85. *Ibid.*, pp. 35–37.

86. *The Spanish Government and the Axis*, no. 1, pp. 3–6.

87. *Fuehrer Conferences on Matters Dealing with the German Navy* (Washington: Office of Naval Intelligence, 1947), 1940, II, conference of July 31, 1940, 9–13. Hereafter referred to as *Fuehrer Conferences—German Navy.*

88. *The Spanish Government and the Axis*, no. 2, pp. 6–7.

89. *Ibid.*   90. *Ibid.*, no. 3, p. 8.

91. *Fuehrer Conferences—German Navy*, 1940, v. II, conference of September 6, 1940, pp. 17–21.

92. *Ibid.*

93. *Ibid.*, Raeder's italics. The importance of "Operation Isabella-Felix" in the minds of the German leaders grew in direct proportion to their realization of Great Britain's determination to continue to fight and of the difficulties attendant on "Operation Sea Lion" (the projected invasion of England). See Langer and Gleason, *Undeclared War*, p. 57 ff.

94. *The Spanish Government and the Axis*, no. 1, pp. 3–6.

95. *Ibid.*, no. 4, pp. 9–13.   96. *Ibid.*

97. *Ibid.* Serrano Suñer's account of his visit to Berlin in mid-September, 1940, corroborates the testimony of the German documents. See Serrano Suñer, Chapter X.

98. *The Spanish Government and the Axis*, no. 5, pp. 14–16.

99. *Ibid.*   100. *Ibid.*, no. 6, pp. 17–19.   101. *Ibid.*

102. Muggeridge, pp. 393–94.   103. *Ibid.*

104. *Ibid.*, pp. 395–99.   105. *Ibid.*

106. Gibson, entry for October 5, 1940, p. 299.   107. *Ibid.*

108. *The Spanish Government and the Axis*, no. 8, pp. 21–25.

109. According to José María de Areilza, Franco's "no" at Hendaye "saved" the British Empire. See de Areilza, pp. 58–60.

110. The Italians, it appears, launched their attack on Greece with insufficient forces, to wit, three divisions. See *Fuehrer Conferences—Germany Navy*, 1940, v. II, conference of November 4, 1940, pp. 32–36. See also Gibson, entry for October 31, 1940, p. 306 and entry for November 10, 1940, p. 309.

111. When Hitler had declared to Franco at Hendaye that "with the first break in the weather" England was doomed, he was engaging in bluff, for the projected invasion of England had been scheduled for September 19–26 and by October 14 had been definitely postponed. See *Fuehrer Conference—German Navy*, 1940, v. II, conference of July 31, 1940, pp. 9–13 and conference of October 14, 1940, pp. 29–31.

112. See *ibid.*, conference of November 4, 1940, pp. 32–36 and conference of December 27, 1940, pp. 68–80.

113. *The Spanish Government and the Axis*, no. 9, p. 25.

114. *Ibid.*, no. 10, p. 26.   115. *Ibid.*, no. 11, pp. 26–28.

116. *Ibid.*   117. *Ibid.*, no. 12, pp. 28–33.   118. *Ibid.* My italics.

119. *Ibid.* Hitler's italics.   120. *Ibid.*

121. Muggeridge, pp. 419–20. "To us," wrote Ciano, "is assigned the hard task of bringing back home the Spanish Prodigal Son." See Gibson, entry for January 21, 1941, p. 339.

122. Muggeridge, pp. 421–30. Serrano Suñer has written that "nothing important came, or could come," from the Bordighera conference. See Serrano Suñer, p. 263.

123. *Fuehrer Conferences—German Navy*, 1940, v. I, conference of July 21, 1940, pp. 81–82. See also *Trial of the Major War Criminals before the International Military Tribunal* (Nuremberg, 1948), v. XV, testimony of General Alfred Jodl, June 5, 1946, pp. 390–91. Hereafter referred to as the *Nuremberg Trials*.

124. The first comprehensive, if tentative, plan of attack against the Soviet Union had been drafted by December 18, 1940. Hitler's military directive for "Operation Barbarossa" of this date is reproduced in Gantenbein, Appendix I, pp. 1073–76.

125. *Fuehrer Conferences—German Navy*, 1941, v. I, conference of January 8 and 9, 1941, pp. 1–4. General Franz Halder noted in his diary relative to the conference at Berghof of January 8 and 9, 1941: "We cannot knock out England with a landing operation (Air Force, Navy). Accordingly our position on the Continent must be so consolidated by 1941 that we may with confidence face continued war with England (and U.S.). . . . Russia must be smashed as soon as possible." See Franz Halder, *Diaries* (MS), v. 5, entry for January 16, 1941, pp. 83–86.

126. *Fuehrer Conferences—German Navy*, 1941, v. I, Conference of February 4, 1941, pp. 5–24. See also *Nuremberg Trials*, v. XV, testimony of General Alfred Jodl, June 7, 1946, pp. 560–61.

127. *The Spanish Government and the Axis*, no. 13, pp. 33–35.

128. Halder had noted in his diary: "Spain must be written off as a

potential ally." See Franz Halder, *Diaries*, v. 5, entry for January 16, 1941, pp. 83–86.

129. Muggeridge, pp. 434–36.   130. *Ibid.*, pp. 441–43.

131. *Ibid.*   132. *Ibid.*, pp. 443–44.   133. *Ibid.*

134. *Ibid.* Mussolini's italics.   135. *Ibid.*, pp. 445–47.

136. According to a statement made by General Guenther Krappe, German Military Attaché in Madrid from October 1, 1941, to November 30, 1942, and Colonel Hans Renner, German Military Attaché in Tangier from March 1, 1942, to June 1, 1944, it was Germany, rather than Spain, that refused to carry out "Operation Isabella-Felix" in the winter of 1940–41. For the postponement of the invasion of England and active preparation for the invasion of the Soviet Union rendered Spain's entry into the war undesirable. "Spain under the mask of neutrality was more useful to Germany." See United Nations, Security Council, *Report of the Sub-Committee on the Spanish Question*, pp. 83–89. However, I believe that the available evidence does not support the Krappe and Renner statement. What was probably true after the spring of 1941 was not true in the winter of 1940–41.

137. See Foltz, pp. 160–62.

138. Information concerning the Spanish military effort against the Soviet Union is to be found in United Nations, Security Council, *Report of the Sub-Committee on the Spanish Question*, pp. 57–58.

139. *Ibid.*, p. 14. See also Plenn, p. 184.

140. Muggeridge, pp. 449–52.   141. *Ibid.*, pp. 460–65.

142. In the autumn of 1941, W. Horsfall Carter wrote: "To make clear that General Franco and his Government are committed up to the hilt to Hitler is still not to tell the whole story. Spanish policy is motivated first, last and all the time by calculations of national interest. Consequently, Spain has also her alternative policy 'under the table.' It is a countervailing policy, just in case Germany's victory does not materialize." See W. Horsfall Carter, "Spain and the Axis," *Foreign Affairs*, v. 20, no. 1, October, 1941, pp. 175–83.

Bibliography

DOCUMENTS

Constitución de la República Española (1931).

I documenti diplomatici italiani. Roma, La Libreria dello Stato, 1952. Ottava Serie, 1935–1939. v. 12.

I documenti diplomatici italiani. Roma, La Libreria dello Stato, 1953. Ottava Serie, 1935–1939. v. 13.

Documents on German Foreign Policy, 1918–1945. Washington, United States Government Printing Office, 1950. Series D, v. III.

Documents on German Foreign Policy, 1918–1945. Washington, United States Government Printing Office, 1954. Series D, v. VIII.

Documents on German Foreign Policy, 1918–1945. Washington, United States Government Printing Office, 1960. Series D, v. XI.

Fuehrer Conferences on Matters Dealing with the German Navy. Washington, Office of Naval Intelligence, 1947. 1939–1941.

Gantenbein, James W., ed. *Documentary Background of World War II.* New York, Columbia University Press, 1948.

Great Britain. *Documents on British Foreign Policy, 1919–1939,* Third Series, v. V (1939). London, His Majesty's Stationery Office, 1952.

Great Britain. *Parliamentary Debates* (Commons), 5th ser., v. 295 (1934–35).

Great Britain. *Parliamentary Debates* (Commons), 5th ser., v. 317 (1936–37).

Great Britain. *Parliamentary Papers.* (*Accounts and Papers,* Vol. XXVIII). "International Committee for the Application of the Agreement Regarding Non-Intervention in Spain," *Spain No. 2* (*1936*). Cmd. 5300.

Great Britain. *Parliamentary Papers.* (*Accounts and Papers,* Vol. XXVIII). "International Committee for the Application of the Agreement Regarding Non-Intervention in Spain: Resolution adopted by the Committee relating to a Scheme of Observation of the Spanish Frontiers by Land and Sea," *Spain No. 1* (*1937*). Cmd. 5399.

Great Britain. *Parliamentary Papers.* (*Accounts and Papers,* Vol. XXIX). "Declaration by His Majesty's Government in the United Kingdom and the Italian Government regarding the Mediterranean," *Italy No. 1 (1937).* Cmd. 5348.

Le livre jaune français: Documents diplomatiques, 1938–1939. Paris, Imprimerie nationale, 1939.

Le procès de Maréchal Pétain. Compte rendu sténographique. Paris, Éditions Albin Michel, 1945.

Le procès Laval. Compte rendu sténographique. Paris. Éditions Albin Michel, 1946.

Léon Blum devant la Cour de Riom. Paris, Éditions de la liberté, 1945.

Muggeridge, Malcolm, ed. *Ciano's Diplomatic Papers.* London, Odhams Press Limited, 1948.

The Nyon Arrangement and the Agreement Supplementary to the Nyon Arrangement. League of Nations. Geneva, September 23, 1937. League of Nations Publications, C. 409.M273. 1937, VII.

Report of the Seventh World Congress of the Communist International. London, Modern Books Limited, 1936.

Skinner, Walter E. *British Mining Year Book, 1930.*

The Spanish Government and the Axis. Washington, United States Government Printing Office, 1946. European Series 8. Official German Documents.

Spanish White Book: The Italian Invasion of Spain. Washington, Spanish Embassy, 1937.

Trial of the Major War Criminals before the International Military Tribunal. Nuremberg, 1948. v. XV.

United Nations, Security Council, *Report of the Sub-Committee on the Spanish Question.* New York, 1946. First Year, Second Series, Special Supplement.

U.S. Bureau of Foreign and Domestic Commerce, Economic Series— Number 1. Dickens, Paul D. *American Direct Investments in Foreign Countries—1936.* Washington, U.S. Government Printing Office, 1938.

U.S. Bureau of Foreign and Domestic Commerce, Economic Series— Number 20. Sammons, Robert L. and Abelson, Milton. *American Direct Investments in Foreign Countries—1940.* Washington, U.S. Government Printing Office, 1942.

U.S. *Congressional Record,* 75th Cong., 1st Sess., 1936. v. 81, Part 1.

U.S. *Foreign Relations, 1936.* Washington, United States Government Printing Office, 1954. v. II.

U.S. *Foreign Relations, 1937*. Washington, United States Government Printing Office, 1954. v. I.

U.S. *Foreign Relations, 1938*. Washington, United States Government Printing Office, 1955. v. I.

ADDRESSES, DIARIES, MEMOIRS, AND PERSONAL ACCOUNTS

A Year of War in Spain. Speech made by President Manuel Azaña at the University of Valencia, July 18, 1937, first anniversary of the military rebellion in Spain. London, published by the Friends of Spain, 1937.

Álvarez del Vayo, J. *Freedom's Battle*. New York, Alfred A. Knopf, 1940.

—— *The Last Optimist*. New York, The Viking Press, 1950.

Bernanos, Georges. *Les grands cimetières sous la lune*. Paris, Librairie Plon, 1938.

Blum, Léon. *L'Exercice du pouvoir: Discours prononcés de Mai 1936 à Janvier 1937*. 3rd ed. Paris, Gallimard, 1937.

Bonnet, Georges. *Défense de la paix*. 2 vols. Geneva, Les éditions du Cheval Ailé, 1946.

Bowers, Claude G. *My Mission to Spain*. New York, Simon and Schuster, 1954.

Cantalupo, Roberto. *Fu la Spagna*. Verona, Arnoldo Mondadori, 1948.

Casado, Segismundo. *The Last Days of Madrid*. London, Peter Davies, 1939.

Ciano, Galeazzo. *Diario, 1937–1938*. Roma, Cappelli Editore, 1948.

Coulondre, Robert. *De Staline à Hitler*. Paris, Hachette, 1950.

Eden, Anthony. *Foreign Affairs*. New York, Harcourt, Brace and Company, 1939.

Gamelin, General Maurice. *Servir*. 3 vols. Paris, Librairie Plon, 1946.

Gibson, Hugh, ed. *The Ciano Diaries, 1939–1943*. New York, Doubleday and Company, Inc., 1946.

Halder Diaries, The (MS.), v. V.

Harper, Samuel N. *The Russia I Believe In*. Chicago, University of Chicago Press, 1945.

Hoare, Samuel. *Complacent Dictator*. New York, Alfred A. Knopf, 1947.

Hull, Cordell. *Memoirs*. 2 vols. New York, The Macmillan Company, 1948.

Krivitsky, W. G. *In Stalin's Secret Service*. 2d ed. New York, Harper and Brothers, 1939.

Martín Blázquez, José. *I Helped to Build an Army*. London, Secker and Warburg, 1939.

Mitchell, Peter Chalmers. *My House in Málaga*. London, Faber and Faber Ltd., 1938.

Mora, Constancia de la. *In Place of Splendor*. New York, Harcourt, Brace and Company, 1939.

Nelson, Steve. *The Volunteers*. New York, Masses and Mainstream, 1953.

Orwell, George. *Homage to Catalonia*. London, Secker and Warburg, 1938.

Paul-Boncour, Joseph. *Entre Deux Guerres*. 3 vols. Paris, Librairie Plon, 1946.

Rosenman, Samuel I., ed. *The Public Papers and Addresses of Franklin D. Roosevelt*. New York, Random House, 1938, V.

Ruiz Vilaplana, Antonio. *Burgos Justice*. New York, Alfred A. Knopf, 1938.

Serrano Suñer, Ramón. *Entre Hendaya y Gibraltar*. 9th ed. Madrid, Ediciones y Publicaciones Españolas, S.A., 1947.

NEWSPAPERS

Manchester Guardian Weekly.
New York Times.
Le Temps.
The Times (London).
The Volunteer for Liberty. New York, Veterans of the Abraham Lincoln Brigade, 1949.

BOOKS, PAMPHLETS, AND PERIODICALS

Atholl, The Duchess of. *Searchlight on Spain*. Harmondsworth, Penguin Books Limited, 1938.

Altamira y Crevea, Rafael. *A History of Spain*. Trans. Muna Lee. New York, D. Van Nostrand Company, Inc., 1949.

de Areilza, José María. *Embajadores sobre España*. 4th ed. Madrid, Instituto de Estudios Politicos, 1947.

Arrarás, Joaquín. *Francisco Franco*. Milwaukee, The Bruce Publishing Company, 1939.

Beloff, Max. *The Foreign Policy of Soviet Russia, 1929–1941.* 2 vols. London, Oxford University Press, 1947.

Borgese, G. A. "Pius XII and the Axis," *The Nation,* March 11, 1939.

Borkenau, Franz. *The Spanish Cockpit.* London, Faber and Faber, Ltd., 1937.

Brasillach, Robert and Bardèche, Maurice. *Histoire de la guerre d'Espagne.* Paris, Librairie Plon, 1939.

Brenan, Gerald. *The Spanish Labyrinth.* New York, The Macmillan Co., 1943.

Buckley, Henry. *Life and Death of the Spanish Republic.* London, Hamish Hamilton, 1940.

Carter, W. Horsfall. "Spain and the Axis," *Foreign Affairs,* v. 20, no. 1, October, 1941.

Catholics and the Civil War in Spain. New York, Three Arrows Press, 1937.

Catholics Speak For Spain. New York, North American Committee to Aid Spanish Democracy, 1937.

Cattell, David T. *Communism and the Spanish Civil War.* Berkeley, University of California Press, 1955.

—— *Soviet Diplomacy and the Spanish Civil War.* Berkeley, University of California Press, 1957.

Colodny, Robert G. *The Struggle for Madrid: The Central Epic of the Spanish Conflict (1936–37).* New York, Paine-Whitman Publishers, 1958.

Cot, Pierre. *Triumph of Treason.* Chicago, Ziff-Davis Publishing Company, 1944.

Craig, Gordon A. and Gilbert, Felix. *The Diplomats, 1919–1939.* Princeton, Princeton University Press, 1953.

Deakin, Frank B. *Spain To-Day.* London, The Labour Publishing Company, Limited, 1924.

Dean, Vera Micheles. "European Diplomacy in the Spanish Crisis," *Foreign Policy Reports,* v. 12, no. 18, December 1, 1936.

deWilde, John C. "The Struggle Over Spain," *Foreign Policy Reports,* v. 14, no. 2, April 1, 1938.

Dimitrov, Georgi. *Spain and the People's Front.* New York, Workers Library Publishers, 1937.

Doussinague, José M. *España tenía razón.* 2nd ed. Madrid, Espasa-Calpe, S.A., 1950.

General Duval. *Les leçons de la guerre d'Espagne.* Paris, Librairie Plon, 1938.

Dzelepy, E. N. *Britain in Spain: A Study of the National Govenment's Spanish Policy* (by the "Unknown Diplomat"). London, Hamish Hamilton, 1939.

—— *The Spanish Plot*. London, P. S. King and Son, Ltd., 1937.

Ercoli, M. [Palmiro Togliatti]. *The Spanish Revolution*. New York, Workers Library Publishers, 1936.

Feis, Herbert. *The Spanish Story*. New York, Alfred A. Knopf, 1948.

Fischer, Louis. *Men and Politics*. New York, Duell, Sloan and Pearce, 1941.

Foltz, Jr., Charles. *The Masquerade in Spain*. Boston, Houghton Mifflin Company, 1948.

Gannes, Harry. *How the Soviet Union Helps Spain*. New York, Workers Library Publishers, 1936.

Gannes, Harry and Repard, Theodore. *Spain in Revolt*. New York, Alfred A. Knopf, 1937.

Garosci, Aldo. *Gli intellettuali e la guerra di Spagna*. Turin, Giulio Einaudi, 1959.

Garratt, G. T. *Gibraltar and the Mediterranean*. New York, Coward-McCann, Inc., 1939.

Godden, G. M. *Conflict in Spain*. London, Burns, Oates, and Washbourne, Ltd., 1937.

Gordon, David L. and Dangerfield, Royden. *The Hidden Weapon*. New York, Harper and Brothers, 1947.

Hamilton, Earl J. "The Decline of Spain," *The Economic History Review*, v. VIII (1938).

Hamilton, Thomas J. *Appeasement's Child*. New York, Alfred A. Knopf, 1943.

Hodgson, Robert. *Spain Resurgent*. London, Hutchinson and Co., Ltd., 1953.

Hughes, Philip. *Pope Pius the Eleventh*. New York, Sheed and Ward, 1938.

Jellinek, Frank. *The Civil War in Spain*. London, Victor Gollancz, Ltd., 1938.

Klotz, Helmut. *Les leçons militaires de la guerre civile en Espagne*. Paris, 1937.

Lambda. *The Truth about the Barcelona Events*. New York, Workers Age Publishers, 1937.

Langer, William L. and Gleason, S. Everett. *The Challenge to Isolation*. New York, Harper and Brothers, 1952.

—— *The Undeclared War*. New York, Harper and Brothers, 1953.

Loveday, Arthur F. *Spain, 1923–1948*. London, The Boswell Publishing Co., Ltd., 1948.

Madariaga, Salvador de. *Englishmen, Frenchmen, Spaniards*. London, Oxford University Press (Humphrey Milford), 1928.

—— *España*. 4th ed. Buenos Aires, Editorial Sudamerican, 1944.

Manuel, Frank E. *The Politics of Modern Spain*. New York, McGraw-Hill Book Company, Inc., 1938.

Matthews, Herbert L. *Two Wars and More To Come*. New York, Carrick and Evans, Inc., 1938.

—— *The Yoke and the Arrows*. New York, George Braziller, Inc., 1957.

Monroe, Elizabeth. *The Mediterranean in Politics*. London, Oxford University Press, 1938.

Morrow, Felix. *Revolution and Counter-Revolution in Spain*. New York, Pioneer Publishers, 1938.

Mosca, Gaetano. *Elementi di Scienza Politica*. 2d ed. Torino, Fratelli Bocca, 1923.

Ortega y Gasset, José. *España Invertebrada*. 2d ed. Madrid, Calpe, 1922.

Padelford, Norman J. *International Law and Diplomacy in the Spanish Civil Strife*. New York, The Macmillan Company, 1939.

Peers, E. A., ed. "A Diary of the Civil War," *Bulletin of Spanish Studies*. Institute of Hispanic Studies at the University of Liverpool, v. 13, no. 52, October, 1936. This is not a diary in the usual meaning of the word but a chronological listing of events.

—— "Documents of the Civil War," *Bulletin of Spanish Studies*. Institute of Hispanic Studies at the University of Liverpool, v. 13, no. 52, October, 1936.

Peers, E. A. *Catalonia Infelix*. London, Methuen and Co., Ltd., 1937.

—— *Spain in Eclipse*. London, Methuen and Co., Ltd., 1943.

—— *The Spanish Tragedy*. 3rd ed. New York, Oxford University Press, 1936.

Pertinax [André Géraud]. *The Gravediggers of France*. Garden City, New York, Doubleday, Doran and Company, Inc., 1944.

Plenn, Abel. *Wind in the Olive Trees*. New York, Boni and Gaer, Inc., 1946.

Richards, V. *Lessons of the Spanish Revolution (1936–1939)*. London, Freedom Press, 1953.

Rippy, J. Fred. "The Most Profitable British Mining Investments in the Hispanic World," *Inter-American Economic Affairs*, v. 8, no. 2, Autumn, 1954.

Romulus. "Dopo un anno di guerra Spagnola," *Nuova Antologia,* August 1, 1937.

Salvemini, Gaetano. *Mussolini Diplomatico.* Bari, G. Laterza e Figli, 1952.

—— *Prelude to World War II.* London, Victor Gollancz, Ltd., 1953.

Salvemini, Gaetano and LaPiana, George. *What To Do With Italy?* New York, Duell, Sloan and Pearce, 1943.

Schmitt, Bernadotte E. *From Versailles to Munich, 1918–1938.* Chicago, The University of Chicago Press, 1938.

Schuman, Frederick L. *Europe on the Eve.* New York, Alfred A. Knopf, 1939.

—— *International Politics.* 3rd ed. New York, McGraw-Hill Book Company, Inc., 1941.

—— *Soviet Politics at Home and Abroad.* New York, Alfred A. Knopf, 1947.

Sencourt, Robert. *Spain's Ordeal.* London, Longmans, Green and Co., Ltd., 1940.

Simone, André. *J'Accuse!* New York, The Dial Press, 1940.

Smith, Rhea M. *The Day of the Liberals in Spain.* Philadelphia, University of Pennsylvania Press, 1938.

Spain, a semi-monthly publication of Spanish War Events edited by Francis X. Connolly, PhD., May 1, 1938.

Strong, Anna Louise. *Spain in Arms—1937.* New York, Henry Holt and Company, 1937.

Taylor, F. Jay. *The United States and the Spanish Civil War.* New York, Bookman Associates, 1956.

Thomson, Charles A. "Spain: Issues Behind the Conflict," *Foreign Policy Reports,* v. 12, no. 20, January 1, 1937.

—— "Spain: Civil War," *Foreign Policy Reports,* v. 12, no. 21, January 15, 1937.

Thomson, David. "Third Republic *versus* Third Reich," *The Contemporary Review,* v. CLIX (1941).

Van Paassen, Pierre. *Days of Our Years.* New York, Hillman-Curl, Inc., 1939.

—— *That Day Alone.* New York, The Dial Press, 1941.

Welles, Sumner. *The Time for Decision.* New York, Harper and Brothers, 1944.

Werth, Alexander. "France and Spain," *New Statesman and Nation,* September 11, 1937.

Index